Archery World's Complete Guide to Bowhunting

ARCHERY WORLD'S COMPLETE GUIDE TO
BOWHUNTING

Edited by GLENN HELGELAND

PRENTICE-HALL, Inc.
Englewood Cliffs, N. J.

Photos by:
Frank Vanfield, Canadian Wildlife Service; Dennis Ballard;
Brian Donovan; Judd Cooney; Saunders Archery Co.; Erwin A. Bauer;
Russell Tinsley; Tom Walker; Len Cardinale; Leonard Lee Rue III;
Charlie Ash; Robert Brashear; Dave Richey; J. Robert Davis;
Wisconsin Department of Natural Resources.

Archery World's Complete Guide to Bowhunting
Edited by Glenn Helgeland
Copyright © 1975 by *Archery World* (H. Lee Schwanz, Publisher)
Printed in the United States of America
Prentice-Hall International, Inc., London
Prentice-Hall of Australia, Pty. Ltd., Sydney
Prentice-Hall of Canada, Ltd., Toronto
Prentice-Hall of India Private Ltd., New Delhi
Prentice-Hall of Japan, Inc., Tokyo

---

10 9 8 7 6 5 4 3 2 1

Library of Congress Cataloging in Publication Data
Main entry under title:
Archery world's complete guide to bowhunting.

1. Hunting with bow and arrow. I. Helgeland,
Glenn./II. Archery world. III. Title:
Complete guide to bowhunting.
SK 26.A72   799.2′ 15   75-17942
ISBN 0-13-044024-8
        0-13-044016-7 pbk.

This book is dedicated to my parents, who – among other good things – showed me the pleasure and excitement available in interesting reading material and also taught me to stop, look and listen not only at railroad crossings, but also in the woods, streams and lakes of northwestern Wisconsin where I grew up. No finer upbringing could a man have.

ACKNOWLEDGEMENT

Our thanks to a fine group of expert bowhunters/writers from throughout the U.S. The total of their years of bowhunting experience is exceeded only by what they've learned over those years. We have attempted to draw it all together for you here. You will note that the various experts basically agree on the aspects of technique in archery and in bowhunting. We have deliberately retained much of this repetitiveness, for the correlation of their thinking and experience will hopefully help smooth and speed your way into the mainstream of bowhunting.

A special thanks to five top guys: *Archery World's* co-hunting editors Russ Tinsley and Judd Cooney and co-technical editors Len Cardinale, Al Henderson and Bob Skiera. Their contributions, guidance and expertise have been invaluable.

Glenn Helgeland
Editor
Archery World magazine

THE CONTRIBUTORS:

Jay Massey, "Bowhunting in the Age of Ecology"; Al Henderson, "Hunting Bow Sights"; Brian Donovan, "Optics for Bow Hunters"; Judd Cooney, "Nowhere Without Footwear"; Opal Enlow, "Why Women Hunt, And How They Should Begin"; Len Cardinale, "Fine Tune Your Hunting Bow"; Russ Tinsley, "Games Bowhunters Play"; Bob Skiera, "Ready to Hunt in the Rain?"; Russ Tinsley, "Brush Up for the Hunt"; Dave Harbour, "*ABC*'s of Tree Stands"; Bob Skiera, "Mastering Tree Stand Shooting"; Dick Ahlefeld, "Scents Make Sense"; Judd Cooney, "Hunt the Edges for More Game"; Keith Schuyler, "Within Sound of the Church Bell"; Jim Stone, "Are You Deer Blind?"; Russ Tinsley, "Finding the Big Bucks"; Judd Cooney and the late Dutch Wambold, "Late Season Deer—West and East"; Judd Cooney, "Mule Deer *Do* Have Brains"; P. J. Hughey, "Think Like a Desert Muley"; Russ Tinsley, "Moment of Truth"; Russ Tinsley, "Where to Aim"; Jim Stone, "After You've Hit Your Buck"; Dutch Wambold, "Bugling Them In"; Bob Irwin, "Bear Hunt That Got My Goat"; Charles Farmer, "Pronghorn Challenge"; Russ Tinsley, "Let the Game Hunt You" and "The Many Steps of Varmint Stalking"; Jim Tallon, "Javelina 'How to' "; Jim Stone, "Bushytails, The Big Little Challenge"; Robert Brashear, "Hip-Deep in Ducks"; Marvin Tye, "Turkey, The Big Game Bird"; Brian Donovan, "Carp Hunting, *A* to *Z*"; Dave Richey, "Carp in the Dark"; Keith Schuyler, "Shooting at Underwater Shadows"; Eric Cameron, "Trophy Care for Taxidermy"; Russ Tinsley, "Bowhunter as a Biologist".

All other material produced by *Archery World*.

CONTENTS

CHAPTER ONE

THE HUNTING ETHIC

●

BOWHUNTING IN THE AGE OF ECOLOGY

Many of us have heard the expression ''the balance of nature'' so often it has almost lost its meaning. While thumbing through a Canadian wildlife publication recently, I came across a black-and-white photograph which illustrated the concept precisely and left an indelible, unforgettable impression on me.

The photograph was an aerial shot taken from two thousand feet over a great herd of migrating caribou. From that height the thousands of animals appeared like a swirling mass of ants. The center of the mass was a circular opening perhaps one hundred yards wide. Directly in the center of the opening was a single black dot—a wolf.

The caption beneath the photo indicated the caribou nearest the wolf were all alert and watching him intensely. On the outer perimeter of the mass many animals had lost all interest in the wolf and had bedded down. The caribou seemed to know the wolf was far enough away to pose no threat.

It occurred to me that the single black dot could just as easily be a bowhunter, for the caribou were just out of bow range and just beyond ''wolf distance.'' Those often-heard words ''the balance of nature'' rang home with a resounding clarity.

All predators—with the exception of man—are natural conservationists in that they are all restricted in their ability to bring down game. The caribou/wolf relationship is a good example of this. The wolf can occasionally get a caribou if he works hard enough. However, the wolf rarely poses a threat to game populations because a healthy

1

Chased by a wolf, a herd of caribou react in a characteristic fashion. Those who are closely followed by the wolf are running for their lives; those a little farther off, watchful but not yet panicked, make a detour; and those in the distance are in no hurry at all.

caribou can usually outrun a healthy wolf. The wolf is in balance with nature.

Man's superior intellect and his technological advancements have thrown him out of kilter with the natural world. He is no longer a natural conservationist, as is demonstrated by our saddening experience with the passenger pigeon and by the near-disasters of the American bison and musk ox.

Aldo Leopold, the father of wildlife management, once defined conservation as "a state of harmony between man and nature." All across the country today, people are awakening to the basic principle that man should strive to be a part of nature and live in harmony with the earth.

Since man is dominant, he must use this dominance wisely to achieve the necessary balance. In many instances man has replaced the natural predators which originally maintained the correct balance. But man has also learned that he cannot subvert and bend wildlife to his will by an overflowing show of force. He must instead fit smoothly into the balance, improving habitat where he can, cropping only as much as needed and not cropping where not needed. This is how man can become a natural conservationist.

The environmental and ecological awareness movement that is sweeping the country is a partial reaction to man's automated, spoon-fed, industrialized and success-motivated world. Everywhere there is a growing hunger for simple, more natural things.

With an ever-increasing amount of leisure time man is rediscovering the old magic when portaging a canoe along a winding path in the crisp morning air was an exhilarating experience; or when a snowshoe trek through the soft winter light of a northern forest left one relaxed and filled with a sense of personal satisfaction.

As archers, some of our most nostalgic memories relate to some of our most humble experiences. Just wandering the woods with a bow allows us time to reflect—to savor that exciting, intangible quality that binds us to the outdoors.

Archers, perhaps better than anyone else, understand the satisfaction from doing things the hard way. The game we get is dearly paid for in hard work, sweat and great sacrifice. As the wolf must work for the game he downs, so must the archer work for his.

One such instance is forever imprinted in my memory. It concerns a weekend caribou hunt timed with the crossing of several thousand caribou on the Denali Highway in the Alaskan interior.

The Denali is open country—great swells and rolling hills clad in knee-high dwarf willow. The caribou were moving through in groups of 10 to 200 animals, flowing over the rolling country in their mile-eating gait toward the timbered wintering range to the south. Stalking a band of ever-moving, migrating caribou was impossible. The only method for a bowhunter was to first locate a band of animals, then attempt to intercept them.

Hours later, I had seen more than a thousand caribou. On several occasions I had managed to set up my position where they would file by, but never was able to get closer than 80 to 90 yards. After hours of alternately spotting moving bands of animals, then struggling to intercept them, I was approaching exhaustion.

These caribou would not have been as much of a challenge with a rifle. In fact, for three hunters I met when I returned to my car the season was over. They had filled their limit of three caribou each, and they were lamenting the fact that the hunt was over for them.

This is why I chose the added challenge of the bow. The herding caribou were an environmental experience in themselves. Maybe the other hunters were inexperienced and believed that their hunt would be more of a challenge than it proved to be.

For them, a true challenge would have been a two-week hunt high in the mountains for an isolated sheep or goat trophy. They then would have experienced the environment—the rugged stalking, the weather, the frustrating movements of free-ranging game animals, the high-country camp at which they would regroup, replan and discuss the challenges ahead.

For it is the individual challenge, the personal challenge, that nearly all hunters feel—not always to take a trophy, but to meet the environment face to face and understand and appreciate it well enough to successfully cope with the hindrances.

A man crawling across a freezing shale slope feels it, no matter what hunting method he is using. And he thrills to that feeling.

The inequality of the caribou situation was produced by man's technological progress, not by a difference in hunting styles. The wolf and grizzly worked hard for the few caribou they took. The ancient Ahtena Indians who had roamed this harsh land for thousands of years worked hard to survive. But technology has crept up so unnoticeably that man can bag some species with great ease.

Today, all of us—no matter how we hunt—are faced with a greater problem. In fact, the method of hunting is immaterial.

Today there is a backlash developing. Everywhere people are questioning man's right to take game in fair chase. But as all hunters know, hunting is not just killing. Hunting is an instinct in man, it is a working *with* nature, it is a finding of self and a communion with self. Hunting is a perpetuation of the species, a predatory instinct that exists in all of humanity, but has chosen different ways to show itself.

The total environmental and ecological awareness that is sweeping the country today is a partial reaction to man's "progress." There is a back-to-nature movement in which man regards himself not as superior to nature, but as blending in harmony with it. Such a movement offers the opportunity to create a *true* understanding of the value and need for all hunting. But even more, it offers the greatest opportunity archery has ever witnessed. The time is ripe for the promotion of an ancient sport wherein man is able to keenly experience the outdoors on its own terms.

Every one of us—every bowhunter and archer in every state across the country—can help promote the concept of man's being in balance with nature through hunting with the bow.

Fortunately, we have developed beyond the point of disagreeing between bow and rifle hunters. Both methods are recognized by the states. There is no right or wrong, there is simply a freedom of choice. The only right involved is the right to hunt.

We love our method of hunting, so we quite naturally promote it. We can point out the aesthetics, pleasure and satisfaction from hunting with the bow. For an infinite number of reasons we have chosen to stack the odds against ourselves in hunting success. Most of us have slowly trickled one by one into the growing ranks of archery. With the current mood of ecological awareness that is moving across America, there is no reason why this trickle should not become a torrent.

What's in it for us? Plenty. Suppose, for example, the development of weapons became so sophisticated and our hunter population so great that only a few hours hunting could be allowed each year for various species of big game. Of course this is far-fetched, but it is not inconceivable.

With our growing population and ever-increasing numbers of hunters, combined with diminishing amounts of wildlife habitat, there is work to be done.

We must have a reasonable human population control to preserve the quality of our environment. We must use our resources better. We must work to create more, and better, habitat—and make better use of the land we need for human occupation.

With our intellect and dominance we can wisely do this. We have brought the whitetail deer to higher numbers than ever before because the habitat has been improved and we have hunted them wisely. We may not be able to increase the numbers of *all* game, but we can ensure that we have the healthiest herds possible for the amount of habitat available.

We cannot preserve each and every animal—as some would mistakenly believe—because nature has ways, more harsh than any we could devise, of eliminating over-population. But we *can* preserve a species.

Without the development of more and better habitat, without the understanding of the need for human population control, and with more hunting pressure, our choices may some day be limited to only restrictive choices. Restricted hunting season length, restricted numbers of hunters through lotteries or permits, or restricted methods and means of hunting. If I were forced to pick one, I'd pick voluntary restriction of methods and means of hunting. But we shouldn't need to do any of them.

What we *can and must do* is set a good example of sportsmanship and a sense of respect for our wildlife. We don't have to harp continually on the merits of bowhunting. We need only to maintain our own high standards of respecting animals and game laws by using proper equipment and cooperating with wildlife agencies who manage fish and game resources.

We can—and should—join and participate actively in conservation organizations. Many of the newer members of such organizations have been attracted because conservation is the ''now'' thing or because they have been made aware of the need for conservation. Many of these people do not understand or appreciate the role of hunting in nature's plan. If we are to continue to enjoy hunting, we must educate such people in the *whys* of hunting.

If you yourself do not fully comprehend the hunter's role in nature, or if you feel you cannot effectively communicate with the anti-hunting critic, then go to the nearest public library and check out a book on the basics of wildlife management.

If you want to drum up enthusiasm, set up speaking engagements with various clubs and organizations or present slide talks on your hunting trips to local sporting groups. Chances are you many find a surprising number of persons who have been considering taking up the bow.

If you are not a convincing speaker, then learn how. I once met an extremely dedicated archer who joined Toastmasters International so he could better communicate to others the attributes of archery. He went on to become president of his local speaking club and a dynamic force in the promotion of archery in the state of Oregon.

The world's human population is growing at an alarming rate and is continuing to encroach upon and crowd out our wildlife. Unless we are careful, we may wake up fifty years from now to discover the only wildlife habitat left is on small game preserves and that the only hunting allowed is one hour each year to keep the game populations in check.

It doesn't have to be this way. Millions of Americans are longing to discover the simple pleasures in nature. We can help them develop a feeling and a concern for our environment—through the simple pleasures of the ancient sport we call archery.

CHAPTER TWO

GETTING STARTED THE RIGHT WAY
●
WHAT TO TELL A NEW BOWHUNTER

There's a lot of difference between a man in the woods with a bow and some arrows and a bowhunter. Some people say as many as 60 percent of the people carrying bows in the woods aren't really bowhunters. They're just there with some sort of archery gear because it seemed like a pleasant thing to do for a weekend, because their brother-in-law was going hunting and they wanted to tag along, or because they just never started properly.

But there's no reason for heading into the woods ill-equipped or under-equipped. Such a guy scares the beejeebers out of knowledge-able hunting companions, and in the rare instance he's unlucky enough to plunk a game animal (usually a deer, because this is the game most neophytes head to the tall timber for) he too often does little more than wound the animal—if he even hits it.

So if you are the encouraging brother-in-law, or one of your buddies has said he'd like to go along with you this fall ''just to see what it's like,'' or your son or daughter or a youth you know wants to start bowhunting, here are some tips to make sure that person is at least a rudimentary bowhunter and not just a person in the woods with a bow.

First, get the new bowhunter enthused. Enthused enough to really care about knowing what to do and then doing those things properly. Tell him how you have expanded your time in the outdoors through the extended seasons most states have for archery deer hunting. Tell him how great the weather is during the early and mid-autumn when leaves

Dwarfed by Ponderosa pine, this bowhunter enjoys the beautiful natural setting, the timelessness of being in the woods during the hunting season.

Tent camping during bowhunting season is a relaxing way for a family to enjoy a weekend.

To determine your master eye and thus determine whether you should shoot right or left handed, form a triangular opening with crossed fingers and thumbs, arms extended. Without changing the size of the triangle, look through it at a specific object and draw it back to your face. The triangle will automatically come directly to your dominant eye.

begin to turn and the air has a crisp coolness. Tell him that it's just as exciting—sometimes more so—to have a near-miss, and watch the deer bound away with tail-waving alarm, as it is to score a kill.

Tell him that bowhunters have this advantage over firearms hunters: they're in a quiet woods with unspooked deer, there aren't hordes of red-clad guys roaming all over the scene, and you as a bowhunter are little, if any, disturbance to non-hunting people around you.

Tell him that it's a time to have a leisurely weekend of great companionship.

Tell him that during this time of year most of the campers are gone and you can have great chunks of public land, and often private land, with few "no hunting" signs around, all to yourself.

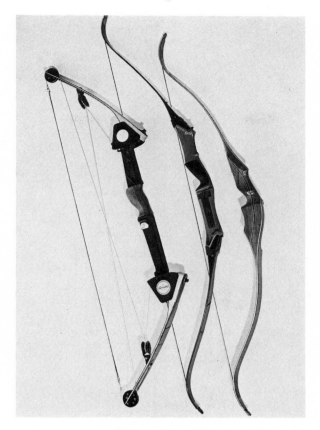

The three basic types of hunting
bows. From left: one-piece recurve,
take-down recurve and compound.

Then, get a set of your state's archery hunting regulations from a
local sport shop or archery shop, help him buy the necessary license
and begin getting him outfitted for the hunt.

Begin by showing him how to determine his master eye and
whether he should shoot right- or left-handed. Have him extend his
arms in front of him, form a one-inch circle with thumb and index
finger of each hand, and look at you. The eye you see will be his
master eye. If it's the left one, he should shoot left-handed; with a right
master eye, shoot right handed.

Show him a selection of good hunting bows. Explain that, since
he's basically looking for a hunting bow, he should look for something
in the 48 to 64 inch length, preferably 56 to 64 inches. These shorter

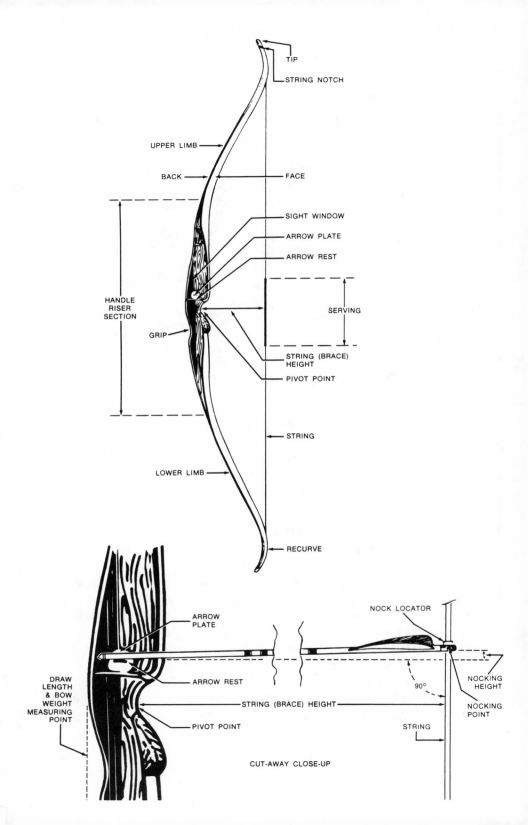

TIP

STRING NOTCH

UPPER LIMB

BACK

FACE

SIGHT WINDOW

ARROW PLATE

ARROW REST

HANDLE
RISER
SECTION

SERVING

GRIP

STRING (BRACE)
HEIGHT

PIVOT POINT

STRING

LOWER LIMB

RECURVE

ARROW
PLATE

NOCK LOCATOR

ARROW REST

DRAW
LENGTH
& BOW
WEIGHT
MEASURING
POINT

STRING (BRACE) HEIGHT

90°

NOCKING
HEIGHT

NOCKING
POINT

PIVOT POINT

STRING

CUT-AWAY CLOSE-UP

bows are lighter and easier to handle in brush than target bow lengths of 66 to 72 inches.

Remember, though the shorter bows are more convenient, they also are more critical to shoot because they magnify errors in shooting form more than do longer bows. A longer bow is more stable and consistent; thus, the 56- to 64-inch bows are a good compromise for stability and ease of shooting.

Impress upon the new bowhunter that it is important to get the *heaviest draw weight bow that person can handle accurately*. Tell your future bowhunting partner, if he's an average adult male, that he ought to look at bows in the 40- to 50-pound draw weight range. Emphasize that *it is more important to get a bow that he can handle well than it is to choose the heaviest bow he can pull*. Try a bow. If he can draw it to a solid anchor and hold it steady for a few seconds—around five—then he can reasonably be expected to handle it well.

Bow Weight Recommendation Chart

	20 lb. & under	20 lb.	25 lb.	30 lb.	35 lb.	40 lb.	40 lb. & over
Children 6-12	X	X					
Teen (girl)		X	X				
Teen (boy)		X	X	X			
Women—Target		X	X	X			
Men—Target				X	X	X	
Hunting							X

(Standards of the Archery Manufacturers Organization)

Proper Number of String Strands

8 — bows up to 25 lb.
10 — bows 25 lb.-35 lb.
12 — bows 35 lb.-45 lb.
14 — bows 45 lb.-55 lb.
16 — bows 55 lb.-70 lb.
18 — bows 70 lb. and up

Point out that a too-heavy bow makes him a poorer shooter because he can't draw it fully, can't aim well, can't hold it steady (or long, if the game is looking at him). Make sure he understands that a slightly lighter bow which can be handled well is a much more efficient weapon than a big bow used poorly. After all, it's performance, not draw weight, that kills game.

Check your state's minimum draw weight laws. If your potential hunting partner is a woman or child, bows in the 30- to 40-pound range are best. But some states may have minimums of 40 pounds. Then you have a problem, unless the beginning bowman can learn to handle a bow that meets the law.

If he or she is just beginning, something in the $30 to $60 range is best. Another good guideline is to get the best he (or you, if it's your youngster) can afford.

Now your partner needs matching arrows. Be sure he understands the absolute importance of the word "matching." No matter how well he can handle a bow, mismatched arrows will ruin everything. Help him pick out a dozen arrows matched—spined—to his *draw length* and *bow weight*. (You can quickly, and quite accurately, determine his draw length by placing one end of a yardstick against his chest and having him place both arms, hands and fingers straight, against the stick. His draw length will be close to the length his outstretched fingers reach on the stick.)

If he can afford aluminum hunting arrows, fine; they're longer-lasting and give unbeatable performance. Glass is less expensive. Wooden arrows are cheapest, and probably best for a beginner; but get a good matched set of them. Don't buy cheap schlock stacked in barrels; they're not hunting arrows anyway.

While you're at the arrow counter, take the time to explain and show him the differences between broadheads, field points, target

---

Selecting Correct Arrow Length

Spread-arm measurement	Arrow length
57"-59"	24"-25"
60"-62"	25"-26"
63"-65"	26"-27"
66"-68"	27"-28"
69"-71"	28"-29"
72"-74"	29"-30"
75"-77"	30"-31"

(Length of the arrow measures from bottom of nock slot to back of head.)

Determining Proper Arrow Spine at Your Draw Length

1. For draw lengths *shorter* than 28″:
    A. Divide bow's draw weight at 28″ by 20.
    B. Multiply this number by the inches or inches-and-fraction that your draw is shorter than 28″.
    C. *Subtract* this number from bow's draw weight at 28″. This will give your draw weight at your draw length.
    D. Match arrow spine to the final draw weight number.
Example: Bow weight = 44 lb. Draw length is 26½″.
    44 lb. ÷ 20 = 2.2 lb.
    2.2 lb. × 1.5″ = 3.3 lb.
    44 lb. − 3.3 lb. = 40.7 lb. at 26½″ draw length
2. For draw lengths of 28″: Match spine to draw weight given.
3. For draw lengths *longer* than 28″:
    A. Divide bow's draw weight at 28″ by 20.
    B. Multiply this number by the inches or inches-and-fraction that your draw is longer than 28″.
    C. *Add* this number to bow's draw weight at 28″.
    D. Match arrow spine to the final draw weight number.
Example: Bow weight = 44 lb. Draw length is 30½″.
    44 lb. ÷ 20 = 2.2 lb.
    2.2 lb. × 2.5″ = 5.5 lb.
    44 lb. + 5.5 lb. = 49.5 lb. at 30½″ draw length

points and blunts. He should realize that no one hunts medium and big game with anything but broadheads—*sharp* broadheads.

Point out that broadhead arrows kill game by cutting and hemorrhaging. One close look at field and target points should show the ridiculousness of going afield with them during hunting season. (But some people do.) Explain that blunts are strictly a small game head, when the impact is usually enough to kill.

You might suggest that your buddy get a half-dozen arrows with field points which weigh the same as his broadheads and use them for beginning practice. They should weigh the same so he will be fully familiar with arrow performance at that weight.

Explain instinctive and sight shooting. You might suggest, particularly if he has done little or no bow shooting, that a simple one-, two- or three-pin hunting sight could help him immeasurably, particularly since he isn't familiar enough yet with the sport to adequately judge arrow performance at various distances and isn't used to gauging distances over the point of an arrow.

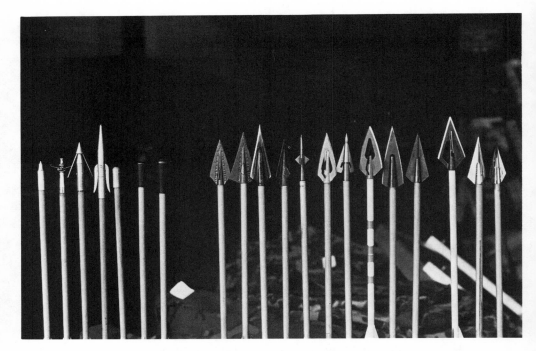

From the left: field point, bird point, two fish points, three blunts, a series of two-, three- and four-blade broadheads of various designs. Some four-blade heads have four fixed blades, others have an insert to be affixed through a slot in the primary head.

Maybe one of the sights which have varied gap spacing on pin fingers for easy range finding would help a beginner. And if he uses this style, make sure he gets the sight mounted right side up with the widest finger spacings on the upper pins.

Now he needs accessories. An armguard and finger tab or glove. Armguards obviously protect the bow arm, but they do more during hunting season—they also hold back a bulky sleeve that otherwise could catch the string and ruin a shot. A tab or glove for the drawing hand protects tender skin and helps you shoot better. (No one should experience pain when shooting, particularly a beginner. So just tell him that it hurts like hell to shoot a hunting bow without finger and arm protection, and let it go at that. He'll find out soon enough anyway.)

Point out the necessity of camo sleeves or camo sticks for the bow, camo clothes and grease for the skin—maybe a headnet if he wears glasses that could shine—and brush buttons and string silencers for a bowstring so it won't catch on twigs or twang on release.

From left: three flu-flu fletching styles, two three-fletch hunting arrows, and two four-fletch hunting arrows. Flu-flus permit swift arrow flight for a short distance, until air resistance to the large fletching area becomes dominant. Such arrows are excellent for bird and small game shooting. The long three-fletch style is the most common for bowhunting uses. The four-fletch style can use smaller fletches because the total stabilizing area is similar to three larger fletches. Also, with four fletches you don't need to look at the arrow as you nock it because either way is correct. Fourth arrow from the right has straight fletching. Third arrow from the right is slightly offset; this will decrease speed somewhat, but adds stability. Second arrow from the right has 75°/105° four-fletching; it also has a Bjorn-style nock. All others are outfitted with standard speed nocks. Arrow on the right has four fletches attached 90° from each other.

Get at least two bowstrings—no one should get caught in the middle of a hunt with a busted bowstring and no spare—and have the dealer clamp a good nocking point locator on each.

He'll definitely need a small stone or file for field sharpening of broadheads. Maybe he'll want some scent to hide his presence in the woods.

You should have a finger tab, as shown here, or a shooting glove; armguard to hold the sleeve and protect your arm; camouflaged bow; arrow holder to hold the arrow in place on the rest; a solidly mounted quiver of whichever design you prefer. Some bowhunters like the security of a bow sling which fits over your bow hand and gives you security, while allowing you to shoot with an open hand—which helps produce a better shot.

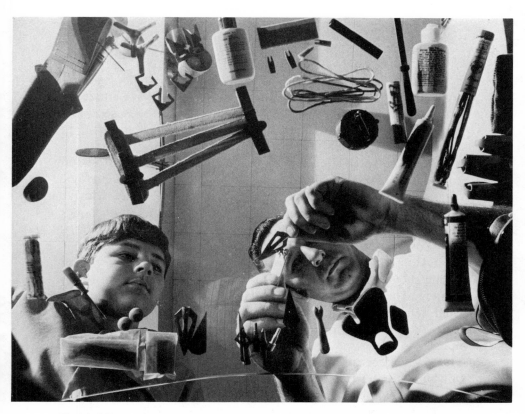

To be fully equipped, you should carry in a small belt pack the extra items shown here—spare string, nocks, silencers, brush nocks, arrow rest, file or stone, nock and fletch glue, extra tab, spare broadheads, scent. Standard material in your field pack will also include a knife, camouflage paint or grease, possibly a plastic bag to carry heart and liver, maybe a lightweight rain jacket and pruning clippers to help build an instant blind. Carry as much as you feel you need to be prepared for field repairs to your hunting gear, and also, to be equipped for sudden weather changes. Some hunters need a small backpack and/or belt pack, especially Western hunters who are more likely to encounter fast weather changes when hunting higher altitudes and when hunting farther from base camp.

Show him back quivers, bow quivers and hip/belt quivers. He can pick his own, but most guys use bow quivers because they protect arrows well and have them right out there, easy to grab for a second shot, if needed. Point out that it's highly recommended that broadheads on any quiver be covered and protected—for his sake, should he stumble or fall, and for the sake of broadhead sharpness.

Finally, buy a bowstringer—the best way to go until he's familiar with stringing, and maybe best afterward, too—and have him learn to string the bow. (Don't chuckle. "Hunters" have been seen in the woods with bows strung backwards and bows so powerful they couldn't unstring them.)

Now he should practice, practice, practice—from all shooting positions and elevations imaginable. Try targets, do some field roving, then some broadhead practice at game cutouts. Practice with your future partner. It's more fun this way, and you can tell him about the uniqueness of actual bowhunting.

Bowhunting is close work. Really close! The average shot is around 20 to 25 yards; plenty are made a lot closer. You try for definite killing shots because there's very little of the shock value of firearms hunting. There *is* some shock involved, but broadheads kill primarily from hemorrhage after cutting veins, arteries and other vital organs. And your follow-up methods are most likely quite different from anything he's known before.

As a general introduction, outline the three basic types of bowhunting—stalking, standing and organized driving. Tell him that if you and he will be in a large group, a drive may move the most game and be most successful. With small groups, standing or stalking or a combination of both may work best. And if he wants to hunt alone, standing is most certainly the best way for a beginning bowhunter to see and kill game.

If he prefers to try a couple of hunting methods, point out to him that standing in early morning and late afternoon when the game is feeding is a good way to hunt. Stalking or drives usually work best in midday when the game is lying up in cover.

Finding good game areas is a science unto itself, and more than you can reasonably be expected to outline now. If he's hunted before, he'll know this part—or should know it.

If your friend decides to take a stand along a good trail, help him set up. Suggest he measure distances from his stand to some of the most obvious shooting spots where game will appear. Walk the distance, try a couple of practice arrows. And do this as soon as you get him to his stand—you've already made some disturbance, so a couple minutes more won't hurt now and could easily mean the difference between kill and miss.

Remind him again that a broadhead kills by hemorrhaging, so it's important that he know exactly the vital spots on a game animal and shoot at them. He should try to let the animal walk past him so he has a quartering shot away.

This makes sense for two reasons. First, he'll get a clearer shot at the heart/lung area—the largest single vital unit on game. Second, there's always a certain amount of movement involved in drawing and shooting, so if the game is past him somewhat, his movement will less often be detected, and it will also be tougher for the game to jump the string. Make certain he realizes the importance of resharpening a broadhead that has rattled through some brush on a missed shot —resharpening it on the spot before he does another thing.

Make sure your new hunting partner fully understands the need for patience after he's hit game. A medium or large game animal must be given plenty of time to go off and lie down and lose blood. This can vary from half an hour to five hours depending on where the game is hit. (A good lung, heart, kidney, liver or major artery hit will have a deer dead within seconds, but it's best to wait and not take chances on spooking the animal.) Any relatively vital hit like the heart/lung area, kidney, or one of the major arteries can be trailed after 30 minutes to an hour. Wait the longest 4-8 hours on a gut shot deer because the animal loses strength slower, and the broadhead needs time to work in the animal. Trail leg hits immediately.

If your friend starts trailing the animal, he should first mark the spot where it disappeared from view. And then, if he kicks it out, he should know that it's best to stop and wait some more.

He should have studied the body hair of the game being hunted. The type of hair found can tell him where he hit the animal. He should also check other signs if he's uncertain where he hit the game. He should know how lung blood, heart blood and kidney blood differ and how blood mixed with stomach fluids looks. He should try to find the arrow and study the blood on it. He should check on the ground close to the trail and away from it and on bushes near the trail.

At the end of all this work, he should find a fine trophy bagged in fair chase on a good hunt. And he will fully realize the value of sharp broadheads; dull broadheads could easily mean the difference between a trophy and a wounded, escaped animal.

By this time, he also should know the basic safety factors of bowhunting. He should know that you don't climb trees or obstacles with exposed broadheads. He should also know his capabilities and the capabilities of the gear he's using. He should know the game he seeks, his state's laws and the rules and ways of sportsmanship.

Sure, some of this information is as basic as you can get. But it's valuable information.

It pays dividends to be well grounded in basic bowhunting skills. It pays you, me and every other person who hunts with a bow. A person with the intention of hunting with a bow owes it to himself and every other bowhunter to be correctly outfitted, well prepared, and sportsmanlike. And he owes it to the game, too.

BASICS OF BETTER SHOOTING

The steps shown here illustrate the classic archery shot—standing up straight, coming to full draw, checking your shooting form, aiming well and then releasing the arrow in the classical, picturesque manner.

This type of shot rarely happens in bowhunting. But you must know the fundamentals of the proper shot before you can advance to the twisted, turned, shoot-at-moment's-notice type of shots you'll often get in bowhunting. Knowing the proper basics helps you develop good shooting form and confidence—both of which you'll need to rely upon almost unconsciously at the moment of truth in the field. You'll be more assured of maximum performance from your hunting tackle and from yourself. And with good fundamental knowledge, your mind will be free to concentrate on the seeking and finding of game.

There's nothing as satisfying as getting the game in your sights and then coming through in the clutch. Your confidence swells. *You're a complete bowhunter!* How sweet it is.

1. Stance

   open stance
   feet apart, shoulder width
   weight divided evenly on both feet

2. Nock an Arrow

   double nocking point
   nock fits string snugly
   odd feather points away from bow

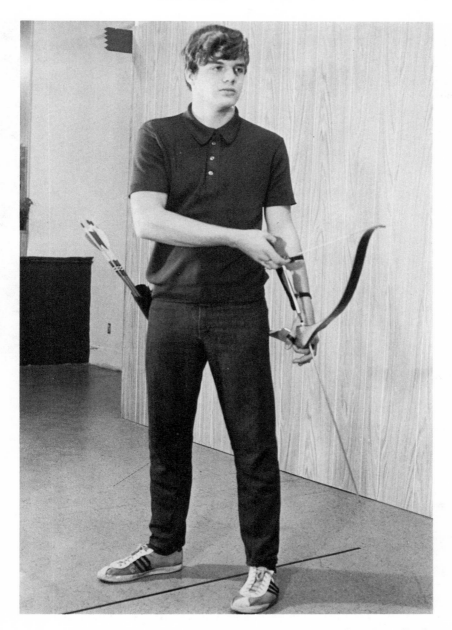

Your weight should be distributed evenly on both feet, bow firmly seated in the web between thumb and forefinger of your bow hand, string hand fingers hooked on the string near the first joint. You should begin concentrating on the target even before you begin to draw.

"Gap space" aiming looks like this before you draw. The closer the target the larger the gap; your first impression will be that you're aiming way below the target, but you won't be.

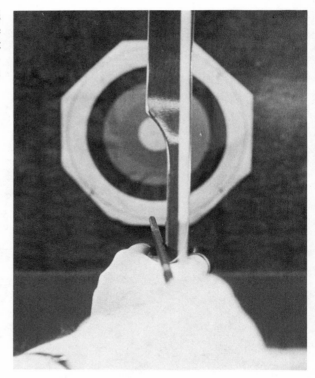

3. String Hand

> forms Boy Scout salute
> string DEEP in first crease of finger joints
> fingers curl around string, forming HOOK, turn tips of
>   fingers toward you
> keep back of hand straight with arm, relax wrist

4. Bow Hand/Bow Arm

> bow fits in V of index finger/thumb
> index finger/thumb form loose ring around bow handle
> bow held against muscular pad below thumb
> wrist, fingers relaxed
> turn bottom of bow arm elbow away from string and
>   hold elbow stiff (locked, if possible)

5. Head Up/Shoulders Back

> raise head to near vertical
> look at center of target
> bow handle in V, elbow turned out, string fingers hooked,
>   string held deep (this is the *unit*)

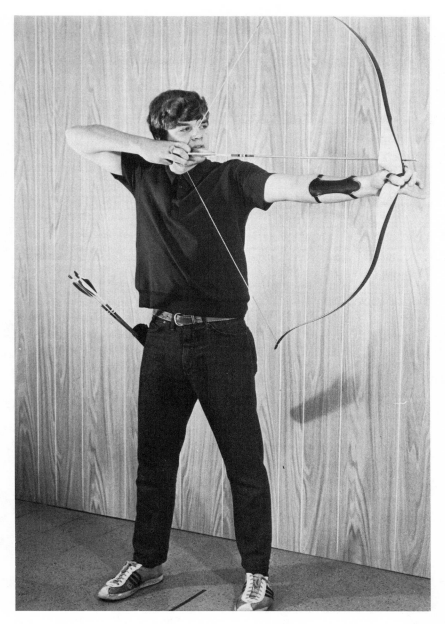

At full draw, your anchor should be solidly placed against a common reference point, such as the corner of your mouth or the base of your cheekbone. Your arms should basically be in line, shoulders level, bow shoulder locked down and away from the string to give better clearance, and bow elbow rotated out of the way of the string path. Your bow hand should grip the bow loosely. A firm grip will cause you to twist the bow upon release. Your bow hand wrist should also be in line with all other bone elements of your bow arm and should be firm enough so your bow hand can relax.

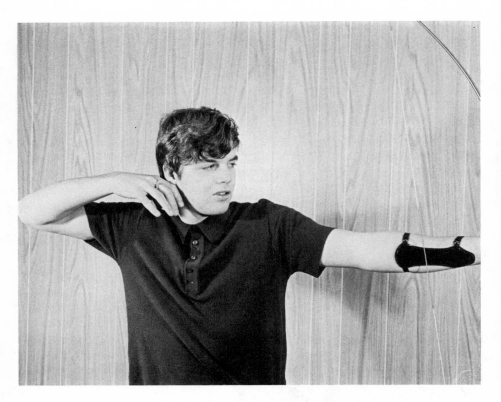

For most consistent aiming, release and follow through results—a more accurate shot—maintain proper tension in your drawing arm shoulder muscles and slightly increase back muscle tension to release. This will help relax the fingers on the string, and they will feel as if the string is going *through* them instead of rolling off the tips. This gives you a cleaner release. After you release, keep your bow arm up and your eyes on the target until the arrow hits. If you drop your bow arm, you'll shoot low.

6. Raise Unit/Pre-Draw Aim

   raise bow arm and draw arm to shoulder height

   Instinctive Aiming
   with both eyes open, position tip of arrow about 18″ below target
       center (using a 36-inch target face, standing 20-30′ from
       target)
   shift eyes to center of target; concentrate on *center* without mov-
       ing unit
   Sight Aiming
   place sight in middle of target and maintain general sight location

7. Full Draw/Side Anchor

   bow arm straight and locked, maintain pre-draw aim or sight
       position
   draw string by pulling with shoulder and back muscles
   pulling elbow slightly higher than shoulder
   to anchor, touch corner of mouth with index finger while thumb
       slides along and drops behind and under jaw

8. Hold and Aim

   bow pre-aimed, so concentrate on center of target, maintain sight
       position in center of target
   constant feeling of tension in drawing-arm shoulder and back
       muscles
   hold for slow count of "three"

9. Release

   eyes concentrating on center of target
   anchor firm along jaw
   start pulling shoulder blades together and elbow back
   as shoulder blades pull together and elbow back, relax string
       fingers

10. Follow Through

   eyes continue concentrating on center of target
   string fingers slide along jaw and touch side of neck
   bow arm remains in line with target
   hold follow through until hear arrow hit target

TAKE-DOWN HUNTING BOWS

Big question: I can only afford one bow; what's the best? *Answer:* Get
a bow that's more than one bow. Consider the take-down.

Take-downs have definitely arrived. They have been on the scene
for just a few years and have seen growing interest among target
shooters and hunters. Some of the impetus has come from manufacturers, some from shooters. In fact, quite a bit from shooters. Earl Hoyt,

whose standing in the archery ranks is renowned, explained it this way: "Demand from the market. People are traveling more. No question about it, the take-down has everything its way."

The take-down was an inevitable evolution for several reasons. (1) Archers forced this evolution because of their hunger for a multi-use bow design. (2) The diversity of limb combinations with a single handle that fits the archer made the old one-bow archer obsolete. (3) The compactness and portability of such a design were needed by the growing numbers of bowhunters on the move, not just within their own state, but from state to state and on longer special hunts involving a diversity of transportation—backpacking, camping, cycling, flying —all demanding compactness.

This style bow also has a bit of a building tradition about it. It can be (and is) a fine instrument that can be pridefully handed down from father to son the way family guns have been handed down and cherished.

This is a heritage factor that has never before existed in archery, mainly because the materials were neither as permanent as they are today nor as diverse. The bows should have the lifetime of a rifle because the new materials won't break down under long service.

For instance, the metal-handled riser or specially-processed wood riser is stronger, and the interchangeability of limb weights allows father and son to use the same basic handle for hunting, field and target work—lighter limbs for training and target, heavier limbs for hunting.

An added bonus to this take-down construction is the better dynamic balance created by heavier and stronger materials like vacuum-impregnated wood, ebonite or other composite materials and metal—which means it is no longer necessary to have a heavy handle (to control riser twisting). The bow can now be dynamically balanced where the weight does the most good during the shot—out on the ends of the riser. Handles can be thinner, too, and they're easier to hold and torque less. With the weight on the ends of the riser, vibrations from the shot come down the limb and are dissipated at the limb attachments, thus smoothing the shot and making the handle nearly vibration-free.

The other thing that has happened is that with the advent of the stronger, twist-free metal and special wood handles, centershot is no longer a problem. So the bows are much easier to set up and will shoot several arrow sizes, including the heavier arrows, without any special setups.

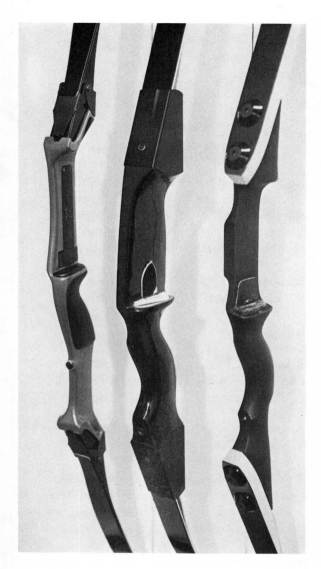

Various types of locking units of takedown bows. The left bow is a grooved unit with a hinged latch; middle bow simply has limbs sliding into a firm pocket; right bow employs two bolts on each limb attachment. Other systems include folding bows and a two-piece unit with metal teeth and a locking pin which comes apart just above the grip on the handle.

Actually, there are two basic concepts of these bows: take-apart and take-down.

The take-apart concept involves the use of special tools to attach the limbs to the handle and usually necessitates the use of Allen wrenches, box wrenches or a coin. This style of attachment takes longer to assemble and disassemble. The take-apart design is a positive attachment that allows the limbs to be changed with ease and the bow to be stored compactly, although you will find that on a day-to-day basis the archer will usually be using a long case to carry his bow.

The take-down bow has the same features as the take-apart—easy limb interchangeability, compactness of storage and positive limb attachment—but has the added feature of quick assembly and disassembly without the use of any tool. It can be taken down or set up in just a few seconds and is usually carried knocked down between shooting times.

Some models are drilled and tapped for bushings to accept hunting stabilizers, screw-in fish reels, hunting sights and quivers. On others you can mount a hunting quiver under the limb hookup bolts. A couple have broadhead cutouts so you can keep your hunting arrow length the same as your target arrow length. Some will also accept a pressure button.

Some have one standard riser length; others have two or three riser lengths. Some have optional grip styles, customized and standard; a couple of models have removable and interchangeable grips. All are available in the normal ranges of limb weights and lengths.

The details are too many to give in the space available here. Suffice it to say that when you start looking at take-downs, you're going to have enough goodies to choose from to keep you enjoyably occupied for quite a while.

COMPOUND HUNTING BOWS

James Dickey, in speaking of compounds, said the human mind is diabolical in what it can develop. He also agreed that compounds are basically ugly—although some new designs are trimmer—and they shoot like blazes. Dickey and countless other archers around the country are fascinated by them.

That fascination ought to grow, because the compound bow scene is changing and growing. There are new compounds being introduced by major manufacturers. The existing ones are slicking up, trimming down and doing something about that inherent ugliness.

But beauty wasn't uppermost in H.W. Allen's mind when he began fiddling with the idea of a bow working off a block-and-tackle effect in 1961 and 1962. "My son and I had missed a couple of deer and decided we wanted some kind of a bow that would give more foot-pounds of energy and more speed. I'm not a professional engineer, but I worked in engineering fields in World War II and the Korean War, and I decided to make use of what I knew.

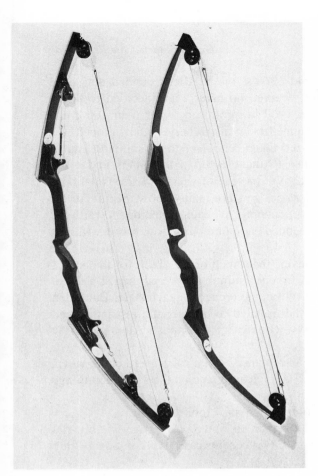

Latest trend in compound bows are the less expensive, stripped-down versions. They are lighter in weight and generally have fewer adjustments. Some models anchor the cables at the end of the limbs; others don't.

"We started working with concentric pulleys and sawed off recurves. In 1965, we went to eccentrics. As we progressed, we charted the stored foot-pounds of a compound against the stored foot-pounds of a recurve. We found that the compound because of shorter limbs had less limb inertia to worry about, and we could get the desired draw length and lightened anchor weight from the unwinding of the eccentric pulleys.

"And since you're holding less than the bow is delivering, this is why you can shoot a lighter arrow from the compound than you can from a recurve of equal draw weight. On the compound, the arrow is already in motion when the peak weight is reached, so there's not the sudden blast of released energy like there is on a recurve."

But all this was basically on paper and in the form of a couple of rough compounds in the mid-1960's, when Allen sounded out some archery manufacturers. He received no takers, and decided to begin producing them himself. In 1967 he produced fewer than 100 compounds. "And they were banned from all archery organizations."

Tom Jennings recognized the potential of the compound and in 1967 bought the first license to manufacture compounds under the Allen patent. He had been active for several years in various national and regional archery organizations and as a recurve bow manufacturer. He and Allen, working independently of each other but toward the same end, considerably expanded the compound bow scene within a couple of years.

They both say, however, that much of the credit for the acceptance of the compound bow, first as a hunting bow and then as a target bow, is due to the efforts of individual archers in each state. But Allen and Jennings also worked and traveled to counter the restriction and objections they encountered—Jennings more so than Allen—and the work paid off.

The compound gained acceptance, some rules were changed (in both directions, pro and con), the release came on the scene and things began to jell.

Is the compound as complicated as it looks?

"The compound can be tough to tune," Allen says, "but it's largely a matter of balancing the two eccentrics at the limb tips so they turn over at the same time.

"The adjustable pressure point helped ease tuning, too. The compound needs that and a strong flexible arrow rest to get that smooth arrow.

"Releases, of course, because of their crispness, eliminate string plucking and thus help remove almost all the force which creates arrow paradox.

"Those items, all put together, were what helped produce the shooting results you heard and read about. In the same manner, and for the same reasons these items also helped improve recurve performance."

There have been myths—that the compound could shoot absolutely flat at 100 yards, that the compound was 100 percent faster than recurves, that you could shoot a 100-pound bow yet hold only 20 pounds.

"The first two are absolutely untrue, and the third is totally impractical, at least at this time," Allen says. "You could get 50 percent relaxation, but you couldn't get a decent release. The string wouldn't have enough tension.

"All I was trying to develop was a bow that would get an arrow to a 10- to 25-yard target—a deer—before that target could move, with less physical discomfort and less practice for the archer."

You can get a compound to about 50 percent faster than a recurve of equal draw weight, but not with the same arrow and not with the same fletching. For instance, if you were to properly tune a 45-pound compound, with the hold weight at around 31-36 pounds (figure about 20 to 30 percent relaxation for most compounds), you would have an arrow spined for 31-36 pounds, and you'd be using a smaller plastic fletching that was attached straight and not offset—all these factors are recommended to minimize drag on the lighter arrow—then you could get 50 percent more speed.

The smaller fletching is also necessary to minimize contact with the arrow rest. This is why Allen feels that peg type or other solid projection rests are not as good as flexible rests on the compound. Smaller fletching is easier to stabilize a faster arrow without getting a parachute effect from the fletches.

Allen also believes that a properly tuned arrow would generally shoot best off a nocking point straight on or no more than ⅛-inch above 90° on the compound. But, as with all bow tuning, this depends on how you shoot as an individual.

Summing up, the critical points in tuning for speed are these: adequate tension in the anchor so you get a good crisp release; the right nocking point height; as small and as straight a fletching as possible; proper clearance between string and sight window so the arrow is pointed exactly straight ahead—especially with releases. All these things combined will minimize drag and paradox and maximize speed, stability and accuracy.

In target shooting, all this business about lighter arrows is fine. But what about the heavier hunting arrow?

"The extra foot-pounds will give added penetration and speed, but not the great speed of the target arrow," Allen says. "I believe a bowhunter would get best results with a compromise between the speed and the heavy arrow. Something in the 400-450 grain weight would give you a good fast arrow and still be heavy enough to give good penetration. If you go lighter than that, you're in danger of losing penetration."

Jennings adds, "Arrow spine and weight in target and hunting

uses depend a lot on the individual's archery form. The recommenda-
tions all compound manufacturers give for proper arrow/bow matching
are just rules of thumb. Archery is still a personal, individual thing;
your gear must fit you.''

Most common abuses of a compound bow come from trying to
make it do what it wasn't intended to do—like cranking a bow five or
10 pounds past its recommended limits for the eccentrics and limbs on
the bow or drawing it past the recommended draw length limit.

Most compounds of the original Allen design need thicker limbs
because the block-and-tackle principle produces a three-time reduction
in draw force. To get a 50-pound bow, you need limbs that are actually
150 pounds in resistance. This three-time principle is always in effect,
so shooters with different draw lengths and draw weights will need
different limbs.

The addition of ''speed brackets''—projections anchored at each
end of the handle riser, on which the cables are anchored—have moved
the cable pressure out from the base of the limb and thus somewhat
reduced the high stress on the limbs. Some manufacturers use these;
some don't.

When you change the size of the eccentric wheel to get a different
draw limit, you need to know whether or not you also need to change
limbs. The space here doesn't permit a critical look at the various
characteristics of each and every compound on the market, so when
you start comparing them, be aware of these factors and ask about
them.

One other point on draw weights and lengths: eccentrics merely
determine the limits; the final adjusting to your personal specifications
is done with turnbuckles or keys or whatever they may be called. If you
don't understand compound turning, *do not experiment*; consult an
expert. So to answer the question asked much earlier: Yes, compounds
can be complicated. But as you gain familiarity, they're less complex.

Most compounds are of the basic style, yet each has its own
modifications in plate attachments, eccentric design and mounting
style, handle design and material and finish, tuning systems, draw
length and weight adjustment limits, and available options (stabilizer
inserts, sight mounts, pressure-button drilling, arrow rests, number of
eccentric sizes and limbs available, and so on). A couple of models
have solid fiberglass hunting limbs available; the rest have wood/glass
laminated limbs. They all have target and hunting models.

Hunting models range from 48 to around 52 inches, axle to axle. At full draw, string angle is generally considered to be equal to a recurve 10 inches longer.

Many later entries to the compound bow scene have models with partial working recurves. They are generally trimmer than the original design and usually don't have cumbersome-looking side plates and fist-sized limb/handle attachment systems. (All manufacturers are working to bring down the physical weight of their compounds and make them easier for the hunter to carry all day.)

There are a few variations on the basic limb-and-cable design. One has four limbs—two working recurves and two fixed metal arms on which are anchored the recurves, with the kidney-shaped working cam at the tip of the metal support arm. This bow can be adjusted for a great variety of draw weights, 30 to 65 pounds, and different draw lengths by changing the settings of the cam. Thus, one bow fits all archers.

Another significant feature of this bow is the system of fitting the cables in the grooved metal handle and cam supports. Because of all this metal, the bow has a physical weight of 5½ pounds or slightly more. The bow also has a positive draw check in the cam/support limb arrangement—at full draw the cam hits a metal stop—so you cannot overdraw.

Other designs have taken the eccentrics from the limb tips and placed them at or near the ends of the handle section. This becomes a cam-type limb-lever. Some of these can be adjusted over a wide range of draw weights, and others are the normal 10-15 pound range. Some have a positive draw check system.

A few of these latter bows are longer than 52 inches, reaching almost to 60 inches.

The latest changes in the continuing evolution of the compound bow are less expensive models which don't have as many adjustable features as the earlier compounds.

They are priced in the $150-$170 range; the top-line compounds with all features generally are more than $200, reaching as high as $295. However, there are compounds in almost any price range from around $110 up to $300; so if you're looking at compounds, be sure to shop carefully and become knowledgeable enough to understand what you're looking at.

Main features in the new, less-adjustable compounds are, obviously, the lower price plus a general streamlining. Most will not have adjustable weights—you will buy a compound set up for 50 pounds, and that will be it. But it will have the letoff-at-full-draw feature of all compounds; in many instances these bows will have a letoff of 40 to 50 percent at full draw. Because of this increased letoff, they will store less energy and thus be somewhat slower than the more expensive models.

However, because they have few adjustments, they cannot get out of tune. As tuning is a big and often troublesome factor of the more adjustable compounds, this feature is highly desirable.

They will also have step eccentrics, with one groove smaller than the other. The small one acts as a partial replacement of the idler system on regular compounds.

They will have fewer working parts and very little hand finishing, thus helping to lower the cost. And because they are stripped down, they will also be lighter in physical weight.

Because they are generally non-adjustable and always tuned, they are also always in balance. You can place your bow hand below the grip, your draw hand several inches below the nocking point, and still have them draw smoothly.

The only way you will be able to change draw weights on most of these is by changing the eccentrics and cable system.

Probably one of the major design changes is the system of attaching the cables at the limb tips instead of at the ends of the handle section. This permits a more even stress flow over the limbs and helps them work more, a la the recurve limb. This places the cables closer to the bowstring, but the bows are cut far enough past center-shot so that there should be no problem getting arrow clearance.

What lies ahead in the evolution of compound bows? It's hard to tell, but some people are predicting there will be compound-like features of relaxed weight at full draw without the need of eccentrics and cables. Others predict that most major changes will appear in the region of higher letoff at full draw without decreasing the performance of the bow. Time will tell.

HUNTING BOW SIGHTS

You have wondered many times, and you have heard the question asked in a crowd, on the telephone or over the counter, "Does a sight

that stump and count your steps, 15 yards to that ditch, count it out, 42 yards up that hill, and so forth.

Shooting successfully with a bow sight means that you will have to think more than you did shooting instinctively, and you also will be shooting a little bit slower. Using a sight, I am convinced, can be practiced until it is very much the same as instinctive shooting—you will become proficient in judging distance quickly and then using the correct sight pin almost automatically. Besides judging distances, practice with your bow canted at varying angles because canting definitely changes where you'll hit.

There are quite a few aids on the market in the form of rangefinders and sights that have rangefinding qualities built in. Due to the rough treatment any equipment gets while we are hunting, the sight should be made of sturdy material, heavy enough to take the abuse. The windage and elevation adjustments should be held by a positive lock device that can't be moved when bumped on a tree limb or brush. Friction-held adjustments on a sight are a gamble that I don't want to take. Why spend time and money to go hunting and discover too late that your sight has been bumped and moved? I believe the sight should be solidly attached to the bow with screws. Taping the sight on a bow (except in an emergency) is not the most ideal way to go.

Saunders has a hunting sight that is self-adhesive and has a copper backing that bends to the contour of the bow and holds the adhesive in place. This works fine and won't come off; however, the sight pin adjustment is friction held. The Pro-Bo hunter sight is a good sturdy one with positive lock adjustments, as is the D/J and the Merrill. I find no fault with any of these for that reason. The Bear Premier hunting sight is unique because it is recessed into the handle riser at the sight window—which gets it out of the way. The sight pins are friction-held, but can be tightened up after sighting in for hunting purposes.

Another unique hunting sight is the one used on the old Golden Eagle hunting bow. This is a super positive arrangement because the sight pins are installed right through the aluminum handle riser in holes drilled and tapped to receive them. You have an adjustment for windage, but the elevation cannot be moved. They are about ⅝-inch apart and you, of course, must practice until you find at what distance they hit, then judge the yardages to fit them while hunting. Although this may sound complicated, it is not; you just may not be working on a 10-20-30-40-yard setting.

Several sight manufacturers have incorporated a distance-judging feature to help the bowhunter. These range-finding types, I think, are very workable. The reason a good many hunters think they are not is because they are too lazy to practice and think while using one. The Scanner sight, the Vee sight, the Range-o-matic and the Rain-Bow sight are a few that have rangefinding features that work.

The Rain-Bow sight rangefinding device, including the sighting pin adjustment and the body itself, is of good design and material and is a bulldog for punishment. It has a heavy plastic rangefinder with graduated black lines and colored dots. Using the principle that a deer's body fits into the space between the lines, you preset the pin (of the same color as the dot) at home by using a 16-inch square of cardboard to represent the chest area of the deer. Doing this for each graduated space and setting the corresponding colored pin so it hits the square of cardboard makes the unit ready for hunting. (One thing on colored pins—the fluorescent ones are easier to see in low morning and evening light.)

With patience and lots of practice you can become very efficient with any one of the sights on the market. Read the directions furnished and really give it a try. Sights on a hunting bow are not a new fad of today; they have been around for some time. Hugh Rich, that West Coast patriarch of hunting, fishing and archery wholesaling, had an adjustable hunting sight years ago that really worked for him. He had three distances: near, far and medium. Through trial and error, practice, guts and ingenuity he made his system work. He carried the sight set on medium at all times. When his animal was near he pushed it up; if it was far he pulled it down. All fine adjustments for in-between yardages were calibrated in his head. Traveling from state to state just hunting, Hugh scored many trophies using this method.

So don't tell me a sight on a hunting bow can't help a bowhunter. Try it—you'll like it!!!

OPTICS FOR BOWHUNTERS

There comes a time in the career of all successful bowhunters when they stop hunting just deer and start trophy hunting. At that time, if you haven't done so before, it's also time to make use of optics as a tool of the hunt.

It isn't difficult to mistake the animal in question if you've spotted it in the distance with the naked eye. But with the help of an extension of your power of vision, in one of several forms, you can avoid wasting time and effort making a stalk on a buck that proves to be a doe—or at least something less than you thought he was.

Consider, therefore, the inclusion of binoculars, a monocular or a spotting scope among your hunting equipment.

The terrain and vegetation will determine which optical aids you will need. There is a wide variety to fit all needs, from spotting scopes for Western hunting to the lighter units for more brushy areas and close-range work.

When you start thinking about buying binoculars, check specifications for them. There is a series of numbers and other details that you may not fully understand. The first number in the series, such as on a pair of 7×50 binoculars, indicates that glass has seven-power magnification. It will enlarge the image you view seven times the normal vision. This is probably the most popular and widely used magnification.

The second figure, the *50*, indicates that the objective lens will have a diameter of 50 millimeters. These two figures will vary according to the optics. For example, you might find 7×26, 8×30, 10×50 and so on. These figures all mean the same as in the above example —except that the powers of magnification and size of objective lenses are different.

The first urge is to purchase the most powerful glasses your budget can afford. This is often a sad mistake. It has been proven time and again that you can't hand hold a magnification over eight-power with success. You will have better success with the seven-power glasses for field use. Eight would be considered top, and if you do get a fantastic buy on a ten-power, you will need to carry a tripod or find a rock, tree or other support to be able to use this high-powered optic aid. When you increase power, you also increase all the little movements of the arms, natural breathing and any wind factor at the same time. Your viewing image will jiggle, and you will probably end up with a headache.

True, a six-, seven- or eight-power glass doesn't give as much magnification, but it won't give you problems in the field.

When you pick up a specification sheet on a pair of glasses, you will notice further statements such as "field of view of 375 feet at 1,000 yards." What this means is that the diameter of the circle you view will measure 375 feet across at the 1,000-yard distance. There are several schools of thought on the field of view. One says you should keep the field narrow and sweep the glasses back and forth to cover the area. The other advocates the wide-angle view that takes in more area from the same distance so you will see more in the same viewing time. For example, instead of a 375-foot field of view, you might have a wide-angle pair with 500 feet.

Here again the choice will be up to you. The proper way to use binoculars is not to scan rapidly, but to place the field on an area such as brush or a crossing and hold them in that position. Move the eye around that field of view checking for signs of your quarry. Don't look for a full-sized deer. You will usually find only an ear, a tine of an antler or merely a brown spot in the foliage. You would never find these sections of game with the naked eye, and only after you spooked them would you know they had been there. Or they could ease out as you approach, and you would never know.

The size of the objective lens—the large exposed glass in the front of the optics—can be important. If you plan to hunt at night for varmints, which is legal in some states, you will need the bigger objective lens such as the 50 mm. This is usually as big as you can buy. If you plan on day viewing while deer hunting, you won't need these bigger objectives. The smaller objectives won't gather as much light; the bigger the glass area, the more light-gathering power.

Another advantage of the smaller objectives is that the entire unit can be constructed much more compactly. To an archer this is important since the last thing you want is to have the bowstring snag on the field glasses as you shoot.

When it comes to compactness, the single tube or monocular is hard to beat. They don't give as wide a field of view, and you use only one eye instead of two which means movement is hard to control. But they are the most compact of the optics in the store. Also, the price of monoculars is accordingly lower than the two-lensed units. This is a factor many consider. There are monocular units on the market that strap on the wrist. When you want to view an area, all you do is bring up the arm, place the eyeball to the exit pupil, and you have instant image-enlargement.

Depending on how serious you are about quality trophy hunting and quality optics, you may want to buy the best on the market. You may prefer to stay with the binocular style, or you might prefer to move one step higher in viewing ability to the spotting scope. These, again, are available in various sizes and powers. Some scopes now on the market have electric power zoom to bring the object in closer after you locate it at a lower power setting. Power zooms are quiet and efficient, but most have no manual override. If you hunt in very cold areas, the electric power system drops drastically in efficiency as the temperature drops. Consider this before you buy one.

The more common and, some say, the more trustworthy units have one size objective lens and a selection of exit lenses to increase or decrease the power of the unit. You could carry two objectives, one of

20-power and another of higher power such as 30- or even 40-power. If you are scanning a new area you might prefer the lower power for a wider field of view. If you spot something that looks promising, you can quickly and easily change the eyepiece to the higher power and really check the game.

The biggest disadvantage of the spotting scope is the bulkiness of the unit. You can, however, buy or make a carrying case to sling over the shoulder so it causes no problem moving through an area and is still reasonably accessible for use. You also need a form of support when using these higher-powered units. The scope usually is purchased with a small folding tripod that will carry easily. Or you can lie down on a rock, rest the scope on your hat and scan an area. The spotting scope is bulkier and must be rock steady in use, but if you are after a Pope and Young rack, this unit will save you many hours of working in on a bedded buck to find he is too small.

Prices on optics will vary. You'll be able to understand this price variance if you pick up a pair of $20 binoculars and, looking through them, see a double image—one for each objective lens. These two circles will never come together. If you pick up a $50 or $100 pair, you will be able to bring both circles together into one large, evenly-illuminated circle. This is easier on the eyes and will prevent eye fatigue and headaches.

Monoculars are the least expensive units since there is less material used in manufacture. The spotting scopes will be higher priced, up among the better binocular prices and higher. You get good optics only if you pay for them. One method of checking optics is to see if you obtain a reddish ring along the edges of the field of view. If you do, beware of these glasses.

When I first started bowhunting, optics weren't considered necessary. Then javelina hunting became a seasonal jaunt and optics became important since the grey ghosts are hard to find any time. I purchased a pair of surplus 7×50 glasses and they saw plenty of abuse during the ensuing years. They are big, bulky and cumbersome—but they give a bright, even image with no red halos and have never produced headaches.

After a few years of bowhunting, the compact 7×26 Bushnell Custom Compact replaced the old glasses, and it has proven an excellent choice. It can be placed inside the front of the hunting shirt, will not catch the bowstring and offers no problem in carrying. The Bushnell Custom Compact is another excellent light piece that carries easily inside your shirt.

The urge to bust a big one has also taken hold, so I added a Bushnell Sentry II spotting scope to my optics locker. This has two exit lenses, one of 20-power and another of 32-power for tighter viewing.

I also tested—and found adequate—the small monocular wrist unit made by Ranging Inc., called the Wristscope. It is a 6×18 monocular, easily straps to the wrist and works nicely in thick brush where other optics are handicapped.

Another item to check is the Bushnell Expo model, an 8×30 binocular made with a fiberglass body. It's waterproof and floats. Great for the rainy season.

The addition of a pair of field glasses or other optics will add enjoyment to your hunting. You will be able to see more game—and pick and choose if you are a trophy hunter.

Buy glasses that fit your budget or, better yet, stretch the budget and obtain a pair of good glasses which will last for many years with no problems. Optics should be a basic field unit for bowhunters. They not only give you extra vision, but also improve your chances for success.

Ten Things to Look For in Binoculars

Compare brands and types. Take your time. As prices increase, you'll get better lenses, better prisms with better installation, improved lens coating, better hinges and mechanisms, improved sealing, better cases and sometimes lighter weight.

- Size, power, field of view.
- Brightness—the higher the ''exit pupil'' or ''twilight factor'' number, the greater the brightness.
- Image quality.
- Alignment—proper alignment will eliminate headaches and double images.
- Workmanship—lenses well clamped, nothing loose inside; swing barrels on hinge to check smooth, but firm, movement.
- Focusing mechanism—rotate firm and smooth; roughness or looseness means poor moisture protection and quick wearing.
- Lens coating—coating reduces glare and reflections and transmits more light. Catch a white fluorescent tube in eyepiece and objective; coated optical surfaces will reflect amber, blue or magenta, uncoated will reflect white.

- Feel—controls convenient, grip and viewing comfortable, balance good.
- Special features—things like retracting eyecups, fast focusing, variable magnification must be useful, not just gadgets.
- Maker and dealer—pick a dealer that will let you try before buying. Check guarantees in terms of repair and replacement and service length of the optic.

NOWHERE WITHOUT FOOTWEAR

My three Plott hounds were telling me in no uncertain terms that they finally had put an end to the three hour bobcat chase and had Mr. Bobtail where he wasn't going any farther. The dogs had worked hard during the three preceding hours, cold trailing the cat for two and a half hours before finally jumping it from a rock pile where it had laid up for the day. The four inches of nice fresh snow that had fallen the night before made trailing the cat fairly easy, but any time you work a bobcat in the rocks you have problems.

I had been plodding along with my bow, following dog and cat tracks all this time, and the racket of them treeing a half-mile up the canyon was a welcome sound. The snow on the ground was great for holding the round cat tracks and scent for the dogs to run, but it made things a bit treacherous for me to follow them. I was about 200 yards below the dogs and could see them bawling and raising havoc around the base of a large, gnarled old juniper tree where they had treed the cat. All I had to do was cross a small, snowcovered rockslide and go up a little ridge, and I would have a nice cat pelt for my den wall.

I hadn't gone 20 yards across the rock slide when my pacs slipped on a snowcovered rock and I jammed my foot, topped by all 210 pounds of me, down between two jagged rocks. Luckily, I hadn't broken my ankle, but I had two very large and painful bruises on both sides of my ankle. This little mishap certainly took the fun out of that particular hunt, and even though I got a nice trophy for my wall, the walk back was anything but fun.

This little episode points out one thing—there is no one piece of footgear on the market yet that will fill all of a bowhunter's needs.

That morning while I was getting dressed, I was trying to decide which pair of boots to wear hunting. I had a pair of Reiker mountain climbing boots that were great in the rocks, as they are fully padded and give your foot and ankle full protection from rock bruises and twisting. Unfortunately, they only come slightly above the ankle and I would have had to wear something to keep the snow from getting down into the tops of them. I chose instead a pair of leather-topped, rubber-bottom, 12-inch pacs that I knew would keep my feet warm and dry and would be comfortable over a long haul. If I had worn the climbing boots I would not have bruised my ankle, but instead would probably have come down with pneumonia from wet feet before the day was over.

The old saw about an army traveling on its stomach is so much hogwash. I spent a couple of years as one of Uncle's beetlecrushers, and on any long jaunt we lost about a third of the guys due to sore feet. You can go a long way on an empty belly, but you can't make it across the road on a pair of blistered and sore feet.

To a bowhunter, picking the proper footgear for his type of hunting could be far more important than choosing a bow or arrows. A bowhunter planning a trip for moose would be in sad shape with a pair of tennis shoes, and by the same token, a hunter headed for a south Texas deer hunt would feel pretty uncomfortable in hip boots.

If a bowhunter will just spend as much time picking out his footwear as he does selecting his other equipment, he will find that he can enjoy his hunts far more. Perhaps it will even make him a better hunter.

As I said earlier, I don't believe there is one type of footgear on the market that will serve all the needs that a bowhunter might have. If a bowhunter is a specialist and hunts only one area and one type of game and uses only one method of hunting, perhaps this would be possible. There certainly aren't many of us who fall into that classification.

Take a hunt to Alaska or Canada, for example, where you are going to pack in on horseback and try for sheep or goats and maybe a moose or grizzly. This type of trip should be planned at least a year in advance—which gives you plenty of time to not only select the proper footgear, but also time to have them properly broken in long before you leave.

For a good hint as to the type of footwear to select on any such outing, take a good look at the critters you are going after. Each animal has its own unique type of footgear and tread design. A sheep or goat's feet are designed to keep it from slipping in the rocky terrain it calls home. A moose or caribou's wide-splayed hooves help them traverse the bogs and tundra that they like so well.

It would indeed be foolish to think you could get around well in a mountain goat's habitat with a pair of slick, crepe- or leather-soled hunting boots. True, you could possibly make it, as I am sure many have done, but it would be a darn sight easier and more comfortable—not to mention safer—if you had on a good set of vibram-soled hunting or climbing boots. This same set of boots wouldn't be worth a darn for stalking a big old bull moose in the middle of some alder and willow swamp where every step you take is going to carry you ankle- to knee-deep in the mire and muck. True again, you can do it with the same footgear but how much easier and drier it would be with a good pair of proper fitting, lightweight hip boots.

So now that you have the proper footgear for stalking the game, how about while going to and from camp on horseback? Oh, you can get by just fine with your lug-soled climbing boots or even a pair of hip boots stuck in a stirrup, you say. Well you had better hope that old nag they gave you is just that and doesn't have a jump left in her. Were she to unseat you, chances are you would find yourself hung by a set of lug soles tenaciously holding your foot in the stirrup, while you were being dragged along near the horse's hooves—not at all the best place to watch a spooked horse from, let me tell you! It would be much easier to wear a decent set of slick-soled western boots or even Wellingtons while in the saddle and carry your hunting boots in a saddle bag or tied to the saddle horn until you need them. It's much safer and not enough extra trouble to warrant griping about, and I guarantee you will feel much better for it at the end of a day's hunting.

I recall a guide who took several friends of mine after bighorn sheep high in the Colorado Rockies. They all started out from camp wearing western boots and on horseback looking for a good spot to glass for sheep. Both hunters carried good lightweight lug-soled hunting boots with them. When they tied up the horses and started hunting in earnest on foot, of course, the guide had to accompany them also on foot—but in his western boots. After several hours of rock climbing and hiking over the rocky terrain, glassing likely looking sheep habitat, the hunters had to give it up and help the guide back to his horse. His feet were so blistered and sore he could hardly walk. I'll bet he is one guide who will either invest in a good pair of hiking boots to carry with him or quit taking crazy sheep hunters out.

Even though there is no one boot on the market that will adequately fill the bill in all types of terrain and hunting situations, there are many excellent boots being made today, a combination of which should prepare you for anything.

The hunting boot for general bowhunting is the one most of us are going to use most often. It's a good boot for all-around hunting. First off, it must be made of leather that is tough enough to withstand the hard miles you are going to put on it. If you do much hunting in the south, it must withstand cactus spines and other such niceties as well. It must at the same time be light enough so all-day jaunts after cottontails don't leave you feeling you have five pounds of lead on each foot. The sole of this boot should be suited to the type of terrain you most often hunt and should be soft enough to provide you with a "feeling" foot so you can avoid breaking branches and twigs and otherwise making your presence known to your quarry.

My personal preference for this boot is one made of Kangaroo or other tough ultra-light leather with speed laces and soft, thin vibram soles. These boots are tough and will give you many hours of comfortable footslogging. And they will last a long time if you take care of them.

If I am going into rockier terrain, I want a good, heavy pair of hiking boots, also with vibram soles. This time, heavy, stiff soles give me the footing I need in the rocks.

Often, for general still hunting and stalking, I will use a pair of tennis shoes. This is probably the quietest type of footwear available. I have a good friend who carries a pair of leather moccasins with him to wear when it really gets down to the nitty gritty. These are fine if your feet are in shape, but they can be pure murder on tender tootsies.

If you do lots of winter hunting you are going to have to get some footwear that will protect your feet and keep them dry as well. I have tried all sorts of winter footwear and finally settled on a pair of leather-topped, rubber-bottom pacs. These are not insulated, as I don't have too much of a problem keeping my feet warm. If you do lots of sitting, the ideal boot for winter is one of the newer types with full felt liners. They will keep your feet toasty warm and dry in the coldest weather. The only disadvantage to them is that they are fairly bulky and heavy for much long-distance walking. I would suggest getting several felt liners; you can always start out with a warm, dry pair in the morning while you let the previous day's pair dry at camp. These boots are great if you are using a snowmobile, and are much better for all-around use than the regular snowmobile boot, which has a nylon upper and rubber bottom.

The pacs and felt-lined boots both make an excellent boot to use with snowshoes, although I still prefer the pacs for their lighter weight. I also have a loop sewn onto my boots just above the rubber bottom. This loop is to put a strap through from my snowshoes and keeps the strap from slipping up or down. This can also be done on all rubber boots by simply having the service station vulcanize the loop onto the back of the boot.

Earlier I mentioned that there are times when it is necessary to wear a pair of hip boots as your main footgear. Hip boots are difficult to get used to and can cause some real problems if you do not have a pair that fit properly. Hunters that are relatively careful about buying good, proper fitting footgear are apt to just walk in and buy any old pair of hip boots for their trip north. When selecting a pair of such boots, make sure they fit you well around the ankles and foot. If anything, get them on the snug side, as walking through mud and tundra will pull off loose fitting ones. There is nothing worse than to be hopping around a bog on one foot, trying to pull your other hip boot out of the mud.

Once you have decided on the type of boot, then comes the choice of getting the right size. Many people advocate getting your hunting boots a size larger than your regular shoe. The theory behind this being that your feet will swell during your hiking and the boots will fit better. My suggestion is to get the boots to fit exactly and get your feet and legs in shape *before* you take to the woods. I have a good friend who has a pair of lead-shot-filled spats similar to those that football and track men wear to get their legs strengthened. He puts these on six months ahead of hunting season and wears them all day long under his trousers to condition his legs so that when he puts on his hunting boots his legs are already used to the weight.

Once you have the boots, the next step is to break them in to fit your feet. This can be done by wearing them for a month or so with the same weight and kind of socks you will be wearing while hunting, or it can be done much more easily by the following method. (This was told to me by an old German cobbler who specialized in mountaineering and ski boots, many of which he handmade.)

Take the new boots and fill them full of hot (not boiling) water and let them stand for five full minutes. At the end of five minutes, dump the water out and turn them upside down over a broom handle or stick to drain for another five minutes. When they are drained, put them on over the same type and weight socks you will wear hunting and wear the boots for four to eight hours or until they are dry. If you do not want wet feet, put a baggie or some very thin plastic over your socks to keep your feet dry. Needless to say, this method is for leather boots only; it works on insulated as well as uninsulated ones. When the boots are dry, give them a good coating of some waterproofing compound and you have a pair of boots that will fit your foot perfectly.

Before I get into the proper care of your boots, I think a word should be said on the proper care of the feet that you put into those boots. This is often sadly neglected by even the best woodsmen. It is foolish to spend good money on a pair of boots, then try to get by with old, worn-out dress socks because you know that after a hunt or two they are going to be thrown out anyway. They put everything but the kitchen sink into material for socks nowadays but still haven't come up with anything that compares to *wool*. A wool sock will, no matter how wet it gets, still stay warm. The most important thing you can have is warm feet. I have several pairs of hand knit virgin wool socks that set me back about $6 a pair five years ago. They get many a mile put on them each year and still look like they just came off the store shelf. For most of my hunting I wear a light-weight cotton sock under my wool ones even in fairly warm climates and have yet to get a blister or have sore feet from all-day hunting.

It is a good idea to carry along several changes of socks. When you sit down for a rest, you can put on a dry pair, and when you get to camp in the evening, you always have a nice dry pair of socks to put on.

When I turn in at night, if I am sleeping out, I always put my socks under my sleeping bag, between the bag and the mattress. In the morning they are dry and warm. Nothing is as discouraging as having to put on wet socks first thing in the morning. It is a good idea to also throw into your duffel a pair of fleece-lined or similar type of slipper to loaf around camp in. These will give you a chance to dry out your boots if they get wet. And your feet will feel better if you change socks and footgear as soon as you get back to camp.

Taking proper care of your boots is almost as important as getting the right fit and selecting the proper boot. The leather in boots, if not properly treated, will dry and crack and lose its water resistance in a very short time. I have tried most of the boot dressings on the market. I used to think that plain old neatsfoot oil was about the best, but thanks again to the old German cobbler, I have found something that will waterproof the leather and make it pliable, yet not soften it too much. This stuff is called Sno-Seal and is more of a wax than an oil. It contains silicone for preservation of the leather.

To get a complete job of waterproofing, I warm the boots over the stove until they are warm enough to melt the Sno-Seal, then I work this semi-solid wax into the leather, holding them near enough to the heat to keep them warm but not close enough to scorch the leather. When they won't absorb any more, I rub off the excess and they are ready for a winter of hard use. If they start to show scuffing, a light coat of this stuff well rubbed in will have them looking like new in no time.

A good way to judge a bowhunter is not by the trophies he has on the wall or by the fancy bows and arrows he has in his den, but rather by the type, kind and shape of his hunting footgear. The bowhunter can take a lesson from the animals he goes into the woods after. Never has there been an animal of any sort in the woods, mountains or desert without the proper footgear to make his goings and comings as easy and comfortable as possible. Why should a bowhunter be any different?

WHY WOMEN HUNT, AND HOW THEY SHOULD BEGIN

There probably are few women married to bowhunters who have not been invited to go along on a hunt. There are dozens of reasons *why* he'll ask you: Maybe some other guy was bragging about his wife's hunting enthusiasm, maybe he would like someone along who can do something with a hamburger other than make a burnt offering of it, or maybe he's feeling guilty about leaving you at home so much.

Whatever his reasons, why didn't you go?

I can guess; I've heard all the excuses. You say you can't shoot a bow. You're afraid of the woods. You have too much work to do. You don't want to leave the kids. And always: you don't think you could shoot one of those beautiful animals.

Now listen to some reasons why you should go. The most impor-

Not all women enjoy hunting, but those who do find it more enjoyable when they are fully accepted as a member of the hunting party and not treated as a fragile quasi-guest.

tant is that he asked you. If your husband really wants you to go along, he'll help you adapt. He's asking you to share something he really enjoys. He is showing you he is proud to be married to a woman who will do some of the things he likes. He's letting you know he respects you as an individual as well as a homemaker. And that's important.

It isn't feminine? Be honest; there were times, years ago, when it wasn't ladylike to play tennis, go to a movie or get a sun tan. Why should it be unladylike to fish or hunt?

Excuses are just that—excuses. You ought to at least be willing to give it a try.

It's true, most women are not hunting- or woods-oriented. The scene is almost totally foreign and somewhat frightening. There are monsters lurking behind every tree, right? Everything unfamiliar is scary.

So how about going along with another couple, or several couples? You and your husband already have friends who hunt, or the husbands do. It obviously helps if the women have some similar interests. You will be together, talking and feeling that you're sharing part of the hunting trip.

If you're not ready to camp out, stay at a resort or a motel near the hunting area. A cabin is even nicer because you can settle down and relax by the fireplace, have a couple of drinks, tell stories—and listen to your husbands tell their hunting stories—and just make it a joy to be away from home for a weekend.

A motel room generally has a television, and that one-eyed electronic monster can ruin the whole reason you're away for the weekend—to have a change of pace.

If you won't be doing your own cooking, set aside some money for a restaurant breakfast and supper, with sandwiches in between.

If you don't want to get up before dawn to go into the woods, sleep in. You're here to learn about the total aspects of bowhunting —the fun of sharing experiences, of getting excited over something besides the problem with the bank account, of relaxing during the evening and recounting what you saw and did during the day—whether or not you were hunting.

These are the elements of hunting, too. Not just the bagging of a deer.

Okay, now you've become partially familiar with bowhunting trips. What about going into the woods?

You're not ready to hunt, not just yet? So don't hunt. There are plenty of things to see and do. The woods are alive with interesting wildlife and flowers and things.

You can start by going with your husband on a midday scouting trip. Or go for a drive and look for deer; just seeing one is exciting!

You and your husband can build a blind within walking distance of the cabin, maybe overlooking a field where you will have a good chance of seeing a deer. Even if you see a deer 100 yards away, you're thrilled. And *you'll* have something to talk about when you get back to camp; you won't have to just listen to everyone else.

By remaining within walking distance of the camp, you can walk back and not disturb anyone else's hunting if you get tired of sitting or you get cold.

Don't let your husband drop you off in some thickly wooded area where you can't see more than a few yards. You'll feel cooped up if you're not used to the woods. Who wants to be cooped up in the woods when you've been cooped up in the house all week? And if you're not familiar with all the sounds and rustlings of a woods on an autumn afternoon, you'll not enjoy them because they'll be strange and somewhat unnerving.

But while you're sitting in that blind, you *will* learn of the wildlife. You will see and hear squirrels, chipmunks, raccoons, songbirds, maybe a grouse and maybe even deer. You'll soon learn that the noisy ones *aren't* the deer and that the quieter you can sit in a blind or walk in the woods, the better are your chances of actually seeing deer.

On that midday walk, how about collecting flowers to dry, or looking for edible mushrooms, or identifying and counting songbirds? This is a great way to become familiar with the woods—learning that there is no rational reason to be frightened.

You really would like to try bowhunting? If you're at this stage, you should already have done several things to prepare for it.

You should have begun with the proper bow and other tackle, a bow that *you* can draw—not his old discarded hunting bow—and arrows of the proper weight and length *for you*. Start with a light target bow (probably around 20 pounds of draw weight) and practice on targets. Most women do not have the strength to draw more than that at first. But as you practice and learn proper shooting form you will also gain strength. Then move up in bow weight.

Begin your shooting with a *qualified* instructor, if at all possible. Three or four lessons should get you started properly; if you want to continue lessons, fine.

Do your practicing at 10-15 yards. You want to be close enough to hit the target regularly—it's more fun that way. And you will spend less time looking for missed arrows than if you were shooting at a target 50 yards away.

While you are practicing at this close range, your husband should also practice at this distance, polishing his shooting form or maybe trying a new technique he has seen.

As you develop the strength to shoot a hunting-weight bow, check your state laws. Some states have a minimum bow weight specification for hunting. Even if your state does not have a minimum-weight law, you should practice until you can shoot a 35-40 pound bow. This bow weight is about the minimum for effective arrow penetration in most types of shots.

The compound bow is a boon to women and youths; it allows you to shoot a heavier bow with less holding weight than a recurve of similar peak-draw weight.

Now that you have practiced until you are skilled with a hunting-weight bow, read up on the laws of the area you will be hunting. Read about the animal or animals you will be hunting. There are lots of books and magazines telling how to hunt everything from squirrels to elephants. And listen to your husband and his friends. There isn't a hunter alive who can resist talking about it. That's because it really is that exciting. Ask questions, too.

As you continue, you will hear the funniest and wildest tales ever told. It's not just killing your trophy that makes hunting exciting. It is also being there in the woods and the anticipation of waiting, then the thrill of seeing and, with luck, shooting your game. Even a miss can be the thrill for seasons to come.

As you begin hunting, you will probably want to be relatively close to your husband, maybe in a blind a few hundred yards away. When you're building those blinds, help him. Study how a good blind is built and where it is built. Walk with him as he scouts; learn what deer or other game sign to look for. You'll enjoy the woods and the hunt more.

Along with all the proper hunting equipment, you must have the right clothing. If the weather gets rough, it will be a great temptation to chuck it all and stay in bed the next morning. It will depend on what, when and where you are hunting.

During deer season I find it handy to have plenty of thermal knit clothing and even a pair of battery-heated socks and good insulated boots for the really cold days. Sitting still for a long time slows your blood circulation, and you can get awfully cold.

I got so cold one morning I swore I would never go hunting again. I meant it. But that was about ten minutes before I got my first shot at a deer. A buck, at that. I missed, but it was so exciting I spent the next couple of days in even colder weather trying to find that deer again. I never regretted another minute of hunting, no matter how cold or tired I got, because I knew someday I would get another chance.

Buy your own hunting clothing; don't expect to borrow clothing because you're "only going out for a little while." You don't have to look like a queen or a tramp. Buy men's thermal underwear; they are of better quality material and better workmanship than women's thermal clothing. They also will fit more loosely than women's clothing and will be more warm. Some women wear pantyhose under all this for added warmth.

Wear layers of loose clothing. If you get warm, take off a layer. Don't wear bulky clothing if you can avoid it; it usually is noisy and constricts your movement at the critical time to shoot.

Boots must be *comfortable* as well as warm. Wear a light cotton sock next to your skin and a heavier wool sock over that. Have enough room to wiggle your toes freely; anything tighter than this will get you cold in a hurry.

Wear warm mittens and/or gloves. A hand warmer in a coat pocket will keep your shooting hand warm, but won't inhibit the touch when you must shoot. You bow hand must also be warm, but you should not have such a bulky mitten on it that you lose the feel of the bow. If your bow has a metal handle, wrap some thin foam packing around it or cover it with leather. This will help keep your hand warm.

If you're still a bit leery about hunting on the ground, where something *might* get at you, try a tree stand. It is the best way to see and get a shot because the tree stand lifts you above the game's eye level and lessens the chance of your being seen or smelled. If it is difficult to climb a tree, try one of the climbing tree stands. I have one, and it takes only a little practice to become skilled at it. Just be sure you're safe; tying yourself in loosely with a small rope will help. Just loop it around the tree and your waist.

Carry a compass and flashlight, just to reassure yourself. Be prepared.

If you think you could never actually shoot an animal, don't worry about that until the time comes. Enjoy the hunt. After hunting a while, I don't think you will feel totally hesitant. It is much more cruel to see animals starving from lack of food during the winter—and few people would argue about the meat being welcome. Hunting is a real challenge; it is placing yourself totally in the game's home ground and seeing whether you are equal to a challenge. Respect the game. Get to know its behavior, where it lives and doesn't live. We are part of the same biologically governed factors that control animal populations. We are important individuals, but we are also only a small part of the entire scene. We have only so much living space and so much food; it is the same with game. Some will be taken so others may live healthily.

True, there may be a misty, guilty feeling about taking a game animal. But if you know the total scene and respect the game as did the Indians—who spoke to the game they took for food after it was taken, acknowledging its position and the interrelationships of each—then you will have gained an understanding of the subtleties of hunting.

No matter with what intensity you hunt, once you begin to learn and understand more of Mother Nature and how she works, you will never get bored. Couple that with the fact that the unexpected, the unprogrammed, is usually what occurs. There are a lot of people telling you how to hunt, when to shoot, where to shoot. The truth is, when your moment comes, it takes a lot of skill and a lot of luck. Some people hunt miles from home and end up taking their deer almost in their backyard. Others practice and practice, figure they have it down cold, and then at the moment of truth get so excited they miss an "easy" shot. Given the capacity with which humans can get excited, there are no easy shots in bowhunting. And you might fill your tag in the last minutes of the season as you walk back to camp, when it all seems over for another year.

Whatever it is, you will enjoy telling about it for seasons. Bowhunting is like nothing else, an experience you and your husband will enjoy—and enjoy remembering—for years.

YOU ARE THE KEY TO BOWHUNTING SAFETY

As with any form of hunting, bowhunting safety is mainly common sense and a knowledge of your equipment. First, seek competent bowhunting and archery instruction. Then always inspect bow, arrows and string before shooting; damaged equipment is dangerous. And remember that a bow's range is 100 to 200 yards, but its effective range is much shorter (most deer shot with a bow are closer than 25 yards). When you're hunting, horseplay is out! Most accidents occur from foolishness, carelessness or a lack of knowledge about archery equipment. Above all, maintain the high ethics of sportsmanship already established by competent bowhunters. Bowhunting has long been a challenging sport; it's up to you to keep it a safe sport.

The Bow

- Use a bow stringer. It's more secure and won't twist limbs.
- Leaning on the tip of a strung bow can unstring it—with disastrous results. There is nothing more embarrassing than having a string come off as a large buck strolls by offering a good shot.
- Never draw or release a bow without an arrow; never overdraw a short bow; never draw another man's bow without his permission. These all lead to overdrawing and bow breakage.
- Have arrows that match your draw length; too short arrows allow overdrawing and cut your bow hand. (Tip: broadheads with major blade mounted horizontally will be away from index finger at full draw.) Arrows too long result in a big loss in speed and accuracy.
- A bow with a nocked arrow is a weapon as potentially dangerous as a loaded firearm: treat it with the same respect.

The Arrows

- Never shoot arrows straight up; they tend to come straight back down.
- Don't run with an arrow on a bow; don't cross fences with an arrow on a bow; don't have an arrow on a bow in camp or when not hunting.
- Be sure of your target; never point an arrow at anything you don't intend to shoot.
- Always be extra cautious when handling broadheads; a slip can cut you or a bowstring, damaging you and the bow.
- Re-check arrows each time after shooting for cracks, loose nocks, fletches or broadheads for dullness. (Tip: Always touch up a broadhead after it is shot.)
- Always carry broadheads in a quiver with protection over the head, should you fall or stumble.

Hunting

- Be careful stalking game in heavily hunted areas; if you are properly camouflaged and moving right you will be hard to see and may sound like a deer.
- Be careful when climbing trees; bark is slippery in mornings and during snow or rain.
- Use a rope to lift bow, arrows and other gear up to or down from elevated stands; never carry tackle in your hand while climbing.
- Tie a safety rope around yourself in a tree stand or elevated blind; it is possible to fall asleep and fall out.

- Approach wounded game cautiously. Even a "harmless" animal may charge or strike out with hooves or antlers.
- If you suspect the broadhead is in the body cavity, be careful when cleaning game.

Woodsmanship

- Mark the trail when tracking game so you don't get lost.
- Acquaint yourself with the area you'll hunt; carry maps; carry a compass and know how to use it.
- Carry matches and a survival kit in big country and/or unfamiliar country.
- Carry a small first-aid kit with adequate bandages, compress and tourniquet.
- In big country like desert or mountain, look behind frequently so you'll know what landmarks to sight when coming out.
- Should you become lost, don't panic. Sit down and think, then climb a tree or to high ground to note landmarks before trying to find your way out.
- Be sure you're in good enough physical condition for plenty of walking, climbing and, hopefully, dragging a deer.

CHAPTER THREE

WARM UP FOR THE HUNT
●
FINE TUNE YOUR HUNTING BOW

When fall rolls around and opening morning is just a few days away, that's no time to start worrying about any part of your equipment and how well it's going to work. If you're going to worry, start early so you can do something about it. Get that hunting bow tuned so you know what it will do for you and you will have confidence in yourself.

Dress yourself and your rig with all the gear you'll use when actually hunting. Then shoot under these conditions—you'll know right away if a quiver is slowing bow cast or the string catches in your camo sleeve or the arrows aren't flying right.

First test your arrows the same as a tournament shooter does, with a bare shaft. Match the weight in front (field points will do) to your broadhead's weight. Shoot the bare shaft into a bale about ten yards away. The reactions of the shaft will tell you what to adjust for smooth flight.

Nothing reduces cast—or speed—and penetration like a wobbly arrow. Put a wobble together with a big, flat broadhead surface, and you can see how game is missed or only wounded. If an arrow is flying straight, it is flying at maximum velocity with the least amount of wind resistance. The entire mass weight of the arrow is directly behind the point. This gives maximum penetration.

An arrow's spine—or stiffness—determines what the shaft will do after it leaves the bow. If it is too light or too stiff, the broadhead planes and compounds the error more noticeably than a field point. The sooner the arrow straightens out, the less are your chances of planing broadheads.

61

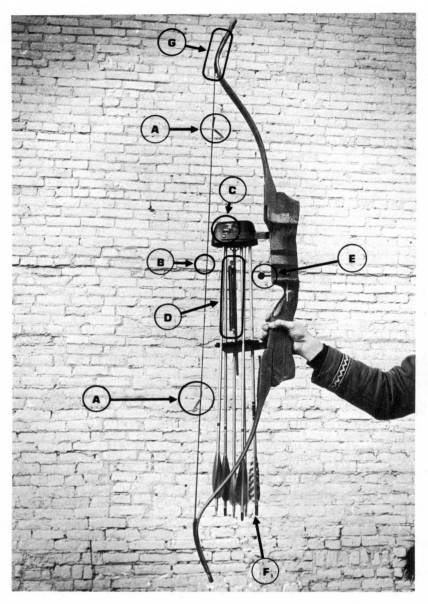

A camouflaged hunting bow, ready for use. String is outfitted with silencers (A) and nocking point locator (B). A spare arrow rest (C) and string (D)—which is also set up with proper accessories—are taped to the bow quiver. The bow is fully camouflaged and has an arrow holder (E) for security so you won't need to hold your finger over the arrow all the time. This hunter carries only one spare arrow (F) for plinking or practice shots; some hunters carry three or four if their quiver is large enough.

Limbs have rug-type material (G) glued on to act as brush deflectors and silence the slap of the string against the bow upon release.

People who shoot with sights are generally not aware of arrow flight, so it's essential that they have someone watch their arrow flight for them. A sight shooter should *not* see his arrows fly—if he does, he's peeking.

If you use a sight, just concentrate on shot and form and let the other guy tell you what happened to the arrow. If you're an instinctive shooter, you will see your arrow flight, but it's still a good idea to have a second person watch the arrows so you can concentrate on the shot.

If your bare arrow tails to the left, build your arrow rest out from the bow (all suggestions pertain to a right-handed shooter, just reverse the adjustments for a lefty). If it tails to the right, take away as much as possible on the arrow rest.

If you can't correct it this way, try arrows the next spine lighter. For example, if 45-50 spine arrows tail, try the 40-45 spine.

If the arrow tails up, lower your nocking point; if it tails down, raise your nocking point. You could also try using a string with more strands or adding brace height if arrows tail left. If they tail right, use less strands or less brace height. You'll have to experiment to find the right combination, but that's part of the fun.

If you use a shelf or hard-surface arrow rest and cannot get proper arrow flight, try one of the "giveable" plastic, feather or brush rests. Don't feel that the weather or delicacy of these units is not worth arrow flight. Just be sure they're waterproof.

No matter what the material, a deer is very sensitive to any noise, so you have to be able to draw the arrow the full length without making a sound. If you camouflage your arrows with a flat paint, be sure to shoot them in practice because the paint will change flight characteristics. Paint will also make noise on the rest as you draw.

Also remember that sometimes after getting the bare shaft to fly straight, your arrow with the big hunting fletch can occasionally wobble. Just raise your arrow rest and match the nocking point to it so the big fletching isn't able to strike the bow shelf.

Noise is a bigger factor than many people realize, and sometimes a lot of work is required to silence a noisy bow. You can't always achieve silence by simply buying commercial silencers and putting them on the string. I've worked for months trying to quiet a bow quiver or arrow holder, using tape, foam, pieces of rubber or anything else that would fit or glue onto string or limb to dampen vibration.

It's important to work out your ideas in a hunting atmosphere, like hunting woodchucks in the summer. Sometimes a rig that seems relatively quiet when practicing at home is intolerably noisy under hunting conditions.

Some bows are rather tricky in silencing string slap. A bow that makes a lot of noise is generally understrung. Try a shorter string or increase the number of strands in the string; the increase in strands will cut cast, but produce a lower pitched vibration.

You can see that in silencing a bow it's a give-and-take situation—you may lose a little cast but you will gain in quietness. It's not uncommon for a deer to completely dodge an arrow in flight (arrow traveling at 180 feet-per-second, sound at 800 fps), thus making it important to trade a little cast for a gain in quietness.

String silencers can be made of many different materials and styles—just look at the variety of commercial models. You can also use cut rubber bands, slim rubber triangles, puffy ostrich feathers—anything that cuts down string vibration. They're placed about six inches down from where the recurve touches the string.

One trick is to use the rug rest from arrow shelves and glue it in place on the inside of the recurve where the string comes in contact with the bow. This deadens string slap.

Brush nocks keep your bow from hanging up in the brush and are also a safety factor. Some guys without brush nocks have jerked their bow out of the brush and, with unprotected broadheads, jabbed themselves in the foot or leg. (Another reason to always use a quiver that covers the broadheads.)

Brush nocks also work as silencers; they keep the string from slapping the bow limb. Take care mounting the nocks so they just touch the bow limbs when the bow is strung. If a nock is stuck between string and limb, it will cut down cast considerably. There are several types; some affix to the string, others to the limb.

The coloration of our beautiful bows is also a prime consideration.

Many are fairly expensive and they all generally have classic lines with laminations, shiny wood and glass. But to hunt successfully, we cannot bring this "furniture quality" bow into the woods and expect animals not to notice it. We must dull it with cloth, tape, paint or even grease or wax. The important thing is that no part of it shines or reflects light in any way.

Try some of the new removable paints. They're light and don't mar the finish. If you hunt with a bow sock, be sure to practice with it because a sock will cut cast (only slightly when dry, but quite a bit when wet). Twist and tape the sock so it is tight and offers minimum wind resistance on release.

When buying a bow quiver, the fi lk thing to consider is whether it fits your bow without inhibiting limb action. The quiver should be attached to the handle riser and not to any working part of the limb. The best types are the ones which screw directly into the bow riser. The simple slip-over-the-limb type is okay as long as it slips down over the heavy portion of the riser and is not on the working part of the limb.

The next point is that the quiver withstand limb vibration at release so it doesn't make any extra noise or vibrate loose or cause arrows to fall out.

Be sure to practice with a bow quiver loaded with as many arrows as you will normally be hunting with. Bow quivers can make a lot of noise simply from feathers touching and vibrating on release. Place them so they don't touch feather on feather.

Some bows are designed for a particular quiver; it makes sense to use the bow designed for your quiver.

A small, forward-mounted hunting stabilizer on a rubber bushing adds to mass weight for lighter bows and deadens sound vibration. You may want to try one.

Arrow holders don't add any effective mass weight. However, in their job of holding an arrow ready, they have a disconcerting tendency to grip an arrow tighter than an excited hunter grips the nock of his arrow. As a result, he can jerk the string out of the nock. This is another reason Bjorn-style nocks are good.

Another remedy is to practice, simulating your shot in whatever style you will use—blind, stalk, tree stand, over your left ear or whatever. Practice to and through your shot, so you build up reflexes that won't let you down.

Shoot with sights often enough so you can have confidence; don't be a last-minute sight artist looking for a false security blanket. This takes practice.

Be sure the sight is rugged and is mounted stably. It must not add noise on release. If you put a rangefinder sight on, be sure you understand the operating principle behind it. Know the distances. Practice!

Have at least three strings—one on your bow and two in a spare pack. All should be set up the same—same strand total, same brace height, same silencer position, same nocking point setup. And all should be shot in. It's also a good idea to tape an extra string to your bow; they're tougher to forget that way.

There are two recommended positive ways of placing nocking locations on a string so the arrow fits snugly, but not tight, and can't slip up or down at the moment of truth. (1) Use two nocking points, just above and below the arrow nock. (2) Double-serve the string above and below the nocking point so the arrow will fit on the string at only one point. Then use a clinch or snug nock—or a soft nock pinched slightly.

In tuning, it's important that you wear clothing you'll be hunting with so you can check string clearance on your arm and don't have protruding pockets or bulky material on your chest that will interfere with the string.

Every year someone gets a deer with a mismatched, untuned, shiny, noisy bow. But that's the exception. Why not have your rig "humming" before opening day. Your chances are a lot better. Take pride in your hunting equipment—enough so that you go into the woods feeling like a competent hunter, not a guy in a lottery. These are old cliches, but true. Know the terrain and the animal you'll hunt, wear correct clothing, practice before the season and, as I've tried to bring out, understand your equipment and use it to its fullest potential.

GAMES BOWHUNTERS PLAY

Practice makes perfect. That's a trite but apt statement which is accepted as gospel. A person learns something, becomes more proficient by repetition, assuming he has mastered the basic fundamentals. Of course the entire theory is founded on the premise that a person is dedicated to practicing regularly. Few bowhunters are so inclined. Many will go afield this fall with a minimum of pre-season practice, if any at all. And those that do practice probably will set up a target, step back a couple of dozen yards, and simply fire arrows as they would in a competitive round. Stance just right, draw to the proper anchor point, hold steady for an accurate sight picture, and release correctly. Arrows fly straight and true.

There is just one drawback: few shots in the field come in this classic position. So about all range practice accomplishes is to condition muscles and fine tune the draw, hold and release motion.

At least, I have convinced myself this is true, for I hate to practice. Hunt, yes; practice, no. But I realize that practice is necessary for success, so I tolerate a certain amount of it.

There is no reason for practice to be dull, however. Play games with your bow as you practice and have fun at the same time. Games of movement teach the archer to make snap decisions, take quick shots, and learn to adapt so he can shoot from practically any position.

When improvising games I think in terms of one arrow, putting the premium on that first shot. In bowhunting there seldom is the luxury of a second chance. Learn to put one arrow where you want it; that's all you will need!

In my backyard I have a crude range. Occasionally I'll take my bow, walk outside and impulsively release an arrow from just about any position imaginable. Just one arrow, no more. The idea is to condition yourself to think positive, to try to make the very best shot possible with this one arrow. In bowhunting, that is the only one which counts.

This is a simple game I play with myself, based on a scoring system with ten points for a bull's eye hit and graduating down to nine, eight, seven, and so on to one. I score on the basis of ten arrows, maybe shot during a week or perhaps even a month. The time-span really isn't important. The points for ten arrows are added; then for the next ten I try to surpass this. The system makes me concentrate, for I know that each arrow is important to the overall score. It is sort of like trying to beat par in golf; the bowhunter can't fool himself, he knows exactly how well or how poorly he has done. This game doesn't involve much time or effort, but for me it accomplishes a need: trying to make the very best shot possible with one arrow, the first arrow.

Anyone with imagination can improvise similar games, based primarily on available practice space. To make them more fun and sporting, they can be competitive.

Like, for example, what I call the rubber-ball game. A small soft-rubber ball (the size really isn't important) is attached to a piece of cord about 15 inches long. The ball is suspended forward of plain cardboard on my backyard paper bale. I like the contrast of a bright-colored ball against the dull paper, where the eye can easily follow the movement.

One person sets the ball swinging, then gets out of the way while his buddy tries to hit the ball during its back-and-forth motion. It is like trying to lead a bird, picking an imaginary spot and trying to anticipate where ball and arrow will meet simultaneously.

Another fun game is bow-birding. A person could make his own throwing disc, to simulate a bird in flight, but I prefer to use the inexpensive target made and marketed by the Saunders Archery Company. This is a tough, 15-inch reinforced-cardboard disc with a three-dimensional center which rises about six inches above the base. One person throws the disc, another with a bow tries to hit it with an arrow. It is that rudimentary. Some sort of scoring system can be devised, if you prefer—or like in trapshooting, you can simply count the number of hits on, say, 25 thrown targets (of course using the same target to throw time and again). This erratically thrown disc is a challenge to hit, particularly if any wind is blowing. It is good practice if you ever hope to try wing-shooting birds with your bow, and it also is a lot of fun. Use flu-flu arrows, the largest fletchings you can find where arrows won't travel too far, and make sure you have plenty of room, like a football field, where distance is an accepted safety factor.

Another simple game is to inflate balloons, put them on fairly smooth ground when a fairly stiff breeze is blowing and try to hit them as they skitter about. Just be sure there is an adequate backstop. A similar game, much more difficult, is to put a cardboard insert in an old tire and have one person roll the casing down an incline while a bowman tries to hit the erratically bouncing target. If you think you are pretty good with a bow, try this game sometime. It has a way of deflating an over-sized ego.

The game I call "Hunt" is one of my favorites. Several lifesize animals are painted on chunks of cardboard (you can use standard animal targets as an alternative). One person goes down a trail and positions about a half-dozen targets at different places, then the bow-hunter follows the same trail, trying to see each animal as quickly as possible and get an arrow into a vital area. The idea is to pinpoint each target to create difficult shots, perhaps on a knee to get under a low-hanging limb, or trying to put the projectile through just a narrow pencil of opening.

If you want to make this game competitive, designate certain point values for hits in vital areas, putting a premium on accuracy. But don't actually mark a point area; this negates the basic reason for playing the game—learning to mentally find a vital area on an animal and pinpointing an arrow there. A deer, for instance, doesn't have a prominent spot just behind the shoulder for aiming purposes, as many neophyte bowhunters ruefully find. The tendency of the inexperienced hunter is to simply shoot at an animal rather than a small, specific spot. The "Hunt" game is designed to teach a person to spot-shoot.

If you wish, at one target a step-ladder can be placed on the trail. The shooter must climb it to get a shot, firing from an elevated position, as he would from a tree stand. Even in simple backyard games, shoot occasionally off a ladder. Try shooting from a tree stand, and you'll understand the value of this practice.

Games can assume practically any shape or fashion. They are limited in scope only by a person's imagination. I've seen bowmen try to hit claybirds thrown with a hand trap, or large rubber balls bounced along the ground. I once saw a unique target made by attaching a slanting wire between two trees and rolling a cardboard disc held by a ball-bearing pulley rapidly down the wire. Archers attempted to hit the moving target.

Games are fun and sporting, not dictated by any season. They teach a person to become a more proficient shot in unorthodox situations, which is what bowhunting is all about.

BACKYARD HUNTING PRACTICE

As hunting season approaches, your practice sessions will get more serious. Then you must simulate a hunt, matching your hunting clothing, tackle and practice shots as closely as possible to the conditions you'll encounter in the field. This is the time to hone your shooting form and find out which hunting gear works best for you. This is the time to practice every shooting position imaginable and overcome one of the most common failings in bowhunting—failure to come to full draw before releasing the shot.

Why all this preparation? *Because that first shot must count!* In hunting, there is rarely any warmup, and very few good second shots are ever offered. Iron out all the details on your practice range and you'll go into the woods a better bowhunter—one capable of producing the best effort possible, capable of the skill the game you hunt deserves.

Practice—under the proper conditions—helps you groove your

Practice in full hunting gear, and practice as many unorthodox shooting positions as you can. Load your quiver with arrows—for a bow shoots differently then, as compared to its performance with an empty quiver. During early practice, you may wish to mark the vital heart/lungs area; as the season nears, you should remove this marking because you won't find a game animal in the woods with this handy aiming device. Remember always to concentrate on as small an aiming spot as possible. This will aid concentration. Too many hunters get excited and look at the entire animal; this usually brings nothing more than a clean miss—which is better than a bad hit, but still not what you intended.

shot, develop your concentration and build the confidence that will give you the ability to make that first shot right. For when it comes, you may be slightly shook; but your practice will pay off in trained muscles and instant response. You'll come to full draw and utilize the full power of your bow. You'll *know* where that shot is going.

YOUR CLOTHING

Wear that new camo suit; break it in and get the crinkles out of it. Wash it a couple of times. Find out whether there are baggy pockets which get in the way of the string upon release. If so, remove them. Clothing must fit loosely enough to allow easy movement, but not be baggy.

If you'll be hunting in cold weather, put on the proper clothing and determine whether what you have will allow smooth, silent movement and a clean shot, or whether you crackle like a burning bush.

Wear a camo headnet—if you're going to use one when hunting —and see whether eyeholes are cut properly for straight ahead and peripheral vision, whether it interferes with anchoring or release or whether eyehole positions change at full draw.

Practice with and without gloves, especially if you'll be hunting in cold weather.

Decide on the headgear you prefer. It must serve its purpose, but it must not interfere with the string as you reach full draw.

YOUR TACKLE

Use the same quiver as when you will be hunting. If this is a bow quiver, you'll become familiar with the bow's performance with the added mass weight; and be sure the quiver is loaded with as many arrows as you will carry when you're hunting. A bow shoots much differently with a full quiver than with an empty one. If you're using a hip or back quiver, you will groove your reach for the arrow with minimum movement. Basically, your equipment will become part of you and you won't fumble around at the moment of truth.

Use your hunting bow; be sure the field points are the same grain weight as your broadheads and be sure arrows are matched to your bow in spine and weight. As zero hour approaches, shoot plenty of practice arrows with old broadheads of the same type you will be using on the hunt. Broadheads sometimes fly differently from field points, even when they are the same grain weight.

As you practice, you will make adjustments to silence a noisy quiver, adjust string silencers for best performance, and set up and break in that spare string which you will *always* carry when hunting.

If you're going to use a sight when hunting, practice with the various types, and begin this practice early. (Archers often exhibit a crazy habit—those who shoot target without sights all year often suddenly decide to put a sight on their hunting bow, and those who shoot target with a sight all year often decide to shoot barebow for hunting. This is not a good idea because your best performance will always come with gear that has become part of your grooved shooting style.) So if you plan to use a sight, find the one that works best for you and install it *now*! Then practice enough so that its use becomes another automatic part of your shot sequence.

If you'll be shooting from a tree stand most of the time, you will need a properly heavy bow that will drive an arrow vertically through bone and extra body depth and give full penetration for a good blood trail. If the broadhead does not go entirely through the body or project out the bottom, the game animal must fill up with blood before you will get a blood trail. A wounded animal can go a long distance before this happens, so you severely decrease your chances of tagging the game.

Practice with the hunting bow until your muscles are totally conditioned to handle the draw weight. Remember: a super-heavy draw weight bow which is shot poorly (from less than full draw and/or with poor aim) is much less effective than a hunting bow of less draw weight but brought to full draw and shot cleanly and smoothly.

Wet weather is the time to check out a silicone spray for feather fletching to repel water—or to switch to plastic vanes and get them set up properly. Any poorly attached fletches will also show more of a tendency to come loose during rainy or misty weather, so check them out now and be certain they will be in proper condition on the hunt.

Wet weather can also affect a bow's shooting performance. A wet bow sock will cause more drag on the limbs, and you will shoot low. Wet feather fletching also slows the arrow. A released string may drag on a damp leather tab or shooting glove. The time to find out exactly how you and your equipment shoot in wet weather is in practice, not at the moment of truth.

PRACTICE SHOTS

Set up a lifesize target and mark the vital heart/lungs area to help your aiming concentration. As zero hour approaches, it is usually best to discard the special markings for the vital area. You certainly won't see the vital areas marked on a game animal in the forest, and by now you should know their exact position in the animal.

As you practice, with or without the vital areas marked, *always* concentrate on the vital heart/lung area. Do not shoot at the entire animal. Practice and concentrate until your senses seem to blot out the animal and all you see is that vital area. Direct that arrow into the proper area almost by force of your concentration and will.

Practice in early morning light and late afternoon; this is when you will see most big game, and your eyes must be accustomed to the game's appearance under these light conditions. Shadows and dim light can drastically change to your eyes the appearance and location of a game animal's body; be ready for this possible shooting condition.

If you're practicing for deer, don't shoot at grass clumps and dirt clods. They're too low for deer, but will help if you're practicing for rabbit hunting. For big game, put the target on stakes or position it at the proper height on the target butt.

Practice in varying terrain, shooting uphill, downhill and flat. Everyone tends to shoot low when shooting uphill and high when shooting downhill. Practice until you know your proper aiming adjustment.

There are two ways to judge distance: either without deliberately mentally pre-judging yardage (usual barebow style); or pacing off each shot (best for bowhunters using bow sights, especially if not yet fully confident in judging distances). The objective, of course, is to develop distance judging skills and get accurate sight settings.

Shoot with your bow canted at varying angles; canting changes your line of sight and affects arrow performance. Shoot when kneeling, seated, crouching, standing straight, standing with body twisted so you become familiar with all possible shooting positions. Shoot from trees to become familiar with various foot positions and learn which unnoticed branches will obstruct your drawing arm and bow upon release. Shoot through holes in brush or branches to learn the arrow's trajectory; with the bow canted to shoot through holes like this, you will find that an arrow tails off to the right for a right handed shooter and to the left for a left handed shooter.

Continually practice shooting from these distorted positions. You rarely get the classical shot in the field.

If no tree is readily available, practice from a ladder or other simulated tree stand, such as a garage roof. If you go into the field and

To simulate tree stand shooting, use any method you can devise to get up off the ground. Try to shoot at a three-dimensional target so you will become familiar with the arrow's path through the entire body of the intended target.

actually use your tree stand, tie a safety rope around yourself so you become familiar with its feel. You will learn how much you can lean against it, whether or not your feet will slip on the tree stand while you are leaning, and whether your tree stand makes noises when you shift position on it.

Practice with your bow canted; canting changes the bow's shooting characteristics and also changes your shooting form until you have grooved this type of shot.

If you are thinking of changing your anchor point, such as from corner-of-the-mouth to cheekbone, now is the time to decide. The anchor must come from force of habit when you have to make the shot on that trophy buck. Some hunters use different anchors—a cheekbone anchor that will permit gunbarreling (aiming right down the arrow) for close shots and a low anchor to give the trajectory for longer shots. Most hunters find it most reliable—and comfortable—to determine the anchor point which works best for them and then stick with it for all hunting shots. This clears their mind and allows them to quickly determine the proper bow elevation and then concentrate on the vital area of the game.

Practice at the distances you will be shooting. If you're an Eastern whitetail hunter planning for a Western antelope jaunt, practice the longer range shots of over 50 yards that are commonplace for antelope, not the 10- to 20-yard whitetail shots you'll get at home. Practice on a lifesize target, so when you see that trophy in the big area out West, you will have a more accurate judge of distance. Those open Western

If you will be shooting from a hole blind, be sure you practice at the proper level. The aiming elevation appears different when you are at eye level with a deer.

areas and the clear air are especially deceiving to anyone who is not familiar with them. Most Eastern hunters find themselves shooting far short the first time they go after Western game. Moose, elk and mule deer are big: you may find it difficult to change your thinking from whitetail sizes to their sizes, and they will appear closer than they are.

As you practice the various shooting positions and ranges, *always* concentrate on reaching *full draw*. Practice aiming deliberately and releasing quickly when everything looks right. Be particularly alert that you do not snap shoot so quickly that you release before you reach full draw. Many times you will get only one shot, so you must be certain you aim properly and develop the full power potential of your bow. This is the only way to assure the arrow will go where it is supposed to go.

Build ground blinds and shoot from them. You will learn the proper height so you can shoot over them with little movement and determine the inside circumference you will need to permit free bow movement. It's generally more than you think.

Put an arrow holder on your bow and then, in the blind, set up a bow holder—a commercial product, cut twig, or anything that works—and practice reaching for the bow, coming to full draw and shooting accurately with as little movement as necessary.

If you will shoot from a hole blind, deer will be at eye level. So practice accordingly.

Stump shooting is an informal, enjoyable way to practice. It gives you a variety of targets and shooting positions.

If you have a suitable backstop and a sloping area, insert a card-board target in an old tire and practice the running deer shot as the tire bounces down the slope.

The results of all this practice, in addition to becoming an accurate shot? During your woods wandering—especially stump shooting, which is an excellent in-the-field practice method and fun, too—you are going to learn something of terrain and the habits of game. All, of course, so you can determine their most likely runway locations, probable escape routes, feeding areas early and late in the season.

Your aim is to get as good a shot as possible. Being a good shot is one requirement; being in the right place at the right time is another. Successfully making the shot and recovering your trophy are the final vital elements.

READY TO HUNT IN THE RAIN?

Why hunt in the rain at all? For several good reasons. One is the necessity of making use of committed time. You've planned all year to go hunting, you've traveled 300 miles to prime deer country, and now it rains. Being equipped with proper knowledge, you can turn the adversity of rain into an advantage.

In addition, by hunting in the rain you'll have less competition from other hunters. The woods are quiet, as the rain deadens sound, and you are able to stalk closer to game because of the wet foliage. The deer and other game are also concentrated in areas of heavy cover and can be approached from several directions because of the deadening of wind and sound. Game is not as alert in the rain. Deer, for instance, tend to turn ears down, like a mule, severely dampening their hearing. The second best sense of warning—scenting—has also been reduced.

But now, before you get all excited about going out and catching pneumonia, there are a few problems inherent in this type of hunting. The most obvious is the drop in arrow flight. Wet feathers weigh down the arrow so that your normal, flat-shooting 25-yard shot will now hit low between a deer's legs. Simple solution: before departing on a wet-weather hunt, waterproof your feathers with the old standard Fletch-Tite waterproofing or Bohning Dri-Tite or use a good quality hair spray.

We might add here that, if you anticipate hunting in the rain, double tack fletching with the old glue tube by putting an extra drop at

Rain and snow act alike on bowhunting tackle. If you plan to hunt under such conditions—and you should because the hunting can be excellent—be sure you have an arrow rest that is unaffected by moisture, and either use plastic fletching or lightly coat your feathers with a water-resistant spray, such as hair spray.

the base of the feather and the end of the feather on the shaft and three or four dots alongside the fletching. The old glue on the fletching may be slightly crystallized from age and the slightest bit of dampness on the base of the vein may be enough to pop the feather off.

A recent wrinkle in solving wet-weather fletching problems is the soft plastic hunting vanes as made by Deer-flight, Precision Shooting Equipment, Ultra and Arizona Archery. They take a little extra effort to set up, but the soft plastic vane sets up a lot easier than the old stiff plastic that didn't work.

Of course, the preferred material for the shaft itself would be fiberglass or aluminum. If you do hunt with wood, be sure the shafts are completely coated with lacquer so they won't warp in the quiver or on the bow itself when in the arrow holder.

Care of arrows also affects arrow drop in flight. For instance, an old trick is to invert the bow quiver and put a plastic bag over the feathers to keep them dry; otherwise the rain runs down shafts and ends up in the bag. Better than a plastic bag is a piece of camo cloth lined with plastic made into a bag—keeps dry, quiet, and has enough weight to stay on and not blow off or get pulled off at the slightest twig tug.

The bag should be loose enough that you can extract an arrow for that second shot if needed. Robin Hood sells a fletching bonnet that looks good.

A couple of dandy back quivers that protect the fletching from the weather are the Cat-quiver and the St. Charles. They'll carry a full arsenal of arrows and keep fletching dry. It is still a good idea for added insurance to spray waterproofing oil or hair spray on fletchings so they won't absorb moisture under high humidity.

When practicing or hunting in the rain, be sure to take particular care of your fletching. Do not grab the fletching when you pull arrows out. When you're done practicing or hunting, shake out the feathers with a snap action. With wood arrows, stand them upright so they don't take a set; dry them slowly, as far from heat as possible. In a camp situation, the best way is upright near the ceiling; near the floor may be too damp, and feathers won't dry.

Spin-dry feathers, rotating the arrow in your fingers. If the feathers have taken a distorted set from being in a back quiver or thrown in a corner while damp, you can restore the fletching by rotating them in and out of the steam vapor of a kettle. Do not overheat the feathers; the idea is simply to help them return to natural shape.

A wet arrow rest can often cause as many problems as a wet arrow. If you enjoy shooting with a feather or rug type rest, be sure to waterproof it with the same material used on fletching, otherwise it will have a tendency to lay down when wet and also cause more resistance against the arrow as it passes over. For best results, treat the rest every time you go out in rain.

A covered back quiver will keep fletching dry during wet weather. And if you're dressed properly, you will stay warm and dry. This hunter was wearing yellow water-repellent pants, but note that they blend in well with the snow in black-and-white—which is how a deer sees things.

We highly recommend the use of some of the new nylon or plastic rests, such as the Hoyt Pro Flex-Rest or the Herters nylon brush rest. Wire rests such as the Flipper or Springy are also good. Finger-type rests are not affected by weather or water conditions and give the cleanest arrow flight because of the least amount of resistance against wet arrow shaft and fletching.

Don't forget the treatment of the business end. One of the first things to corrode rapidly in wet weather is the razor sharp edge. We therefore recommend a treatment of light oil or vaseline. It will keep heads sharp; no need to resharpen them every day of wet weather.

For those of you who hunt with a camouflage bow sock, this material for wet-weather hunting should be wound tightly on bow limbs and sprayed with a good grade of waterproofing spray in the wound position. A wet bow sock will have a dramatic effect on deadening of cast. When hunting under rainy, overcast skies, we recommend that the bow sock usually be removed as reflection of the bow is at a minimum. If you want camouflage, the waterproof tapes and camo paint would be ideal wet-weather aids. In most cases, water on the limbs won't affect cast.

Tabs and gloves can throw you off. When they get wet, they have a tendency to form a deep groove and grip the string, making a smooth release difficult. This wet tab and glove, coupled with swollen, wet fingers, makes a smooth release difficult—and, yes, your hands do swell if they're wet. The trick is to have a side pocket where you can keep your shooting hand as dry as possible. Or use a plastic tab like the Saunders model.

So much for the bow. For yourself, the number one consideration is footgear. It is extremely difficult to be comfortable and enthusiastic when your feet are wet and soggy. So you should have a good pair of sealed leather boots like Browning's Weatherproof or a light rubber boot. The only drawback of rubber boots is that they retain moisture and your feet get logy and sore.

A key item of wet-weather comfort is the rain suit—and by this we mean the type that has pants and a parka top. The light nylonized rubber types that fit well would rank at the top of the list, as they make the least amount of noise for stalking purposes and are generally well enough constructed and vented that they won't conserve moisture in your clothing.

However, there's no totally quiet rubber suit. Many hunters overcome this by wearing rubber or plastic rain suits under some light cotton overgarments like camo clothing, although camo clothing can weigh a ton when drenched. A very light plastic or nylon rubberized undergarment is best, it is light in weight and will be more flexible and less noisy than heavier material.

The best hat is the standard Jones-style sportsman's cap. Pulled down at back and sides, it offers enough protection for eyes and sheds water equally over your shoulders—not down your glasses or your back like some of the wide brimmed jobs do. An additional comfort in head cover is a light waterproof hood that can be pulled over the head to just behind the ears to keep your hearing at peak efficiency. A short, hooded jacket top works fine, not the overly long parka type which is hard to walk in.

For stalking, we prefer the shorter type of rubberized suits because you can zip down the front for better body ventilation. Otherwise, you can get as wet from the inside as from the outside.

If you're hunting from a blind, however, the ventilation factor is not as important as being dry and warm.

The best adapted armguard fitting over all this damp and semi-damp paraphernalia is the long training or hunting armguard that covers the sleeve from just above the elbow to the wrist. A tip on the armguard: do not fasten it so tight it cuts off circulation in your bow arm. This causes rapid fatigue. It should flex with the elbow.

Okay, now you're properly clad and equipped for rainy weather. The next thing is to practice in the rain. Pick the worst day to go to the archery range—you won't have any competition for a target—and field test your equipment several times to familiarize yourself with it under actual rain conditions.

Remember that under rainy conditions you will probably have closer shooting than normal because of the advantages the rain gives; practice in the rain should emphasize closer distances. The need for accuracy in actual rainy conditions is very important. Remember, you're not going to have a clearcut blood trail, so get up close to the target and check out the effects of your new, totally soaked equipment.

What you're looking for in practice is the knowledge of sighting adjustments at various ranges. It is important to let the feathers get as wet as they will under natural hunting conditions before you fire that first practice shot. It is also important, if you hunt with wet tab or glove, to let that leather get as saturated as it does under hunting conditions and see what effect it has on arrow flight. Also, if you are a bare-finger shooter, be sure to let your hands get as wet as under actual hunting conditions.

Of course, you will realize that the lighter bows will be affected more than the heavier equipment; however, they will all be more difficult to shoot because of three factors: the added weight of the wet arrow, its resistance on the rest, and the fact that it's harder to release with a soaked glove or tab. Instinctive shooters must be prepared to adjust mental sightings for changed wet conditions, and sight shooters should realize the differences in settings between dry conditions and wet conditions.

BRUSH UP FOR THE HUNT

It has been said that in an athletic contest one team rarely beats another. Rather, the outcome is determined when one team defeats itself with mistakes.

The same logic applies to bowhunting. Most unsuccessful hunters fail because of their own blunders. These costly errors usually can be attributed to oversight and carelessness. The hunter simply has not done his homework.

Such details are numerous. Here we will delve into ten of the more common ones. If you can read these informal rules and be satisfied that in planning your hunting strategy you have taken each into consideration, then you indeed qualify as a prepared bowhunter. And the "luck" of a kill often is just preparation meeting opportunity.

●   1. Know your hunting territory.

A rudimentary, belabored rule, but perhaps the one abused the most. Any bowhunter who goes into strange country "cold" certainly has all the odds stacked against him.

I've long contended that more deer are killed *before* the season than *during,* which isn't to imply that some hunters rush things. This merely means that the successful archer has scouted his potential hunting territory thoroughly and hunts where he stands the best chance of seeing game.

He has become familiar with game trails, knows how the logging or other trails twist and turn, knows what he will see when he peers up over a ridge, knows how the deer will react in certain areas when they are spooked or just sneaking away. He knows where the deer feed and where they just travel through. He knows where to find the good deer food areas—or bear, javelina, turkey, elk or any other game-animal feeding areas.

He knows where the game rests in hiding and where they are most likely to emerge.

● 2. Pre-season practice.

Most hunters are aware of the need for practice, but they go about it wrong. They simply punch holes in a range target with field points. The wise bowhunter also practices with broadheads—the same arrows he hunts with—and he learns to shoot from all sorts of awkward stances, kneeling and squatting. A broadhead adds more weight to the arrow and it reduces the draw by as much as three-quarters of an inch. These factors tend to make an arrow shoot lower. The hunter must learn to compensate for this. So by all means take some old arrows and practice in the field during the actual hunt, shooting into an earthen bank.

● 3. Have your hunting sites pinpointed and prepared.

This rule is closely akin to the first. As you scout your hunting territory, find places where you can hide in ambush and wait for game. If you select a tree for a stand, prepare a strategic spot prior to your actual hunt. This means a place where you will be comfortable and clear of any obstructing branches. I've seen archers climb into a tree before daybreak and immediately start snapping off limbs—a telltale noise which alarms any deer within hearing distance.

Preparation should have been completed days or weeks before. Game can recognize changes in their surroundings, so it will take them a while to become adjusted to a large new clump of brush or any other camouflaged blind.

Another salient reason for having pre-selected hunting sites is that you know exactly where to go to commence your hunt. Otherwise, you might have a vague inkling of the best spots, but being off in your calculations even a few yards might mean the difference between success and failure.

I've seen hunters during a rifle deer season stomp into the woods before dawn, pick what appears to be a good stand at that time, and then move one, two or more times in dissatisfaction after daybreak. This is not the way to blend into the area.

● 4. Know the hunting laws for the area.

Another very basic rule that often is taken for granted—which encourages mistakes.

A few years ago, I was hunting in Nebraska, seeking deer, when a large wild turkey gobbler walked beneath the tree where I was hiding. I was tempted to shoot the tom but I hesitated, not knowing whether the season was open on turkeys. My hesitation was fortunate; turkeys were

Ground blinds should be large enough to permit free movement. Most bowhunters build them too small and then, at the moment of truth, discover they cannot move without scraping brush. Build the blind so you can see and shoot just over the top and have some vegetation behind you to break your outline. If you have well defined approach routes for game, you may wish to build higher and shoot through openings; this doesn't happen often though, because game do the unexpected. Also be sure you scrape the floor of the blind clean so you can move your feet without crunching leaves. Do this far enough ahead of the intended hunting time so there will be no aromas of freshly turned soil to alert the game.

not legal. But if they had been, I still would have been kicking myself for passing up such a ridiculously easy shot.

You may be familiar with laws on a statewide basis, but these are usually the basic, general rules and may vary considerably within a state or region. Be particularly alert if you plan to hunt near the boundaries of any of these areas with potentially troublesome regional rules. You may cross from one region to another without knowing it, but ignorance of the law is no excuse.

Get the most complete list of hunting laws available for the area or state you will be hunting, study them and obey them.

You can create an instant blind against an isolated bush or other natural material which will break your outline by simply cutting and jabbing leafy twigs into the ground in a semi-circle.

- 5. Learn to judge range.

This rule goes with the second. As you practice, be aware of the capabilities of your weapon and your ability. If you can accurately place your arrows in a tight circle at 35 yards, for example, but find that you are erratic at longer ranges, work for shots within your ability. Far too many hunters take haphazard shots which only encourage crippled game. A true axiom of bowhunting is a yard of range for every pound of bow weight. This means a 50-pound bow is effective up to 50 yards, both for accuracy and for adequate power to give penetration for humane kills. If you hear stories about those "80-yard shots," take them with a grain of salt. Those shots beyond 50 yards are only for the very skilled, and I'm not so sure about some of them.

- 6. Know your quarry.

The moment of truth for any bowhunter is that instant when he draws an arrow and releases. Some animals like the whitetailed deer spook easily; others are not quite as aware. A few seasons back, I missed a once-in-a-lifetime opportunity at a giant mule deer buck in Colorado, one that possibly would have been a new Pope & Young world record. I'd hunted muleys many times with a rifle but I never had stalked one with a bow. I got close to this brute, within 25 yards, when my pants leg brushing against a limb alarmed him. He turned and looked directly at me. Instead of taking the shot, I waited for the buck to turn his head, believing he would promptly spook—a la the whitetail—when I drew the arrow. Only later did I ruefully learn that a mule deer often stands, looking directly at an archer, and takes an arrow without flinching. By not knowing my quarry I pulled a blunder I will always regret.

- 7. Be sure your equipment is ready for the hunt and you have adequate replacements.

Sharpen broadheads before going afield. Double check before you leave home and be positive you have the necessary balanced equipment. I once went on a trip, and as I started to load my bow quiver, I noticed I'd brought along Microflite 6 arrows rather than the Microflite 8's I normally use. In my haste I'd picked up the wrong box. Another time I was hunting near my home when I accidently damaged my bowstring with a sharp broadhead. It required only about an hour to run into town for a replacement, but I shudder to think what would have happened if I'd been in a remote area. If you are going to be far from any civilization and plan to spend several days, buy a cheap "insur-

At zero hour, give your gear one final check and sharpen all broadheads razor sharp. If you're hunting in wet weather, give them a light oil coating to prevent rust and help them hold an edge.

ance'' bow in case something happens to the one you use. Bows don't break often, but they seem to give away at the most inappropriate times.

- 8. Have adequate camouflage.

I once missed a chance at a large javelina because sunlight glittering on a bare bow frightened the animal. The bowhunter can't be too careful. If you're hunting in leafy forest, wear the conventional brown-green camouflage; should it be snow, utilize white garb, even wrapping your bow in white. I even prefer to wear a camouflage mesh headnet and mesh gloves. The bowhunter is foolish not to take advantage of every bit of camouflage that is available, even if his stand is high in a tree fork where he is above the animal's normal line of sight. Sometimes the most insignificant mistakes are the most costly.

- 9. Let hunting aids work for you.

Equip your bow with string silencers. If your hunting jacket fits loosely, place your arm guard on the outside to compress loose folds of

White camouflage material helped this bowhunter get within range of a fine mule deer buck in a late Western season.

cloth that might hang on limbs or strike the bowstring and alarm game. Scent helps counteract an animal's main line of defense—the sense of smell. If your stand is situated where you'll be looking into the glare of a rising or setting sun, wear tinted glasses. Yellow-lens shooting glass-

A stocking cap will keep you warm and will not interfere with the bowstring at full draw. You can make an excellent camouflage headnet from a discarded pair of pantyhose, cutting off the legs and tying the openings shut, then cutting appropriate eye and mouth openings. Clear nail polish coating the edges of these openings will keep them from running. This material also gives added warmth to head and neck. Combine this with a lightweight down vest and a wool shirt, and you are dressed for cold-weather hunting.

Proper camouflaging from head to foot will make you almost invisible. It is important to cover hands and face as well as your body, for flesh tones stand out clearly. Cheekbones tend to shine, without camouflage of some sort.

es brighten the landscape, making it easier to put your arrow in a vital organ of an animal in the gloom of daybreak or dusk. Insect repellent will discourage pesky flies and mosquitos. A bowhunter who is continually scratching and slapping is creating far too much movement and noise. Watch that the brim of your hat or cap visor won't interfere with your shot. If necessary turn your cap around, visor behind, the way a baseball catcher wears his. The little details are the ones which often count the most.

- 10. Warm up before hunting.

A baseball player doesn't take practice throws just to loosen his muscles to prevent injury. He knows this also aids in accuracy. So it is with bowhunting. Just a few random short-range shots will warm and relax those back and arm muscles used in shooting. A small thing, yes, but it might be the ''edge'' that will produce results.

To some bowhunters these ten rules will seem quite elementary, which certainly they are. But often familiarity breeds carelessness. We tend to take things for granted. When this happens, the bowhunter is asking for heartbreak. Quite often, that's what he gets.

CHAPTER FOUR

BOWHUNTING TECHNIQUES
●
ABC'S OF TREE STANDS

Many bowhunters I know still strike out frequently because of carelessness in such areas as selecting the stand site, constructing or equipping the stand, clearing the stand area or sighting in from the stand. They don't get good shots or get no shots at all. For these reasons, I'm convinced that every bowhunter should occasionally bone up on these important fundamentals of tree stand hunting. Accordingly, this review of the finer points of stand hunting was prepared. It is written primarily for new bowhunters, but perhaps it will give even the old pros a few pointers.

The average bowhunter doesn't stand much chance of putting a lethal arrow in a deer unless he is within about 30 yards of his quarry, and unless the deer is standing or walking slowly. Selecting a good stand location is, of course, the first key to getting this kind of shot.

Don't pick a stand site simply because it overlooks an area with a lot of deer tracks—it rarely pays off. Numerous tracks usually indicate an area where deer mill around while feeding, which occurs mostly at night. In addition, a couple of milling deer can leave as many tracks as would a big herd passing through the area. Merely selecting a stand site on a heavily used deer trail is little better, for deer may pass that spot only during the night.

The experienced bowhunter looks for sign indicating the exact spots where deer are likely to be during the early and late *daylight* hours, and he selects a stand site within twenty yards of such spots. One top way to locate these ideal stand sites is to first search for the heaviest cover in your hunting area, then circle this cover until you locate points where it is penetrated by deer trails. Most deer in any area prefer to bed down in heavy cover during the day; they'll usually leave the cover to feed in the pre-dusk hours and return to it by the same trails just after dawn.

You will likely find several points where tracks with promising sign enter any patch of heavy cover. Trails most likely to be used during the next few days by deer will be those with plentiful fresh *and* old sign. A trail well pitted with old tracks indicates the trail is a well established deer highway. Fresh tracks indicate that it has not been temporarily abandoned because of hunting pressure or other factors.

Of course, when bucks are rutting, a stand overlooking a fresh scrape is also promising. Far better, however, is a stand overlooking the *centermost* scrape in a line of scrapes. Scrapes in creek or gully bottoms are poor spots to wait for deer because they are usually made and visited only at night. Instead, look for scrapes on high ridges or hilltops, for these are most likely to be visited during daylight hours.

If your objective is a trophy buck, you'll want your stands to overlook those trails or scrapes with exceptionally large tracks. To increase your odds of scoring regardless of wind direction, select alternative stand sites on opposite sides of heavy cover and scrapes.

A good bowhunting stand must not only conceal the hunter from deer until they approach within shooting range, but also let him raise and draw the bow without spooking his quarry. These requirements can be met to a degree by ground stands, but good tree stands are superior. Deer are not conditioned to expect danger from above; therefore, they rarely look upward. Approaching deer can be seen at greater ranges from a tree stand, and the hunter can be ready for them. The scent of a hunter in a tree stand is less likely to be carried to an approaching buck by a sudden gust of wind different from the prevailing wind direction.

How high should a bow hunter's stand be? All the pros I know agree that, if possible, it should be at least twelve feet above the ground. Some insist that it should be fourteen or fifteen feet above ground. I believe twelve is high enough, but when practical and safe, I go a bit higher.

Tree stands are of two basic types: portable and permanent. Portable stands are legal in almost all deer hunting areas. They can be quickly erected anywhere the hunter can carry them, their use elimi-

Portable climbing tree stands are an aid almost everywhere.

nates complicated blind-building problems and because they are portable they won't be a year-round eyesore in a woods. Several types of
portable tree stands are on the market today.

Many of the old pros I know have designed and made other
ingenious tree stands. Billy Bass, one of the sharpest bowhunters in the
central Florida area, made two light aluminum platforms. Each is
equipped with a light chain which fastens around the tree as the main
stand support, and each has an aluminum support bracket which drops
down from the underside of the platform and wedges against the tree

Some portable tree stands, climbing and non-climbing varieties, have seats which help make your hours on the stand more comfortable and less tiring.

trunk to provide the additional support required. A five-foot nylon rope ladder drops down from each stand. Billy fastens one stand against the tree at his six-foot height and climbs the rope ladder hanging from it. Then he puts the second stand in position six feet above the first and climbs up its rope ladder to the twelve-foot perch.

Permanent tree stands are still legal in a few areas, and they have advantages, too. They can be constructed with larger platforms and

Wedge-type tree stands are light, easily carried and secure when wedged firmly into the proper width opening.

comfortable seats. These factors make it easier for the bowhunter to remain still and quiet and to shoot with greater accuracy. A simple frame of two 2 × 4's nailed to two trees growing three or four feet apart, plus a platform top, makes a good stand.

Every hunter would agree that it is not desirable to rattle the woods with extensive hammering just before you hunt. However, building a tree stand during mid-day at the point where you intend to hunt late that evening or the next morning is not likely to keep your deer from appearing on schedule. Last season, I built two tree stands about a week apart, both during mid-day periods. Both stands overlooked points where good trails entered heavy cover. I hunted from each stand during the late afternoon of the same day I constructed it. And each afternoon, a deer emerged from the scrub just before dark, exactly as I had hoped. I missed one, but killed the other.

Swing your bow around for simulated shots in all directions from the stand and make a full draw in each direction at various vertical angles. Detect and remove all twigs, branches or limbs which interfere with your draw. Two related precautions: (1) Make sure the bill of your new hunting cap doesn't restrict bow movement or draw. (2) Make sure your stand seat is not in your way.

Next, check your field of fire in all directions and at various vertical angles. You can't—nor do you want to—remove every tree and bush around your stand, but make sure you have a reasonable number of open avenues available for shooting, especially in the directions from which your quarry is likely to approach.

First and foremost, the stand should be comfortable so that it is physically possible for you to remain still and quiet for long periods. It is for this reason that all permanent stands should be equipped with seats. You can be still and quiet for much longer periods by alternating between sitting and standing positions. Climbing down out of the stand to get water, food or clothing—or to perform more personal chores—is unnecessary and should be avoided. Take water, food, raingear, coat and a general-purpose waste pail to the stand if you intend to hunt for long periods. If there's not room on the platform for these items, hang them on branches well behind the tree trunk and out of the way.

On the subject of minimizing scents deer hate, use that waste pail! Such offensive scents hanging high in a tree are far less likely to alarm deer than they are if coming from the ground around your stand. And never carry strong-smelling foods to your stand. I once opened a can of sardines in a tree stand and spooked two approaching deer a hundred yards away. Cigarette smoke is particularly alarming to deer and carries long distances. If you must smoke in your stand, space those light-ups as far apart as possible and take only a couple of drags from each.

Range estimation is critical in all deer hunting, and ranges of objects appear very different from tree stands than they do from the ground. In addition, in the shadowy woods most hunters find the ranges of all objects difficult to estimate. Even the size of the deer often causes you to over- or underestimate its range.

Duck all these bothersome problems in advance. Each time you position or construct a new stand, conduct a test-firing session from it. Pick reference objects in several directions and at various ranges from your stand and fire a few arrows at or near each of these objects. Then when a deer sneaks in, glance at a nearby reference object and know exactly where to hold for a clean and lethal hit.

While sighting in from tree stands, it is extremely important to shoot a couple of straight-down practice shots. Actual shot opportunities like this can easily come while hunting from a tree stand, and if you know where to hold, you can break the deer's back and have no trailing problem. Strangely enough, this easy straight-down shot is missed frequently by new archers. The new archer usually sights in at no ranges closer than 10 to 20 yards, then shoots over the deer that suddenly walks under his stand.

Falling off a 12-foot tree stand can kill you just as dead as falling off a 12-story building, so don't take lightly the manner in which you construct or position the stand on the tree. Make sure the support and platform are strong enough to hold your weight. Make sure that access ladders, spikes and steps are strong and safe and that all bolts are tight. It also makes sense to tie a couple of safety ropes around the trunk and yourself. They should be loose enough to allow freedom of movement, but not so loose they are of no value.

It may sound strange to non-tree sitters, but it is easy to lose your balance when perching like an owl for long periods on a small platform high above the ground. If you are allergic to high places, stay out of a tree stand and hunt on the ground. It is also strange—but true—that you can get motion sickness in a tree stand! On a windy day a tall pine trunk will sway gently back and forth just as a ship on rolling swells.

Every bowhunter knows that sharp broadheads can be dangerous. Use a rope or line to haul your bow and quiver up to the tree stand *after* you climb up. And when leaving the stand, lower the bow and quiver to the ground *before* making your descent. It also makes sense to use the rope to raise and lower all other equipment you need in the stand. It is a simple matter to tie your bow and quiver, water jug, waste pail, food and raingear to one end of the rope and haul them all up at the same time—and to lower them in the same manner.

MASTERING TREE STAND SHOOTING

Up there, 8 to 12 feet above the ground, it can be a strange world. Your visual frames of reference are almost totally altered. But repeated practice and experience will solve this for you.

In addition to being viewed from new shooting- and distance-judging angles, the animal may be partially or completely obscured in shadows, and a deer extremely close to your stand—or straight under it—may appear larger than it actually is. This has happened to many bowhunters and often resulted in extreme loss of composure. As a result, the archer either hurries everything, spooks the deer and misses the shot or feels so pinned down by the close presence of the quarry that he or she is afraid to move.

Tree stand hunting has one particular nemesis—over-shooting. Practically every close shot ever missed from a tree stand sailed right over the deer's back.

But this can be cured. In fact, it *must* be cured, for tree stand bowhunting is effective and interesting. In densely brushed areas or early in the season with plenty of foliage still on trees and brush, it may be the only way to hunt.

Shoot as heavy a bow as you can *handle accurately*. You need complete penetration to leave a good blood trail; you'll be shooting through 15 to 20 inches of body depth and sometimes through heavy bone structure.

Use heavy arrow shafts because you don't need to worry about trajectory at this close range.

Use a heavy, strong, multi-bladed broadhead. A long, thin head is not as desirable for tree stand shooting because it could bend on the heavier bones (spine and base of ribs) or deflect and slide over the outside of the rib cage. A multi-bladed head does more cutting and opens up the wound more, for better bleeding.

Be sure the broadhead is *razor sharp* to give best penetration and cutting. File the tip to more roundness so it will be less likely to curl or bounce out.

Use an arrow holder on your bow so the arrow won't fall off the shelf whenever you move. Use Bjorn-type nocks which hold the arrow on the string. These nocks, together with the arrow holder, will keep your arrow firmly in place but won't hinder shooting.

Choose a stand location where you have: (1) good vision of approaching trails, (2) decent shot angles, (3) a comfortable position for long hours of waiting. Position the blind 10 yards or more off the deer trail if you can. This will give you a side angle shot—which is easier to make and offers better opportunities.

Drop deer scent in proper locations on the trail so the deer will drop its head and look away from you to sniff the scent. Try to set the scent position so you get a quartering shot from the rear into the lung area.

Clear the tree for the standard 20- to 40-yard shots, but also remember to clear for the much closer shots almost straight down. Do this before hunting season.

Position your tree stand—and yourself in the stand—so you can move into shooting position with the least amount of movement. A deer extremely close might be able to hear the limbs creak as you draw, hear the wheels turning on a compound, or hear the arrow sliding back over the rest. Tune your equipment to be as quiet as possible during the draw as well as during the shot.

The stand's attachment system must be firm and quiet. Move around in the stand when you first enter to settle it against the bark and remove the chances of shifting or scraping when you move to shoot. Then tie yourself in with a rope; it will hold you in should you slip or fall asleep. You can also lean against the rope for a firm shooting position.

If you're standing on a tree limb, and/or leaning against the trunk, scrape off the loose, softer areas of dead outer bark (but don't damage the inner bark). This gives a firm, quiet stand.

Be sure your face and hands are fully camouflaged. Even if you're up high, your light skin texture stands out noticeably. Wear camo gloves and use a headnet or camo paste on face and neck.

Coat all possible light-reflective areas on the portable tree stand.

If possible, have second and third arrows in ready position; you sometimes get a second shot from a tree stand. Place broadhead tips lightly in tree bark and lean the nock end of the arrows against a branch.

Every time you leave the blind during hunting season, take a practice shot or two if it is light enough to see. This will keep your shooting eye sharp. Retrieve the arrows as you leave.

It's not all sweetness and light though. Tree stand hunting can be dangerous: (1) If you're afraid of heights you'll never relax and enjoy

Bend at the waist when shooting from a tree stand. If you simply lower your bow arm, you tend to heel the bow and shoot high.

yourself in a tree stand. (2) You have to be prepared for falling asleep. (3) You could slip off the stand, or the stand could slip. (4) Wet or icy tree trunks and limbs are especially slippery. (5) You must take extra care bringing tackle into and out of a tree stand. Use a rope to raise and lower the bow with arrows in the quiver.

Remember, the tendency is to shoot high, so compensate in aiming and shooting form: (1) if you cannot stand fully upright, lean forward at the waist, don't just lower your bow arm (if you shoot from a low bow arm position, it will kick up on release, thus kicking your arrow high). (2) Do not heel the bow (on sharply angled shots downward, you tend to put more pressure on the bottom limb, which also kicks the arrow high).

Try a cheekbone anchor, with three fingers under the arrow. This decreases the angle between anchor, eye and point of the arrow. You will thus aim directly down the arrow shaft, just as you would a gun barrel. You will also have less control of the arrow on the string, but if you use a Bjorn-type nock this should not be a problem.

Remember that your arrow tends to rise slightly in the first few yards of a shot, so concentrate heavily on a lower-than-usual point of impact—especially on very close shots.

When deer are extremely close, there's a tendency sometimes to feel that you won't need to come to full draw. This is wrong! You always need to come to full draw for optimum bow performance and full arrow penetration.

Barebow (instinctive) shooters must practice well for all shots, but especially on the extremely close, sharply angled shots. You can't rely on "normal-gap-plus-a-little-more" type of aiming. Until you become familiar with the aiming gap for extremely close shots, you'll feel that you're pointing your arrow at the deer's feet; but you won't be.

Practice with a three-dimensional target cut out of cardboard or foam so you'll become familiar with the general shape of the deer —and the path of the arrow in the simulated deer.

Practice close—everywhere from a few feet out to 30 yards or more.

Don't overlook the advantage of a bowsight at extreme close range; set a pin for the proper elevation and use it. On a 20-yard shot the arrow will be right on target at 8 to 10 feet and at 20 yards, first as the arrow rises, then as it falls slightly. But nowhere in that distance will you be very far off.

When shooting almost straight down, most archers aim slightly off center from the spine so there will be less bone to penetrate. This offers better chances for complete arrow penetration and a better blood trail. And if you strike the spine, the deer is usually downed immediately. Instead of shooting when the deer is directly under you, and almost too close to draw without spooking it, you may wish to let the deer move past you a few steps. Then adjust your aiming spot

TREE STAND SHOOTING

TREE STAND BOWHUNTING is effective because: 1) a deer's warning system is attuned to ground level threat, 2) you're above the deer's normal line of vision, 3) your scent pattern is above the deer, 4) you usually see the deer approaching, and 5) you often get a second shot. In densely brushed areas, this might be the only way to hunt.

However, you'll be seeing the deer from an unfamiliar angle, distance judging is more difficult, angle of shooting is unusual, and a deer very close to you may appear so large you blow your cool.

Practically everyone tends to shoot high, over the animal's back or getting a high hit. Concentrate on aiming low and concentrate on the exact target, not on the whole deer or the antlers.

• SHOOT AS HEAVY a bow as you can handle ACCURATELY. You need complete penetration for a good blood trail, and you'll be shooting through the entire 15-20 inches of body depth. Heavy arrows and heavy broadheads are also advisable, especially for very close shots where trajectory is not a factor.

• CHOOSE A LOCATION which gives good vision of approach-

STAND HEIGHT

Your location, 8-12 feet above the ground, and possible extreme closeness of deer, gives a different sight picture, often makes deer appear larger than it actually is. Compensate in aim and shooting form. Bend forward at waist for close shots; do not hunch over because this shortens your draw length. Do not lower bow arm, do not heel

• TREE STAND MUST BE firm and safe. Tie yourself in with rope, for safety and aid in aiming on straight down shots.

FEMORAL ARTERIES • KIDNEYS • LUNGS • HEART

INTESTINES • STOMACH • LIVER   CAROTID ARTERIES

ANATOMY

When shooting sharply down, most archers aim slightly off center from spine. This offers better chances for complete penetration and better blood trail. And if you strike spine, deer is usually downed immediately. Let deer move past you, then adjust aiming point rearward so arrow will cut down into vitals, not ahead of them. Little left/right margin for error on straight down shots; be sure you have proper string alignment. There are vital organs the length of the deer, so a shot farther back than desired can be effective.

QUARTERING SHOTS

From above, must have aiming spot moved properly forward or back so arrow will slice at full penetration through vital organs. Do not try to visualize standard full side view and vital organ locations; they're different when viewed from above. Shots from the side mean there's less bone structure in the way, and less body depth to contend with. Concentrate on the exact aiming spot, not the entire body.

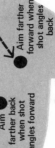

AIMING

For very close shots use a cheekbone anchor, three fingers under the string, and aim down the arrow shaft as you would a gun barrel. Since most archers aim too high on these shots, and arrows tend to rise in the first few yards of shot, remember to AIM LOW.

If you use corner-of-the-mouth anchor without a sight, practice enough so you know the proper gap spacing. Your sight picture will look like you're aiming the arrow below the animal's feet.

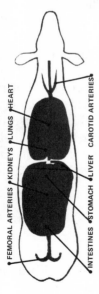

Aim farther back when shot angles forward

Aim farther forward when shot angles back

rearward on the animal so your arrow will cut down into the vitals, not ahead of them. The point of entry may seem too far back, but when the broadhead gets down into the boiler room, it will be right where it should be. Remember, too, that there are vital organs the entire length of the deer, so a shot farther back than desired can be effective. (All these various shot conditions should be governed by one rule: take the *first good shot* you get; it may be the only good shot you'll get.)

Whether your stand is almost directly over the trail or off to the side 10 or more yards, do not try to visualize the standard, full side view and corresponding vital organ locations in the deer's body as you would view them from a ground-level side position; their relative positions are different when viewed from above, or above and to the side. For instance, the closer you get to being directly over a deer, the more heavy bone structure you will have to contend with and the further your arrow will have to travel through the deer to get complete penetration.

On all quartering shots, remember to aim at a point of impact farther back when the deer is quartering away from you and farther forward when the deer is quartering toward you. These aiming adjustments will bring the broadhead right into the heart/lung cavity.

Always concentrate on the exact aiming spot, not on the entire deer.

Don't be afraid to take a *good* shot at a deer facing you or moving directly away. There are vital organ positions from side to side. With shots from behind there's less chance of bone interference. But the arrow *will* have to travel longitudinally through the deer to reach most vital organs and give complete penetration. Again, I emphasize the need for a heavy bow handled accurately. If the deer faces you, aim just above the juncture of neck and brisket. If the deer is facing directly away, aim for the spine about midway in the body length so the arrow will slant down into the heart/lung area.

SCENTS MAKE SENSE

How often have you wished you could come up with the magic formula of success that some hunters seem to possess? And how often have you tried quizzing these people without learning much more than you already knew? In your mind you are quite convinced that these successful hunters have indeed found something magic, and it's a deep, dark, guarded secret.

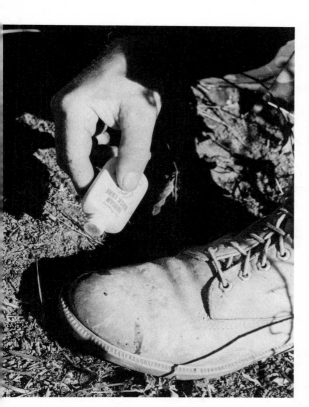

Scents can attract game and mask your own odor.

In reality these hunters probably are no more knowledgeable than you. They do about all of the things any other good hunter does—*except* they may have used a product you've overlooked: the artificial and natural scents.

Most game and predatory animals (except birds) have a keen sense of smell. If conditions are favorable, they are apt to get a whiff of you long before you are within bow range. Human and associated odors readily disclose danger to game animals.

Each individual's scent differs from the scent of every other and is attached to him as long as he lives. In fact, all living creatures from mouse to man have scent, and it can't be disguised by perfume or by wearing another's clothing. It can be masked, however, by the use of scents.

The Indians were well aware of this and used several methods to mask the human smell. They placed great faith in the power of musks and glands cut from game animals. Among the more common practices were such acts as rubbing their body with oils rendered from the fat of prior kills. Another favorite trick was the coating of their body with fresh dung.

Some Indian deer hunters would avoid bathing for several days, spending the entire time swaddled in a deer hide. Their short range bows and limited hunting weapons demanded the utmost in stalking skill. They had simply learned that masking their odor helped immensely in capturing game animals for food and clothing.

The mountain man and the trapper found scents to be of great value. Many of these hunters carefully saved the urine and gall while dressing or skinning out game and fur-bearing catches. They would brew a concoction, let the mixture stand several days, then shake well and scatter a few drops on weeds and ground near the trap set. A little of the scent would also be rubbed on the trappers' gloves and shoe soles to conceal the human odor.

Scents that mask the human odor are of great advantage to the bowhunter who practices the art of varmint and game calling. He will find that the basic reasons for using scents are twofold: One is to use a scent that will actually have some appeal to the animal being called; the other is an attempt to overpower or mask scent which is certain to be human.

Scent applied to shoe soles is of great assistance when walking into a hunting or calling area. Invariably, if there is any breeze at all, your quarry will circle downwind to pick up scent. This is his natural hunting technique to locate forage or his enemies. If his sensitive nose picks up your scent from wind or tracks, he is likely to vanish.

Probably there's not much else that's easier to buy and more often overlooked than scents. Just about every sporting goods outlet offers a variety to choose from. Most mail order houses carry a good inventory, especially those that stock trapper supplies.

One mistake often made by hunters is the choosing of the wrong scent. A hunter should never use the scent of an animal that's not generally found in his hunting area—a completely foreign odor may be just as bad as his own. As an all around man-scent mask, skunk essence is one of the best since skunks are found over much of the U.S.

When you are out calling fox, a fox urine scent should be used. For coyotes, a coyote urine scent. Additionally, mink, muskrat, coon, weasel, and others are available from most dealers.

Paul W. Howard, Jr., of National Scents (Garden Grove, California) had this to say when I quizzed, "How's business?"

"Our business stinks," he said, "but for a good reason. A few short years ago we made animal scents almost exclusively for the professionals, but when the secrets got out, even the novice hunter and trapper began to do things unheard of in the past.

"Some of the odors that emanate from our laboratory are atrocious, but they work. We manufacture over sixty different scent products presented in easy-to-handle, non-breakable polyethylene applicators, and each scent is an exact duplicate or concentrate of the real smell."

One example is National's twin-pack buck (deer) scent that completely counteracts human odors. It contains two powerful scents —their favorite food, apples (a synthetic), and that ever lovin' smell of sex (the real thing). Both are said to be nearly irresistible.

Jet-Aer Corporation (Paterson, New Jersey) has a three-ounce pressurized spray-can labeled G 96 Deer Lure. It produces a pungent natural odor of ripe apples. Sprayed on the hunters' clothes, trees, bushes, rocks, and so forth, it effectively obscures all human odors, carrying on the wind for many a mile. Deer, moose, caribou and similar game are notoriously fond of ripe apples and will follow its tempting fragrance.

Pete Rickard's original Indian Buck Lure is used by quite a few bowhunters. It's made from pure musks, and it won't spoil or freeze. A few drops near the stand or calling station—or on boots and hat while stalking—are all that's needed. And it's guaranteed to overcome all human scent. It is claimed by some to even stop running deer.

Some hunters, particularly varmint hunters, prefer to use cottontail rabbit scent. A hunter I know uses an electronic call and places the speaker about 25 yards from his calling station. The speaker and area around it are treated with the rabbit scent.

He says the speaker cone is scarred from the varmints' chewing and scratching, trying to get at what they believe is a rabbit inside.

Dog training scents work well, too! Such scents as rabbit, quail and pheasant have been used for years by trainers to help develop a dog's sense of smell. These scents work effectively for the hunter, masking his odor and offering a tempting scent to varmints and predators.

Most scents come in a handy polyethylene squeeze-bottle and are easy to apply. Some hunters cut the highly concentrated formulas used for dog training fifty percent with distilled water, placing the cut formula in plastic bottles that have spray applicators attached to their caps. A few squirts on shoes, clothing and brush can pay off.

Many hunters prefer a cloth saturated with their chosen scent, looping it over their belt or fastening it to their clothing with a safety pin. A soft cloth, such as a wash or face cloth—preferably a brownish or green shade that will blend with the natural environment—is best. The important thing is to use enough scent to adequately hide your odor, paying special attention to shoes—including the soles.

Avoid the use of a deodorant, antiperspirant and after shave lotion on the day of the hunt. These can be classified as scents that work in reverse. All they'll do is advertise your presence. Skip the roadside beaneries and similar establishments. The scent of fried foods and tobacco permeates clothing and skin with telltale odors.

New clothing should be washed, rinsed and dried before being worn on a hunt. The fresh store odor might please your sense of smell, but it's apt to ring an alarm bell for the game. Your new hunting boots will need extra attention, too! It'll be necessary to work in a goodly amount of natural scent to overcome the manufacturer's odor. Some hunters store their hunting clothes in a sealed plastic bag that is jammed with broken twigs and branches from brush and trees native to the area. Pine is a favorite because it gives off a great deal of scent.

Thermal drafts also play an important role in the use of scent. Veteran hunters know that early in the morning, usually before an overhead sun, winds push scent downhill. As the morning advances and the sun heats the ground, odors rise. Since hunting above the quarry is the proven rule, keep this in mind constantly.

You can sometimes gain an edge on opening day by scouting likely spots the afternoon before the hunt. When you locate deer sign—fresh tracks and droppings—pick a likely spot for a stand, mark the location and sprinkle the area with musk scent. Go back to the spot just before sunup, settle down and wait for action.

The wild animal can't think, plan or remember in the same perspective with you—but he's got you beat in all the other departments. He depends on his senses and natural instincts for survival and forage. His senses of smell, sight and hearing far surpass that of man.

Your preparedness and success on the hunt will depend entirely on you. You can select the best of hunting clothing, do a lot of target practice, stop smoking several days before going afield and stalk soundlessly—and draw a blank. Had you incorporated scents with the proper use of hunting techniques, you just might have brought all kinds of animals within a few feet of your bow—proving that scents do make sense.

HUNT THE EDGES FOR MORE GAME

I can remember back in southwestern Minnesota when I was a sophomore in high school and had just taken up the sport of bowhunting. In those days I had a 45-pound bow and a fine set of glass arrows and some of the best whitetail habitat in the country in which to use them.

The deer herd at that time was building rapidly along the Rock River. Come late October and November, the state conservation department would open the deer season for bow and arrow only.

We did most of our hunting along the river bottoms, which harbored the main portion of the deer herd. At that time the river bottom consisted of patches of dense hardwoods, patches of alfalfa fields, lush corn fields and small, irregular areas of completely open pastureland.

This patchwork of different cover was great for hunting because we could use two or three bowhunters to drive the deer from one timbered area to another and try to ambush them on the trails coming out of each area. Many a time I had several nice bucks move past me and provide some exciting moments; but, alas, I wasn't too deadly with a bow and arrow in those days.

There was much discussion among local hunters as to just why the deer were adapting and increasing so rapidly in this flat farming country and at the same time appeared to be diminishing and getting harder to come by in the northern Minnesota woods, which had for years been among the top whitetail deer areas in the U.S.

This adaptation phenomenon—big game moving into farmland and narrow river bottoms—was happening not only in Minnesota but also in many of the states that previously had only a limited number of deer within their borders.

As bowhunters, we can be thankful for this little happening of nature, because it has opened up many, many areas to bowhunting that previously had no game in them to hunt—other than an occasional rabbit or two.

The "edge effect" seemed to have created game where before there was none. In reality what happened in these areas was that game animals were migrating into the areas, and because of ideal habitat conditions—sunlit areas for brush, shrubs and grass to grow, cover nearby and probably easy access to water, too—the herds were reproducing at a more rapid rate.

If we go back in history, we can see how this change took place, and how it can continue to benefit us as outdoorsmen in the future.

Before the white man came along, great numbers of birds and animals were basically open-country prairie- and foothills-dwellers. Animals such as the elk, mountain sheep, mule deer and whitetail were most often found in fairly open country where Mother Nature had provided them with an edge effect of her own. Deer in the north were almost nonexistent until the land was logged and brush had a chance to grow. The deep, dense hardwood stands of the East and Midwest and the pine and spruce forests of the far West were still untouched by the axe and saw of civilization and were much too dense to provide enough food under their canopy of leaves and branches to support very many game animals. As man moved westward he logged and cleared areas for his farms and fields. He changed this once deep, dark, uninhabited forest to a patchwork of clearings, brush patches, fields and pastures. This provided game animals and birds with an area of plentiful forage, plants, browse, and good cover within easy reach.

As was the case in northern Minnesota, the deer multiplied rapidly, and hunting was great. Then, however, the new growth in the cleared areas began to mature and the clearings and cut-over areas began to fill with larger trees and brush which in turn crowded out the smaller food species and browse plants of the whitetail. The vast numbers of animals now had less food per deer, and many simply starved to death.

A few hardier deer migrated to areas where there had been but few deer before and multiplied into huge herds. These deer in turn migrated farther and farther south into the farm lands which provided the ideal situation of food and shelter. Small, dense, wooded and brushy areas were surrounded by ideal feed—such as various field crops and plenty of the smaller browse plants on which deer thrive. Now there isn't a state in the United States that doesn't have a deer population.

Deer weren't the only ones to benefit from this edge effect that man created. Pheasants, cottontails, turkeys, elk, bear and many other game animals, large or small—as well as most of the game birds —benefitted directly from this phenomenon.

I have tried to show you the broad effect that the edge effect has on you as a bowhunter. Just how can you use this to benefit you directly when you are actually out after, say, deer or cottontails?

First of all, if you were to pick an area to hunt, you would be wise to pick an area that exhibits a good bit of the edge effect. You will find far more game in the fringes around good feeding areas and open fields

A slingshot will rattle a pellet through vegetation on the side of the game opposite from you and often will cause it to move toward you.

than you will in the deep, dark forest. So if you have to move through big stuff to get to the edges you want, keep alert but don't waste too much time there. As I said earlier, game animals like to move out into the open where they can use their eyesight, hearing and smell to warn them while they are feeding. They will move from the heavy wooded areas to the lesser wooded areas and open fields during the evening to feed. At daylight, the procedure will be reversed. Armed with this knowledge, you will be able to better place your blind or have a better idea which direction would be best to hunt in a given area.

As a test several years ago, two hunting partners and I drove a small swampy patch of pines and alders for five consecutive days. Sometimes we drove it morning and night, but never very early or very late.

The astounding thing was that we saw deer every time we went through.

A close look at the geography of the place gives a good explanation. The area ran along a creek bed for about a quarter-mile, but at no place was it wider than 250 yards. Scrub oak ridges ran along both sides of the valley, dwindling to an open alder and pine clearing at the south end.

This little patch was surrounded by 40 acres of jackpine slashing. The tops and scrap had been piled in rows or left where it fell. A tongue of timber reached within a couple of hundred yards of the northern corner of the swamp, a semi-brushy ridge approached it from the east and an open, mature jack pine stand was within good bow range on the western side.

Deer funneled into—and out through—these natural approach-ways. But they wouldn't move unless pushed hard. And since there were only three of us to stand and drive, we did little more than watch them go out the trail we weren't on. Easy rifle shots, but nothing for the bow.

The part I like best about the whole thing is that no one but us hunted that patch during the five days. It was surrounded by roads, too open around the edges, too small. Or so everyone else thought.

If you are going into an area that is unfamiliar to you, get a map and try to tie your hunting into a place that shows up as a patchwork of openings, brushy areas and dense stands of timber. Look for ridge tops, draws, swamp edges, fire lanes or food patches developed by conservation departments. Your chances of finding game in areas such as this are much better than in an area that is completely open or one that is all dense timber.

Several years ago, I was hunting an area in northern Colorado with a friend of mine for both deer and elk. We left home before daylight, and as we drove to the area, I gave him a good verbal description of the lay of the land. The lower edge of the valley was all broken country with small quaky patches, brush-edged clearings and open meadows, and the upper part of the valley was heavy, green spruce and pine.

We separated just at daylight and hunted separately all day. That evening when we met at the car, my companion said he had not seen a single deer or elk all day. I had, during the early morning hours, seen upwards of thirty muleys and one nice bunch of elk. That afternoon, during the heat of the day, I had jumped four nice bulls and two buck deer and during the evening had seen quite a few does and fawns and small bucks. In further discussion it was brought out that my fellow bowhunter had spent all the early morning hours in the dark timber and had spent the mid-day hours hunting the open areas when he got skunked in the timber. I had hunted the open, brushy areas until about 9:00 a.m., then moved into the heavy timber, where I knew the game would be bedded down, and hunted this until about 4:30 p.m. and then moved back to the open and brushy areas to catch the game moving out to feed in the evening.

This episode points out the value of knowing the game habits and of hunting an area that lets you take full advantage of the edge effect.

In this case we were after deer and elk in Colorado, but the same principles apply to cottontails in Kansas, pheasants in Iowa or whitetail deer in Pennsylvania. Find an area that has good edge effect and you will find the game. Put good hunting practices to use and don't waste time hunting areas where the game isn't. Give yourself the edge by hunting the edge.

WITHIN SOUND OF THE CHURCH BELL

Although the whitetail deer, as it is officially known, is scattered to some degree around the contiguous United States, it is east of the Mississippi that you will find it in greatest abundance. Here it has learned to frequently live as neighbor to the archer who hunts it and preserves it with the same sportsman's dollar. Despite the dissimilarity in habitat, the whitetail has much in common with its western counterpart—the mule deer.

In fact, when you get right down to it, hunting *any* deer in any part of the country varies little *until you take that first step of your hunt*. Your camouflage may be patterned a bit more to the anticipated background, but the same bow and arrows and skill are necessary whether you are working your way through the old farm land thickets of Upper Tupper, New York, or the wide open spaces of Wyoming.

Nevertheless, the dissimilarities in flora and terrain will provide a different story on the average hunt.

Although there are real wilderness areas in the Northeast where you can walk for many miles with no sign of man's presence except the second growth timber and brush which provide ideal deer country, *the best hunting is frequently within sound of the local church bell*. Although basically a woodland animal, the whitetail knows on which side its bread is buttered. And that side is frequently a gentle slope of slashing and red brush leading up to the old ice-eroded mountains of northeastern United States.

There the whitetail proliferates. The fact that in most areas it doesn't reach its full growth potential is due simply to heavy hunting. For example, in Pennsylvania the average whitetail buck is no more than 18 months of age when it falls to the gun or bow. The exceptions to this roam the timbered-over areas of the less heavily populated states where big swamps and thick secondary growth permit the deer to grow to its full size.

But anywhere from West Virginia to Maine and from Maryland to northern Minnesota, it is not overly unusual to find a buck that will field dress well in excess of 200 pounds.

Since the vast majority of deer are taken in farming country, methods used will work almost anywhere there are whitetails. It must be considered that, although hunting the wilderness areas has its plus values, bowhunting in such states as New Jersey and Connecticut may have the approach of the animal muffled by the roar of traffic from a nearby six-lane highway. An indication of just how well whitetails do in the East is the grim total of over 25,000 killed annually by vehicles on the highways of Pennsylvania alone.

F. Rit Heller is a case in point when considering whitetails of the Northeast. Rit downed the biggest deer taken with a bow in Pennsylvania in 1973, a mammoth buck with a nine-point rack that had a 23-inch spread. It scored 139.6 on the Pope and Young Chart. And this one ranks only as the third largest whitetail taken with the bow in Pennsylvania. Four-and-a-half years old, the buck came from the area around the city of Reading, population 87,643.

Although driving deer in the East is most productive from the standpoint of shooting, most hunters prefer to go it alone or with one or a couple of friends. (Deer driving, especially in well-populated areas, creates a gang of people and cars that doesn't enhance the hunters' image.) Deer can frequently be located by traveling farming country in the evening before season. Although the whitetail is basically a browsing animal, feeding heavily on new growth of shrubs and trees, it reverts to grazing where farm fields provide the opportunity. Consequently, it is not unusual to find deer in these fields at the tail end of summer. Once deer are located, it is no great problem to determine their trails. With the knowledge that the deer do travel from the mountain benches to these favorite grazing spots, the smart archer stations himself or herself where he or she is most apt to get a shot as the animals pass through—often taking a stand *100 or more yards back from a field edge* to catch the deer before sundown and when they are less wary.

For this reason, tree stands are much favored by bowhunters in the East. The thickness of brush limits the shots under normal circumstances, and the problems of air movement make it difficult to get close to a deer. It is not unusual for a hunter to station himself in an apple tree and shoot a deer directly beneath him when it comes time to feed. Apples are a highly favored delicacy for whitetails, particularly when softened by the first frost.

A hunt that Rit and I had together with a group of locals from my home town of Berwick, Pennsylvania, is typical of another method of hunting which is a carry-over from the time when deer were not so plentiful in the Keystone State. We divided our small group of eight hunters, two of whom had already taken deer and were volunteering their services, so deer could be funneled to the more likely stations which might provide a shot. On one drive at least a dozen deer erupted from a thicket, and all managed to escape despite a personal shirttail try on a running doe. We hunted scrub brush interspersed with second-growth timber which stands as wooded islands among the surrounding farmlands. Although it was the late season, with snow on the ground, and the deer had been worked over during the full month of the October archery season—plus two weeks for antlered deer with the guns and two days of guns for antlerless deer—we had deer loose on almost every drive.

Driving produces shooting, but whitetails are extremely skittish when they know they are being hunted. They frequently come through at full tilt.

Another method of hunting in the East, which fits in with the deer's habit of feeding in the open from late afternoon to sunup, is the time-honored method of stalking. Because of heavy leaf cover in early autumn when the regular archery seasons are held, it is sometimes possible to approach deer in open fields from the wooded side. Or stalks can be made through high grass. In any method of stalking, the odds are very much with the wary whitetail. It may tolerate a group of noisy youngsters waiting for a school bus, but it is highly suspicious of any stealthy moves. Its habit of lowering its head to feed and then abruptly raising its head to locate an intruder is well known to all experienced whitetail hunters. Or it will stamp a front foot to alert its companions.

Most Eastern deer are shot at ranges well under 20 yards. There are the exceptions, of course, and there are always the "by-guess and by-golly" archers who will fling arrows at any distance to include themselves in the group most detrimental to the sport.

When hunting in the East, it is usually not too difficult to find living accommodations in the vicinity of the better spots. This is particularly true during the month of October when hostelries are begging for business before the later gunning season begins.

One of the toughest problems involved in bowhunting the frequently thick brush and swamps of the Northeast is recovery of even fatally shot animals. It is a far cry from most Western hunting where a deer can be seen with the naked eye for long distances and the ground is such that a blood trail is easy to follow. The broken terrain, often with many years of deciduous and evergreen tree droppings, is a difficult bed on which to pick up blood sign before it melts away or blends with this cover. Even the *best* areas often offer but a few yards of easy vision.

It is not unusual to look long and hard for a deer that drops from a fatal shot no more than a hundred yards or so from the archer. Consequently, a wait-and-watch procedure is in order, even though you *know* that your hit was a good one. Moving after the animal too soon may cause it to draw on extra energy to travel twice as far and double the complications of recovering it. An hour is not too long to wait—two hours if there is any doubt about the probable effectiveness of the hit.

The East is host to many varieties of maple trees. Their leaves, which start to fall after the first good frost, can really complicate following a blood trail. Some of them come in yellow with little red spots which closely simulate blood. And there is a host of other deciduous trees which soon blanket many hunting areas with a variety of colors.

For the most part, regular archery seasons provide shirtsleeve weather, and there is no need to bundle up. On the higher mountains, like 2,000 feet, it can get right chilly in the evening and early mornings. Consequently, it is well to have a light jacket or a heavy sweater in reserve. Since the days will normally be warm, some provision should be made to have such covering available.

October is Indian Summer in the Northeast. Rain comes seldom, but morning dew from cool nights means wet legs and feet unless clothing is worn to avoid it. But days will likely be warm, and wet-proof footgear can be uncomfortable during the midday hours. Unless you are driving deer, however, midday hunting, from about nine o'clock to four o'clock, is largely a waste of time. It is better spent catching up on sleep lost at the poker table the night before.

Whether it is stalking, driving or still hunting, each phase of the sport has its own attractions and drawbacks. The stalker has the intense satisfaction of meeting the deer on its own terms, although he is a minority and needs all the skills at his command. The driver will get more shooting, although the deer will frequently be on the move, but he has the added advantage of ready help in the event it is necessary to search for or trail a wounded animal. The still hunter, who parks himself behind a convenient bush or takes to a tree stand, has the opportunity to see many of the wonderful things of nature unfold during his quiet wait, although he must rely on the deer to come to him. But no matter what approach he takes to his hunting, the successful whitetail deer bowhunter has his pleasure cut out for him. There is no smarter animal afoot. Its ability to survive in the face of advancing civilization places it somewhere in the intelligence category of the fox, the coyote and the raccoon—all of which refuse to retreat.

And it is the sportsman's dollar which makes it possible to regulate seasons and maintain the herds of whitetail deer which abound in the brush, in the forests and on the farms of the Northeastern United States.

ARE YOU DEER BLIND?

While deer hunting several years ago in the vast, swampy acreage of the Mingo National Wildlife Refuge in southeast Missouri, I sat leaning against an old cypress tree and eating my lunch. It was near the end of the season, and it was the last day I was going to be able to hunt before the season closed.

I really wanted a deer, and I had spent the biggest part of the morning—without results—in a portable tree stand I had set up earlier near a particularly good crossing. Before daylight, a couple of deer had come by, but that was all. I had climbed down about the middle of the morning and had still-hunted until noon, seeing two more deer; but it was so thick and brushy I had no shot. Much of the undergrowth in the old swamp was so thick and dense it was next to impossible to shoot through; but the place was full of deer, so I'd hunted it quite a bit that year.

My bow, a stubby Pearson Hunter well suited to the dense cover, rested on the ground beside me as I ate, and in the damp, crisp coldness of the late December day I was enjoying immensely the remote silence of my swampy surroundings. I let my eyes wander from one spot to another while I ate, sipping the hot coffee I'd brought along. As I gazed about, I suddenly became aware of what seemed to be a rather strange pattern of branches in a fallen treetop about 45 yards away. I looked closer.

Sorting out the branches and the outline of the trunk, my eyes saw what seemed to be a pair of giant antlers. I studied the brush pile more, and the outline of the buck's chest and front legs seemed to become clear. So much, in fact, did it seem like a whopper buck standing in the brush that I almost laughed aloud. How the mind plays tricks, I thought, especially when it's the last hunting day of the season and I haven't scored yet. The imaginary buck certainly looked real because, I admitted to myself, I *wanted* it to be real. If I were a novice, I told myself, I'd grab my bow and be looking for a hole to shoot through. I smiled to myself and continued eating. Occasionally, though, I let my eyes stray back to the brushy treetop and its imaginary buck.

I finished eating, carefully folded the lunch sack and stuffed it back into my jacket pocket, reached for my bow and stood up. The figment of my imagination with its brushpile rack still seemed a part of the fallen treetop. I eyed it again. To satisfy a final, infinitely small shred of curiosity, I swung my bow over my head.

What happened? You know what happened. The biggest whitetail I've ever seen—before or since—catapulted from behind the brush and in two jumps was out of sight. I stood there with my jaw hanging open, without even an arrow on the string.

A rare episode in the annals of bowhunting for deer? Hardly. For me, it is only one of many such incidents that have convinced me that deer are the most adroit, evasive animals in the woods. A deer's ability to melt into his surroundings surpasses all other animals in the wild; he can blend perfectly into nearly any kind of cover, not moving a muscle for what seems hours. He'll freeze and let you walk past within a few yards of him, then slip away quietly after you've gone. And he can do this summer or winter, early or late in the day, remaining invisible regardless of lighting conditions. For the beginning bowhunter, this makes scoring particularly difficult. And even experienced hunters, I've found, are often duped.

In fact, after spending considerable time in the woods in pursuit of deer with bow and camera, I'm convinced that quite a few hunters —both experienced and beginners—suffer chronically from what I

Don't be deer blind. Look for unusual angles, lines, irregular bits of white, movement, and so forth. Do not look for an entire deer.

have come to call "deer blindness": the classic ability to walk past and never notice most of the deer in the woods. Most of the time this "blindness" results from looking for the wrong things when it comes to actually spotting concealed deer. Sometimes, however, it has its roots in a hunter's inability to read correctly—or even recognize—deer sign that could ultimately lead him to his trophy. Happily, though, the affliction of "deer blindness" is not a permanent one, and overcoming it is relatively simple. When you start looking the right way, you'll start *seeing* a great many more deer, and you will greatly increase your chances of spotting potential trophies.

The first thing you need to get out of your mind before you enter the woods is any notion of seeing *whole* deer. If you don't you're going to miss seeing most of them. It's rather infrequent, especially during season, that you see a deer standing fully exposed. And if you do, most of the time he'll be well out of bow range. Besides, if you can easily see the deer, chances are pretty good he's already seen you. So, instead of looking for *whole* deer, you need to concentrate on learning to look for *parts* of deer, because when you're hunting the kind of woods that deer favor—thick, dense and brushy—usually that's all you'll see. And you won't see even that if you are not looking for the right things.

One of the main things you need to look for in the woods is any variance in *line* that might suggest, in heavy cover, a deer's presence. And this means any line that somehow looks different. Few horizontal lines exist in nature—except for the edges of rivers, lakes and, of course, small limbs. So if you spy a horizontal line where your experience tells you there shouldn't be one, have a second look. Check it out with binoculars if you're carrying them. Quite possibly what you are seeing is the top of a deer's back or perhaps the bottom line of its belly. If you spot a horizontal line that extends for a couple of feet or more in thick brush, odds are it will belong to a deer almost every time.

If you're hunting hilly or mountainous country, keep a sharp eye directed toward the high ridges on your flanks, especially if the sky provides a lighter background. This is a good way to spot the silhouettes of standing or bedded deer because they constantly look ahead only. Make a habit of searching to either side as you hunt. And frequently look behind you; you may catch a smart deer sneaking off that had let you walk past it.

Not only *line*, but also *shape* will help you spot your quarry when otherwise you might miss seeing him. When you are hunting in a thickly wooded area, your eyes automatically adjust to the confusion of your surroundings. Brush, trees, rocks and thickets, when viewed together, make a kind of "total" impression on you, and you don't naturally isolate many individual objects as you look about. The objects that make up this total impression are for the most part irregular in shape; they are not symmetrical, except perhaps for leaves and cylindrical tree trunks. Therefore, if you see anything in the confused pattern of the terrain that *is* symmetrical, you better take another look. As your eyes sweep your wooded environment, train them to "fix" on anything unnaturally symmetrical. This practice often will find you deer.

What symmetry should you be looking for? The balanced, triangular group of spots created by a deer's nose and eyes is, for example, perfectly symmetrical in shape—and it is totally unlike anything else that exists naturally in the woods. The nose and eyes form black spots that are surrounded by white. And if you see these three black spots fringed in white, you can bet it's a deer facing you directly, probably looking right at you. The symmetrically-shaped ears of a deer are also hard to conceal, and these, too, are marked by white inner hair. Occasionally a hidden deer will show you his ears when he won't show you anything else, especially if he's still trying to locate you. And it's the symmetrical *shape* of the ears that gives the deer away.

If the weather is particularly cold, you should be watching for *steam*. A deer's breath, just like a man's, makes tiny, explosive puffs of steam on really cold days, and you can locate a deer by isolating the source of these small steam clouds.

I recall a hunt in bitter cold weather in Missouri's Ozarks when I located a deer in exactly this manner. I had come up from the bottom of a hollow to cross a ridge, and at the top I stopped a minute to look around. About 40 yards away in a thick stand of pine I could see regularly spaced puffs of steam in the snappy cold morning air. A closer look produced the line of the deer's back and its forelegs, but I couldn't see anything else. I stood still and in a few minutes a fat spike buck stepped openly onto the old logging road that traced the top of the ridge. I would never have seen the buck had it not been for the steam of his breathing. If I hadn't spotted it when I did, the deer would have slipped away and I would never have known he was there.

Sound, too, is a way of locating deer, in spite of the myth that a deer moves without making even the faintest noise. Certainly they can do this, but they don't do it all the time. If you are hunting carefully and slowly with the wind in your favor, often you can get very close to deer without their knowing it. If they are unaware of your presence, you can often hear them as they move about feeding—especially if there is no wind blowing. If you're moving as you hunt, pause every now and then to listen for leaves rustling or for the barely audible soft thud of a big deer's hooves on soft earth. And listen for things like the abrupt scolding of an old fox squirrel or the cantankerous shrieking of a bluejay. Often these are signs that something nearby, perhaps a deer, is moving through the woods.

Movement is, in itself, something else to watch for while deer hunting. Some deer, usually does, will flip their tails back and forth nervously, even while hidden, and the sharp-eyed hunter will detect this tiny movement. You may not want a doe, but her presence often suggests a buck is nearby. Just hold and wait. If nearby deer are unaware of your presence, they will often reveal themselves by movements of brush or saplings as they browse. If there's no wind to confuse matters, always keep an eye peeled for movement. A gently swaying sapling top has led me to more than one browsing deer.

Color is yet another element that will help you spot your trophy, and the color you need to become most sensitive to is white. If you see a white spot, however small, chances are pretty good it belongs to a deer. While some white occurs naturally in the outdoors—birch trees, aspens, limestone, the exposed wood of a broken tree—a flash of pure, brilliant white nearly always signals a deer's presence. The white hair on a deer—especially on its chest, tail and rump—is its biggest weakness when it comes to moving without being seen. White contrasts sharply with virtually everything else in the woods, particularly in the fall when you will be hunting. Just be sure it doesn't belong to some thoughtless hunter who happened to bring along the wrong kind of handkerchief. *Any* color variation from the ordinary might mean a deer: a tree whose bark seems to abruptly change color a few feet off the ground; a curious light spot in a distant shadow; any spot that strangely seems somehow darker, lighter, brighter, duller, grayer, browner, redder.

Having previously scouted your chosen hunting area for deer sign—tracks, droppings, buck rubs, beds, trails, browsing areas, old orchards and other similar indications that deer are actually around—concentrate on *seeing* some of the deer population once you begin hunting. Keep in mind those elements that will help you accomplish this: line, shape, symmetry, steam, sound, movement, and color —especially white. Remember, *anything* that doesn't seem to fit may well signal a deer's presence, and if your eyes and ears are tuned to these things, you'll come a whole lot closer to seeing deer than the hunter who ignores them.

FINDING THE BIG BUCKS

When I first saw the buck, he was standing in a small opening close by, looking directly away from me. As with many deer, the buck materialized on the scene suddenly, with no forewarning. One moment there was nothing; then I turned my head to scan the opposite direction, and when I glanced back, there he stood, the early morning sunlight glimmering on his antlers.

There was plenty of time for a decent shot, but a quick analysis of his antlers told me this wasn't the one. The antlers were wide, all right, reaching beyond his ears, but the beams were light and the points stubby. I knew that much better bucks roamed this area.

Then the buck turned his head and I knew immediately I'd made the wrong decision. But before I could raise my bow he trotted off and vanished into the underbrush.

It wasn't size that made him special. As white-tailed deer antlers go, his were just average. But while Nature cheated this buck on beam, she made up for it by blessing him with points.

A typical 10-point buck—with four tines on each beam, plus a pair of brow points—is something special, of course, but it really isn't uncommon. What is unusual is a 10-pointer with five tines on each beam instead of the standard four. In a long career of hunting I never can recall seeing a buck running loose with the five points on each beam.

That is, not until this one. It seemed incredulous that a buck with antlers no larger than this one had could carry such an abundance of points. I wanted that deer and I wanted him badly and I mentally kicked myself for muffing a golden opportunity.

So I began hunting him in earnest. The private ranch where I sighted him was a long way from my home—almost a 300-mile round trip—which restricted me considerably. I could get there only twice more before the season ended. It stands to reason that the more a hunter can get into the woods where a specific deer is known to roam, the better are his chances of getting a shot at it. Even so, I did see the buck again, but it was just a brief glimpse and there was no chance to release an arrow. The trail forked around a small clump of brush, and the buck took the right route, which put the brush between him and me. If he'd gone left instead, I would have had an easy shot—which proves there often is a very thin line between success and failure in bowhunting.

Meanwhile, I passed up several other bucks, including one nice eight-pointer, in hopes of getting a crack at this specific deer. This brings up one very important point in this type of hunting: the hunter must possess the utmost in restraint and patience. He must be dedicated in his pursuit and not tempted by deer of lesser stature.

John Hershey of Lititz, Pennsylvania, is a crackerjack hunter who has three whitetail deer listed by the Pope and Young Club. Each record-list buck was hunted specifically.

"When I located one that I thought was a good head, I hunted him and only him," Hershey explained.

And in each case, he emphasized, a few "lesser" bucks were passed by to take the larger one.

Stan Zellner took the biggest buck ever killed with bow and arrow in Arkansas. In describing his pursuit of the trophy, he said, "I had several opportunities at average-sized bucks, but I resisted the urge."

Mel Johnson killed the biggest whitetail ever taken by fair chase with the bow. The buck was killed in a soybean field near Peoria, Illinois. He was after a big buck and he hunted practically every evening after work.

"On several occasions, I saw small deer," Johnson said, "but I let them go."

But perhaps we should pause here and define a "specific" deer. It really is a nebulous term which has a different meaning for different people. Hershey was after big bucks. In my case, it was an unusual specimen.

The first buck I killed with my bow was a spike. That broke the ice. Since I'd taken who knows how many deer with a rifle, simply killing for the sake of killing didn't appeal to me. So I set my sights higher and went for a buck with at least forked antlers.

A rancher friend told me about a clump of oaks where many deer were coming to eat acorns. Several times he'd seen bucks in the oak grove—mostly spikes, but there was one six-pointer.

So I climbed one of the oaks, got comfortable and waited. At one time I had three spikes near my tree, all within easy bow range. But I let them be, waiting patiently for the six-pointer.

And the strategy paid off!

Now I was hunting a specific deer. It was not a trophy, agreed, but at the time it was a deer that I wanted.

So how does a person find a specific deer to hunt, perhaps a trophy-sized specimen or one that is unusual?

He gets in the woods and persistently looks for it, that's how! A few big deer are taken accidentally, by the hunter who happens to be at the right place at the right time, but most are killed by archers who are willing to pay the price, to work just a bit harder.

John Hershey said that all three of his record-list bucks "were scouted well in advance." He said he knew long before the season commenced just about where each one would come from and go to and be at any given time. Stan Zellner saw his Arkansas record buck go into a tangle of brush at dusk one evening and he strategically set his ambush point where he could intercept the buck as he came out the following morning. Mel Johnson had seen some very large bucks in the timber adjacent to the field where he took his world-record head.

Anyone who goes after a specific deer—graduating to the master's degree of hunting—obviously knows something about deer and their behavior. A beginner isn't going to discriminately start culling deer. But there is more to hunting a specific deer than merely climbing a tree stand near a trail where sign indicates deer travel and waiting and hoping.

As Hershey revealed, his trophy deer were scouted in advance. That's the key. Look for a specific deer prior to the season, then hunt him. A rudimentary statement that's simple in theory, complex in fact. You just don't head into the woods and locate a specific deer every day, and once you locate one, he isn't always going to cooperate just the way you think he should.

Hershey said one season he sighted a big buck, a real trophy, and played hide-and-seek with the deer throughout the season and never shot an arrow.

Remember: a buck doesn't get old and big by being stupid. A sagacious old rogue of the woods isn't going to be guilty of many mistakes.

White-tailed deer are widespread and abundant. But there are

What it's all about—a fine trophy taken in fair chase with a good weapon. But to find the big bucks, you must search them out and hunt hard.

some areas which yield bigger deer than others. Such places are where you want to concentrate your search. The odds dictate it.

Your primary source of information is the state game and fish department. Once you pinpoint a locale or locales, try to select one within a short drive of your home. The more time you can spend in the woods, the better.

Another salient point: almost all big bucks are killed on private land. Less competition means the buck can escape hunters for several seasons, grow older and develop larger antlers. Many hunters roaming haphazardly might also spook the animal and make him alter his daily routine.

A deer, like humans, gets everyday habits. This is his vulnerability. The observant hunter tries to "pattern" a specific deer, determining which trails he travels, where he feeds and where he beds. Then he pinpoints his stand to take advantage of this pattern—perhaps on the trail where the deer leaves his bed at daybreak or a field where he comes to feed. And the hunter leaves nothing to chance, realizing that no detail is too trivial to ignore.

The whitetail deer is a fairly predictable animal, one of limited range. In a trapping, release and retrapping program several years ago, the Texas Parks and Wildlife Department found that whitetails seldom strayed more than a half-mile from where they were born. In fact, several deer were retrapped in the same traps where they were caught originally many months earlier.

Scouting isn't unlike actual hunting. The scouter hides and looks during the periods when deer are traveling—early and late in the day. Actual sightings are more pertinent than any sign. One deer track looks pretty much like another, unless it is an exceptionally large buck with a track much more pronounced than the run-of-the-mill.

When preseason hunting, I like to carry a telephoto camera. Trying to get a photograph makes me study my quarry more closely. But some hunters prefer to carry their bows and actually practice-pull on deer, to settle their nerves and to learn where to place the arrow if and when an opportunity presents itself during the season.

If a certain deer wanders down a certain trail at a certain time, that might be a coincidence. But if the same deer uses the same trail at the same time on a different day, that is a pattern—an indication of its habits. The actual hunting and perhaps the kill are just the climax. The groundwork, the hard part, has been laid much earlier.

The hunter who is moving about in an area, spooks a deer and sees it bound off, white tail waving, doesn't have to worry about spooking the animal into the next county. It isn't going to run far. This is the deer's home territory, and it won't leave unless it is absolutely mandatory. A whitetail depends more on its innate survival instinct that it does its legs. Unlike the mule deer, which is migratory, the whitetail would rather hide than run. It is the nature of the species.

Hunting a specific deer is a challenge. But it also is hard work. Few trophy-sized deer come easily. There is no shortcut to success. The successful hunter first locates a specific deer, then learns all he can about its behavior and habits and musters every trick he knows to outwit the critter once the bowhunting season arrives. Even so, the odds are in the deer's favor. The bowhunter loses more often than he wins.

But there is nothing quite like going after a specific deer and using all your know-how and skill to produce. It is the ultimate in bowhunting. Few hunters are willing to pay the price.

LATE SEASON DEER—WEST AND EAST

West

The day was beautiful. The sky was a deep, pure blue with white; puffy clouds floating lazily around like cottonwood fluff on a backwoods pond. There was only an occasional, almost indistinguishable breeze, and all in all it should have been an ideal day for a bowhunter to be in the field after a record-book buck—which is just where I was and what I was after.

There was only one slight problem in this beautiful picture, and that was the fact that the temperature where I was hunkered down in the snow was almost down to the 20° below zero mark, and my blood was slowly congealing to the consistency of heavy syrup. The only thing that kept me from freezing solid was the presence of a magnificent buck that was some 60 yards up a slight slope from me in a serviceberry thicket, intent on convincing two sleek, young does that he was the best buck in the whole, wild West.

The buck was broadside watching the does, and I thought that it was either now or never, because if I waited much longer, I was going to be too cold to even unbend at all. I slowly eased up into shooting position, trying to keep the groaning and creaking in my stiffening legs to a minimum and at the same time trying to tell whether I really had my fingers on the string or, for that matter, whether or not I had fingers. They were so cold I couldn't tell where they stopped and the string and nock on the arrow started. It was an effort to get the 65-pound Bear takedown to full draw; just as I accomplished this and looked up to line up the buck, he stepped over the hill and out of sight.

Late-season hunting in cold weather has a whole different set of rules and is a whole new ball game, so to speak. Many states have deer seasons that extend well into the winter, and if a bowhunter has a little know-how, along with the proper equipment, this is some of the best hunting available.

There are several reasons for late-season hunting being better, be it for moose in Canada, whitetails in South Dakota or mule deer in New Mexico.

In most parts of the country the deer go into the rutting season in late November through January. At this time the bucks are interested mainly in does and not bowhunters, so you have one point in your favor right there. The bucks by now also have the velvet polished off their antlers, and you don't have to guesstimate much as to whether or not a buck is a trophy animal. In the northern belt of states there is usually tracking snow at this late date, which will enable the bowhunter to find trails that the deer are using in their daily movement—as well as make the job of trailing a hit animal much easier. And in some areas with relatively deep snow deer will have begun concentrating in areas of good food and cover. If you can find such areas, you'll have hot hunting. Meat spoilage is much less critical during the late seasons, too.

The main problem created for the bowhunter by these late seasons is keeping warm and comfortable. If you are cold and your fingers numb, you sure aren't going to be able to handle that bow and arrow with the same efficiency that you did during the nice, warm August season.

The hunter who hunts exclusively from a tree stand during the winter season is going to need a parka or coat and pants that will keep him warm and cozy for hours on end without his moving. He is going to have to have a pair of boots that are warm and will need to exercise to keep his feet that way. I have found that for hunting where I am not going to be moving around much, a down parka is by far the best. It is light, warm and comfortable, even though I may not be moving for several hours at a time. I have never been able to sit still with wool "long handles" on, but a pair of the quilted Dacron-filled type of undies fill the bill just fine. For footgear for this type of hunting I prefer the felt-lined "snowmobile" boot. Mine are made by L.L. Bean and are leather on top with rubber bottoms and also work fine for walking medium distances in snow and water. This is the warmest type of boot I have found and one that will not "sweat" when you have to walk in to your stand. Some of the better all-leather and all-rubber insulated types work well for this type of hunting, too.

A word of caution about your parka—make sure you have an arm guard that will pull the sleeve back away from the bowstring. I know many good bucks have been missed because the string caught momentarily on a wrinkle in a bulky sleeve.

A bowhunter's hands are probably more important than the rest of the body, and as such they deserve proper care. During cold weather I wear a very light leather glove such as trapshooters or golfers wear. A finger tab or glove will usually fit right over this. If the weather is extremely cold, I wear a heavy mitten over this or a regular snowmobiling glove with padded back and fingers. Just before shooting, it is an easy matter to slip the mitten or glove off—you can still go for a period of time before your fingers do get numb because of the protection of the light glove. This type of glove can also be worn in cool or wet weather with the same effect.

The bowhunter who likes to get out and stalk his game can't bundle himself up like the tree stand hunter, or he will find that he is roasting one minute and freezing his butt off the next. Try to balance your clothing so that you never get hot enough to sweat while hunting. This is hard to do, admittedly, but it can be done. My preference is for this type of hunting, and I usually wear the following clothing when the temperature is way down.

I like a soft, long-sleeve shirt such as a chamois cloth or soft cotton. Over this goes a good quality down vest. This will keep the trunk of the body warm—and normally, assuming your circulation is adequate, if you can keep your trunk warm, your limbs will stay warm. Over this I wear a leather shirt or a camouflage wool sweater. Both of these will cut the wind, and the sleeves are tight enough on both to stay out of the way of a bowstring. If the weather is way below zero, I will wear an Eddie Bauer, Kara Koram parka instead. This is a snug-fitting outfit that has knit cuffs, is warm to 70° below zero and is extremely lightweight and durable. If I had to choose one piece of cold weather gear that I couldn't be without, this would be my choice.

For pants I like a heavy wool cord pair. Here again, depending on the severity of the weather, I wear the quilted long handles under them.

For most of my winter work and hunting I prefer the L.L. Bean rubber-bottom pac with and without the felt liner and with the lug sole for traction. I usually wear two pairs of heavy wool socks and have a felt insole in the unlined ones. I have two pairs of insoles, so I always have a dry pair to put in before I take off hunting next morning.

A good cap is also essential to keeping warm during cold weather hunting. Your head is like the radiator of a car—if it gets cold, your whole body is going to be cold; so keep your head warm and your feet will stay warm.

I haven't found much difference in the way various equipment performs in cold weather as opposed to hot weather, but one thing I have found is this: A bow with an aluminum riser section will get colder than all hell and stay that way all day long. So if you have one of these, it's best to cover it with leather or something that will serve as insulation. I always try to leave my bow outside when I am hunting in cold weather, as constantly going from cold to warm and back again could have some effect on the limbs. Moisture condensing on the bow and your arrows doesn't help any, so if you are in the camp, leave your bow outside under the shed roof or hung on a branch.

Late-season deer hunting calls for some changes in hunting methods. One of the most successful methods I have used for late season whitetails, mule deer and even antelope is driving. Driving is only a fair way to hunt whitetails during early season hunts, and will rarely work at all on mule deer during early seasons. Hunting the late seasons changes this method completely.

Successful drives depend on full knowledge of the terrain and the deer's habits and travel routes. With mule deer, it is best to move your drivers from downhill upward, as the wily buck muley is far more likely to move uphill away from danger. Once the deer have established well-used trails during the late season, they have a tendency to use the same trails when driven from the area.

The same holds true for whitetails. The drivers on this type of hunt should move slowly and make sure they actually hunt their way through likely cover so they don't miss that smart buck that decides to hang back. By moving the game slowly to the standers, you'll give them a chance for a better shot than if the deer are badly spooked. This method of hunting will take more people, but if done right, can provide your bowhunting party with plenty of action.

Using a stand is another method that is extremely successful during late season—if you have a good knowledge of where and when the deer are moving each day. It will be time well spent to thoroughly scout the area for several days or even several weeks to find major trails the deer are using to and from feeding and bedding areas. It is then a simple matter to put your stand or tree blind where it will do the most good. During most late season hunting, deer have a tendency to move to and from the feeding and bedding areas a little later in the morning and earlier in the evening than during early fall hunting.

Stalking can be used successfully if you make good use of your binoculars and are careful to pick individual animals. Even though this is the toughest method for late season hunting, it is still my favorite, as nothing beats the thrill of seeing a bedded deer and then sneaking within bow range. This type of hunting puts a premium on your hunting and stalking ability, as well as on your knowledge of the animal's habits and behavior. The most important single step in being successful at stalking a deer in the late season is spotting the animal before it sees you. Here again, knowledge of the deer's habits and terrain will go a long way.

The weather can be a big help in successful stalking. Usually, the poorer the weather, the more successful is this method.

There are a surprising number of fair-weather bowhunters in the country. On all the late season hunts I have been on, I have never run into any appreciable number of bowhunters in the field—which to my way of thinking is just great. A bowhunter with the proper clothing, hunting gear and a little knowledge, along with a smidgeon of fortitude, can have a great time in the woods or mountains in pursuit of those late-season bucks. Even if he doesn't bag a trophy, you can bet he will be back next season a little wiser and far more determined in his pursuit of the late-season deer.

EAST

When the Thanksgiving turkey is but a bony reminder of what once was a grand bird, there are some who have thoughts of something other than the Christmas season and the new year ahead—late-season bowhunting!

Temperatures have dropped, many areas have snow and all foliage has disappeared, giving the bowhunter little cover for concealment, whether he will hunt on the ground or from a tree.

If you intend giving late season a try in any of the northeast locales, you face preparations completely different in clothes, gear and hunting methods.

Since the amount of clothes worn has a dual purpose—keeping you warm while still permitting sufficient freedom of movement to allow you to draw the bow properly—the answer is to wear as little as possible, but choose warm, light clothes.

Starting on the inside, I prefer longjohns to the padded insulated type underwear to minimize bulk. If you will be moving continually, try a set of silk underwear—they're light and hold heat. But they also hold moisture, so you'll freeze if you wear them in walk-and-stop hunting.

The next layer of clothes should offer freedom of movement, not

Late-season and high-altitude hunting decree wearing adequate warm clothing to give you the patience to get within range of a trophy like this.

be binding when you're walking and be lightweight. This is best achieved by choosing some insulated type of outer garments.

Personally, I have found insulated coveralls the ideal outer clothing. This one-piece outfit fits loosely enough to permit adequate freedom, offers little hindrance for shooting, and the one-piece design keeps body heat inside, while still permitting a body breathing action for utmost comfort.

A light woolen sweater with a crew neck can be donned under the coveralls. For added warmth around neck and ears I have used a sweater bib for many years, and it is ideal.

A sweater bib consists of a turtle neck and small bib front and back that extends about 12 inches over the chest and back area. Made of a heavy wool in various colors, it can be found in many department stores. This piece provides necessary neck warmth without the added bulk a complete sweater places on the arm areas.

Now we come to the extremities. Head gear varies according to personal preference, but after you have tried a stocking cap of the woolen type, chances are you will stick with it for cold weather wear. Versatility is the answer to all hunting clothes, and the stocking cap offers the most—rolled up when moving, and pulled down when the ears get nippy. Pick a woolen knit in a coarse strand; avoid the fine strand for it loses its shape too easily.

The skier sets an example with the combination cap and face-mask version which offers the ultimate in head, ears and face protection when temperatures drop to near zero.

What about hearing when your ears are covered? The woolen stocking cap lets you hear through the coarse knit—but unless you are hunting bare forest floor, your eyesight is more important, for the footsteps of a whitetail are soundless in snow.

When it comes to footwear, there are dozens of combinations used for cold weather. Regardless of which you find warmest, the one thing you strive for is the least bulk for utmost walking comfort. Trudging a half-mile in snow with your feet encased in a combination of inner and outer footwear can be a task.

Again, if you're constantly moving, silk stockings are fine. Then put on one or two pairs of woolen hunting socks and finally the hunting shoes. Whatever you do, avoid tight shoes. And if your feet perspire a lot, silk isn't for you.

Outer shoes should be waterproof to a degree when hunting in snow, for wet feet never can be kept warm. Leather seems best for flexibility and comfort. Proper waterproofing beforehand keeps the feet dry.

If a dry and powdery snow prevails, I have found a combination worn by my Alberta guide ideal and quite warm: First, a pair of silk socks (they can be a pair of hand-me-downs from wife or sister). Then, several pairs of heavy woolen hunting socks, worn to full knee-length and held there with a heavy rubber band. Next, a pair of heavy work-type rubbers are slipped over the socks, with another heavy rubber band slipped over the arch and instep to keep them on. This combination is warm, amazingly light and offers good footing.

Without any doubt, hands are vitally important to the bowhunter when temperatures get on the chilly side.

Shooting with gloves on is practically impossible for utmost accuracy. Since the majority use either a shooting glove or tab, the drawing hand must be kept bare of any other glove or mitten.

About the most suitable rig I have ever seen or used I copied from

Elmer Jernigan (who makes the Copperhead hunting heads) while hunting with him on Fox Island in Lake Michigan.

Elmer wears a pouch on a belt that is large enough to permit slipping his drawing hand inside. The pouch is made of a piece of fur—leather side out, fur side in. For temperatures on the upper side of freezing, the fur alone does the job of keeping your hand warm. When the mercury drops lower, all you do is drop a hand warmer into the pouch for added warmth! There are commercial models of this same type of unit available. Kolpin has a good one.

Although conventional camouflage outer garments have been worn by successful late-season bowhunters, you can increase the odds in your favor by dressing to match conditions. In snow country a white outer color is hard to beat. If the forest floor is bare, try dark gray to blend with brush and trees that are bare of foliage. Hemlock and pine thickets, as well as laurel, take on a dark hue during the dull winter days.

How to go about the white outer shell? If your wife or someone you know is handy with the sewing machine, an old bed sheet makes a fine outer shell for this purpose. You can settle for a parka only or go all the way with pants to match. Cut to fit loosely, they are slipped over outer clothes. You can also invest in a pair of white coveralls. White flannel might be best of all. It's soft enough to prevent twigs from scraping noisily when you brush against them, is tougher than sheet material and is also warmer.

With a stocking cap in white wool, outer garments in white and your bow wrapped in adhesive tape, you will be pulling the old Eskimo trick by blending completely with the snowy background!

Two things must be kept in mind when trying for a late season whitetail: lack of foliage and previous hunting seasons leave the deer somewhat spookier and far more cautious; feeding habits due to available feed and ground cover change movement patterns.

If you intend to brave the chilly temperatures and sit in a tree stand, forget the stands along the edges of feeding fields or apple orchards. Choose a tree stand in timber, preferably in a hardwood stand. If the snow is not too deep, or there's none at all, you may find deer still rooting for ground acorns and beechnuts in such areas.

Deeper snows will find deer feeding in brushy areas where browse is available. Very deep snows find little feeding taking place, and most of that in small areas where visible browse lines will be evident. When such conditions exist, look for a deer trail that usually will lead from water to a yarding spot. Pick your stand along such routes if you intend to play the waiting game.

For many, late-season bowhunting is a stalking game, which not only provides more opportunity, but also keeps you warm.

When dressed all in white with snow on the ground, the average bowhunter can do quite well at stalking, as long as one important requirement is kept in mind at all times—wind direction.

Remember, the deer can see as far as you can. Make your stalk in a wandering manner instead of a direct approach. You not only will make your faint body outline less discernible in movement, but also will use a pattern similar to that of the deer.

If the weather is not clear and any degree of wind exists, don't expect to find deer in open timber. Stalk the thickets and the pockets in small ravines or the protective sides of steep side ridges. Whitetails seek cover when weather is raw, to stay out of the wind and keep as dry as possible.

The least uncomfortable, most enjoyable method for many is to hunt in groups and make drives. Dress can be lighter, and if deer are in the area, action will be frequent.

When on stand or watch on such drives, do not wait on a deer trail; pick a spot alongside, preferrably hidden behind a tree. Step out to make your shot when the deer has passed your spot. This not only offers the best target profile, but also is less apt to spook the approaching deer.

Since drives are of short duration, you might try a tree stand. It offers the least chance of being detected by deer moving ahead of the drivers. When helping on the drives, be ready for shooting—especially when customary noise making is held to a minimum. Whitetails are known to bust back through drivers, especially around the end men.

With snow on the ground, tracking is easy. Many a fresh set of deer prints will direct the stalking bowhunter to a possible shot that may just fill his game tag. When working a track, keep looking ahead as far as possible for sign of the deer, and don't overlook both sides as well as behind, for deer usually circle.

Always be on the alert for bedded whitetails when moving about on wintery days. Midday is the normal time for the bedding habits of the whitetail, and when deep snows or blustery weather prevails, the lack of feed may find the deer bedded for warmth or to conserve strength.

Like the old Maine woodsman advised, "Find a fresh track, follow it and by and by you will find a deer at the other end!" Although winter weather may not be ideal bowhunting, a try at taking a "deep-freeze whitetail" may prove both interesting and successful.

MULE DEER *DO* HAVE BRAINS

The five muley bucks were casually feeding through the oak brush when I first spotted them from a hilltop about a half-mile away. In the late afternoon sun the reddish hides on the muleys glistened almost like burnished copper. I was going to have to hurry like blazes to make a stalk on these critters before sundown. The knoll on which the bucks were feeding was ideal for stalking, and if I could get around behind it, I could come up over the top and be right on them. Theoretically, that is; things have a way of going differently when you take out after a muley buck with a bow.

I quickly donned my camo outfit, grabbed my Wing PII takedown and took off on the dead run to cover the half mile to the back of that hillside. Two bucks were good and one was exceptional—with a 30-inch rack that was an even four to the side. Just right for the den wall and Pope and Young records.

Everything went perfectly, and I was soon easing through the brush at the crest of the knoll, straining both eyes for sight of a buckskin. I didn't have to strain very hard because not 15 yards in front of me I saw the flicker of one small buck's tail and froze in my tracks just to one side of an oak clump. I soon had the three smaller bucks within twenty yards of me, all calmly feeding on the tender oak buds and weeds. In a moment I spotted the largest buck about 80 yards away, moving through the oak right toward me, so I just stayed put to wait him out. I was keyed to the exploding point when out of nowhere the other buck stepped around a clump of oak just twelve feet in front of me and stood staring me straight in the eye. In the instant before he whirled and took off, I saw that he had a heavy, wide rack and decided to try him. He hadn't made more than two jumps when my 2020 Razorhead-tipped shaft took him right between the hams.

I watched as he walked about three hundred yards through oak and laid down for the last time. The time which had elapsed since I left the pickup was one hour and fifteen minutes. Who says mule deer bowhunting is tough!

Before you get the idea that all you have to do is spot a buck muley, walk out and shoot him, let me say that the foregoing buck was by far the easiest muley I have killed and that most of them came one hell of a lot harder. The ones that got away far outnumber the ones that didn't. To kill a mule deer usually takes skill, patience and preseverance.

The mule deer is not a hard animal to get once you find him, but sometimes it takes a little doing to do even that. The most popular, easiest and most successful way of taking a mule deer is by using a tree stand over a natural or artificially-placed scent or salt lick. Many of the successful guides and outfitters here in Colorado formerly used this method, and their hunters took a good number of deer this way. However, the Colorado Game, Fish and Parks Commission passed a law a couple of years ago that prohibits baiting or salting in any way for big game ungulates—which is opening up a whole new ball game for many Colorado bowhunters. Deer can still be taken from tree blinds that are strategically placed on trails and waterholes, but the hunter must now get out and do some scouting and find where the muleys are and what trails and waterholes they are using if he is going to be successful.

The first axiom in mule deer bowhunting is *spot your deer before he spots you.* Whether you are hunting from a tree blind or stalking or several hunters are putting on a drive, if you can see the deer first, you have half the battle won.

Probably the most important piece of equipment you can have —outside of your bow and arrows—is a good set of binoculars. I prefer the 7x35 power because of the relative light weight and good, clear field with ample magnification. Don't scrimp on your binocs. If you use them right, you are going to be spending a lot of time looking through them, and a poor glass will have your eyes feeling like they have a day's growth of whiskers before the day is half over. It is far easier to pick a nice spot and let your eyes do the walking, rather than your legs. It is much quieter, too. Once you spot your quarry you can do all the sneaking and walking necessary to get within bow range.

It always amazes me how few people really use binoculars right. I have spent half an hour trying to point out to fellow hunters a deer that was bedded down with only the rack or a portion of the body visible, but they couldn't come close to seeing it.

When you are glassing an area for mule deer, or any game for that matter, don't look for a whole critter standing broadside in perfect profile; you will seldom see it. Look for an ear twitching or maybe the blacktipped tail or any off-color patch or out-of-context shape in the timber. I probably make more use of my binocs in very heavy timber than any place else. I once spotted an off-color patch that I was sure was a deer, but after fifteen minutes of glassing it, I still couldn't be sure. I finally tried to move a few steps to one side for a better look and spooked a buck that would have made the record book easily. The distance was thirty yards.

If you can't go out in the field and practice glassing on deer, crows, varmints or what have you, then hasten to the nearest zoo and watch the mule deer and other critters. Glass them at various distances, pick out a portion of the body or an ear or antlers and study the shape and color through the binocs. Then, when you get into the woods and see a branch sticking out of the willows, you can tell whether it is growing from a tree or a buck's head!

If you are in open or broken country, a spotting scope is another invaluable piece of equipment. It can save you from sneaking up on a brown rock laying near a cedar tree that suddenly materializes into a buck. It can tell you just how big the buck you are glassing really is. It can also show you the terrain and help immeasurably in picking a route for the best stalk. Again, use your scope as much as possible before the hunt so that you are completely familiar with it. It takes a lot of looking before you will be able to get used to the depth of field of the glass and the piling-up effect it has on the country you are glassing. I have many times spotted deer and made stalks above the timberline that were several miles in distance—deer that I wouldn't have had a chance at without a spotting scope. I have also passed up many deer that the scope showed to be small bucks or does that, without the scope, I would have wasted time stalking for a closer look.

As you can probably tell, my favorite method of hunting muleys is stalking; it has accounted for most of my deer. Stalking requires not only that you find the animal but also that you get close enough to him for a good shot. This takes a knowledge of the country, but more important, you must know every quirk and habit of your adversary.

There are many bowhunters who feel the mule deer is among the most stupid of the game animals—and just as many who feel it is among the smartest. I believe it depends entirely on the situation. I have had bucks let me walk within a few yards of them bedded down one day, and on a different day I couldn't get within rifle shot of them. One thing I will say is that they are completely unpredictable.

Their habits are basically the same as most animals in the wild in that they are the most active shortly after sunrise or shortly before sunset. But don't count on it; I have found them feeding and moving at all hours. I once waited until full dark for a couple of bucks to get out of their beds and start grazing so I could make a stalk, but they never moved. For all I know they might still be bedded down.

In checking back through my records, I discovered that *all* my mule deer bucks have been evening and late-afternoon kills, although this doesn't mean that I haven't seen quite a few at sunrise.

When a mule deer is feeding, he will put his head down; in this position he is virtually blind to everything, so this is the time to move. Watch him closely; just before he raises his head, he will flick his ears back. When he does this, *stop all motion* until the head goes down again. You haven't bowhunted until you have been caught with one foot off the ground, just stepping over a log or some other obstruction, and had to stand that way until you just couldn't stand it any longer. Goodbye buckskin.

Usually a mule deer will bed down facing downhill, so do most of your serious hunting from the highest point to the lowest; this will generally keep you behind your quarry.

In most cases, if you spot a deer and decide to try to drive him he will go up, so make your drives from the lowest point to the highest. A deer coming uphill is one heck of a lot easier to get than one smoking down the side of a ridge.

When working your way through the woods, never cut across clearings of open parks. Mule deer will often bed just off the edges of such areas, so if you circle them slowly with your eyes open, you stand a good chance of spotting deer bedded down. If you spook a deer and don't think it has seen you, don't move. Just get ready to shoot because often a deer will sneak back for a look and give you an opportunity for a shot.

There has been a lot said about bow weights and so on for deer, so I would only add that I feel any bow over 45 pounds is plenty for mule deer as long as your broadheads are razor-sharp and you can place them precisely where you want them at whatever range you choose to shoot.

Bowhunting for mule deer is no different from hunting any other critter with a bow. It is usually the amount of time, effort and practice that you put in before going into the field that decides the success or failure of your hunt. The better prepared you are, the better your chance will be of taking home a rack that will make you the envy of all your bowhunting cronies back home.

THINK LIKE A DESERT MULEY

I'm no mule deer expert. Ten years ago, I had those wily desert critters just about psyched out. Then they started tossing spitballs at me. All my hard-won expertise—based on some beginner's-luck stalking —went right out the old window.

For starters, I made the fatal mistake of listening to every little old thing the game biologists said. Desert mule deer, they solemnly intoned, use a distinct summer and winter range. What the PhD's didn't mention was that muleys are also crazy as hell.

In sleety November the beast should, by all that's holy, be up in timbered foothills waiting for a blizzard. They're as apt to be mucking along lowland washes, munching nonexistent chino grass.

When rain is a seldom thing, they refuse to visit *el waterhole* where bowhunters crouch. No, the foolish creatures are hiding a mile up the draw, and you have to chuck rocks to get them to move. Should Tobosa grass be lush and green down on paintrock flats where intrepid archers patiently lie, the muleys will without exception be somewhere else, browsing the nearest landfill dump.

Crazy? Sure, they're crazy! What you have to do out here is to learn to think muley. It's a matter of water savvy and understanding the mental road map of a flop-eared jackass deer.

Some folks call him the bowhunter's bane and a couple of other things largely because he's so easily located, yet so impossible to get close to. Across desert badlands you see into the middle of next week. And so can he. What he can't see, he *will* hear.

This desert deer is sort of a grown-up big brother of the western blacktail, so called. Technically, they're the same animal. Habitat and forage differences make the desert muley a little chestier and perhaps a little less sane. His summer color is pale tan, matching perfectly the arid wastelands. In winter the muley becomes slate gray and blends right in with bare rocks. He's adept at nimble-footing down the back side of a loose-rock *cuesta* (ridge) with nary a sound—places where you'll come through like a three-legged blind bull amongst granny's china collection. His black-tipped flag on a white rump, dark forehead patch, double-branching antlers and outlandish ears are registered trademarks.

The thing about a mule deer is, he does have those ears. Believe it, brothers, they're not mounted up there for comic effect. Roaming wide-open spaces, he can note the chink of boots on gravel at unreal distances. Any foreign noise will either pique his curious-bone or send him melting away into the confusing landscape.

For prime muley country we could offer with some native pride the far southwest corner of Texas, where the Rio Grande makes its loop south into Chihuahua and then drifts back north around the Chisos Mountains, heading for Del Rio and the Gulf of Mexico. Take a road map and draw a loop connecting Marathon, Alpine, Marfa, south to Valentine, eastward through Presidio to the Black Gap Wildlife Range and you've located a top stalking arena.

The Southwest is laced with muley country. While our northern tip of the Chihuahuan desert extends over into New Mexico, Arizona's Sonoran desert (ever hear of the Kofa Game Range or Cabeza Prieta?) boasts fabulous trophies. And we might point out that while desert rats consider the desert muley as a distinct subspecies, in fact it's basically a mule deer which just happens to make its living in the malpais. Its habits and wacky disposition make it *seem* a bigger and more imposing trophy. Sure, you can hunt mule deer all over the western states. But the desert itself—hottest, coldest, driest, most cantankerous land in the world—will lend added zing to your hunt.

A remarkable and exciting thing about hunting mule deer is that in the southwestern ranges where bucks sprout such wallhanger hatracks, much of the land is publicly owned. Primitive areas, outright wilderness, national forests and BLM acreage amount to a majority of the real estate.

Texas is the sole exception. Here, ranches and private hunting leases are the rule. A note to the West Texas Chamber of Commerce (Abilene, Texas 79603) or any local Chamber of Commerce will net you a list of ranchers with vacant leases. Be sure to specify that you're a bowhunter, as some hunting areas feature rimrocks and graveled flats where a .270 is considered a ladies' weapon.

Plan on spending from $100 to $250 for a good Texas muley lease. Some ranchers do offer special archery or day-use rates, since they can scatter more archers than gun hunters per thousand acres.

Incidentally, Big Bend ranches are *big*. A small ranch is any plot less than 25 sections, and a section of ground is 640 acres.

If your budget or conscience dictates that you hunt on public land, start by writing the federal agency in control and request information on specific areas: Forest Service (USDA, Washington, D.C. 20250); Bureau of Land Management (Dept. of the Interior, Washington, D.C. 20240). They'll send general information, regulations and the address of regional offices or game managers you can contact for maps or local information. An additional request to state game agencies will bring news of local hotspots to your mailbox, along with license data. Remember, these people are in the business of promoting hunting in their bailiwick, so don't be bashful when asking advice. While mule deer range through most of western North America, the states of Arizona, New Mexico, Texas, Colorado and Wyoming boast the major trophy action.

The new all-time Boone and Crockett buck muley—an 11-point with a 33-inch spread—fell to Texan Doug Burris, Jr., in 1972. Burris, a rifle-toting gent, whacked his record buck while stalking at close range in the Rolling Hills area of Colorado's San Juan National Forest. Public lands and inexpensive non-guided hunting can pay off big!

Last spring, I stalked Chihuahuan muleys with a camera, a *vaquero* named Jesus and another guy. I needed pictures for my photo file. As it turned out, I needed lots of practice. Scrambling up a slickrock ridge studded with spidery ocotillo shrubs and spike-leaved yucca, my razor-honed eye focused on the all-time genuine superstar mule deer, well hidden in the angular flora.

"Ain't he a *big* 'un, though?" I breathed.

"Madre de Dios," moaned Jesus.

"O gawd," muttered the other guy, "you're outa yer skull."

My Nikon's shutter click didn't spook the fabulous animal, so I crept closer, knees shaking. Again I took aim, focused and my world record muley magically dissembled as a cunning assemblage of desert foliage.

"Nice shot, P.J., you big jerk," drawled the other guy. Jesus snickered something untranslatable. The Great Desert Muley Oaf had done it one more time.

The reverse of my Mexican fiasco points the way to expert spotting of muleys in their native camouflage. Consider a typical case, because this is important stuff.

A hotshot bowhunter drives a couple of hundred miles to the

hunting area while idly watching the skeleton shapes of "spanish dagger" yucca plants flash by the window. He gets out on a gravelly *cuesta,* just stalking up a storm—and never sees that 10-point rotter of a buck hiding amongst the angular dagger leaves. The poor dolt has hypnotized himself with visual logic:

(1) "I have seen ten million bifurcated shapes today." (2) "They have all been yucca leaves." (3) "Therefore, any angular thing I see today will be another damned yucca."

You need to develop an extra sense of sight, something akin to ESP. Call if "odd-spotting." Without it, you'll never stalk close enough in this brushy, highly geometric cover.

Odd-spotting? It's simply the art of mentally taking in the entire scene while a hidden corner of your brain watches, waits and pounces when *anything* not natural appears. Among sword-like yucca foliage, watch for odd lines running across the parallel leaves. If you're into timber, don't look for stumps—look for stumps which seem different. Check even remotely suspicious shapes to see if they sport long ears above or skinny piano legs below or a smoothly rounded rump off to one side where no stump's rump should be. At the same time, keep firmly in mind the idea that some hunters may display skinny legs, long ears and a smoothly rounded rump, too.

Just don't go into desert cover expecting to see the awesome whole-body silhouette of a trophy muley outlined against the Roy Rogers sunset. Muleys being muleys, things seldom work out that way. Look for odd bits and pieces of muleys projecting from behind things.

Everything else being equal, water's your key. Desert lands seem to lack topside water. Oh, there's no shortage. The desert is blessed with the precise endowment of liquid it needs in order to be a desert. Just that and no more. There's often an ocean beneath the hobgoblin rocks, but seldom a running stream up above. You could die of thirst out there, yet mule deer and other critters always find enough to get by.

Watch the doves. In the evening they'll fly toward a waterhole and circle it. Follow along the flight path, hoofing it or in a jeep. As you begin to zero in on the watering spa, you'll notice a lot of game trails. They radiate out from the waterhole like wheel spokes, and you can follow them right in the rest of the way.

If the birds let you down or you can't follow, climb up on the high ground and look for a patch of dark green vegetation. On the desert, extra chlorophyll means extra water. It may be a rock *tinaga*—a natural catch-basin. It may be only a damp spot in a brush-choked gully, but animals and desert rats can find enough moisture to live on. Slip in there at dawn or dusk, and you should be near muleys.

If you're prowling a ranch, one of the hands will likely point out the waterholes. He may even show you a blind on a game trail. However you locate that water, hunt it out properly before you give up.

Hunting methods are partly personal preference and often dictated by the terrain. If you feel more comfortable in a blind, by all means build one. Use the native brush—greasewood or creosote bush, whitebush (chaparral), Mormon Tea, mesquite thatched with beargrass. For open spots, go ahead and use that fancy camouflage netting, but for heaven's sake keep it low! A four-foot net fortress looming above a bare rocky place is just a shade pretentious. Muleys are by no means blind or stupid. Your best bet in the open stuff is a low pile of rocks in front of a scraggly bush.

To really hunt a muley, you ought to stalk him out. There are some advantages here—and a bunch of problems. A desert deer is forced by the scanty food supply to keep moving. He's not so predictable as the humdrum whitetail. Even though a buck muley may visit the waterhole like clockwork, he's apt to arrive by a different route each trip. Yesterday's artfully built blind may be on today's barren trail.

Like all animals living a marginal existence, the muley has developed tremendous powers of observation. This makes him a tough cookie. But he's also curious, and a good stalker can work this trait to his advantage.

Show a low profile at all times so you'll resemble a browsing animal. This means the old duck-waddle, head low, dropping to all fours when the cover thins out. It hurts, but that's why they make liniment. Stand and relax those spasmed muscles *only* when there's a small tree to break your outline. Once you've spotted a good head of horn, move in at a snail's pace in a pendulum route. You need to appear as an idly feeding animal, moving nowhere in particular, ending each swing just a bit closer to your quarry.

Keep in mind that a solitary muley buck is rare, indeed. They like company, and that buck you're stalking will certainly have friends spotted around in the brush. Spook one of these unseen sentries (or girl friends), and you're through for the day. If it takes 20 minutes to move 50 yards, you're moving just right.

Desert muleys are as curious as the proverbial kitty. A buck in the rut may very well charge if you give vent to a whistling snort. Try it if he's spooky and inclined to bolt. It can be hair-raising. Just clench your teeth and blow so hard your sinuses ache.

On occasion, they'll come running to a distress call. Give a whinnying little scream, exactly like a kid goat being strangled. If you've never been favored with hearing a garroted *cabrito,* I can't help much. Just use your morbid imagination. Don't overdo any call—twice is plenty. Antler rattling is seldom productive out here. It takes no special expertise, but too often it sounds like loose stones rattling—a sound guaranteed to send a muley to hell and gone out of there.

On any southwestern desert, there's one bit of plant life you can't help noticing. *Agave lechuguilla* is a runty member of the amaryllis family. Its short, recurved spines are just ankle-high, so wear heavy boots. Clusters of needle-sharp lechuguilla cover the acreage on many slopes, and most mule deer have chronically swollen fetlocks as a result. But this hindrance can also be a big help. Dry summers and wet autumns often cause the lechuguilla to send up its seven-foot bloom-stalk as late as January. Deer go nuts for the succulent flower heads, so watch for chewed-off stalks. They can answer perplexing questions when the muleys aren't where logic tells you they ought to be. Think muley.

When the silly beasts don't respond to waterhole hunts, cast your red-rimmed eye toward higher elevations. They may have felt a coming lull in the weather, or they may have simply discovered a patch of watered browse. (Desert rainfall is spotty and scattered.) So adjourn to the headers, the top ends of draws and gulches. Creep up the outside slopes at an angle, and go easy in loose rocks. Crawl across the ridgetop, and work the inner slopes over with glasses. Always climb at an oblique angle to any slope. Animals always take this route (it's easier), and any noise you might make going straight up a hill will be quickly spotted for a phony.

If stalking seems a losing proposition on the open slopes and the deer begin to move away, you have two options. One is to back off down the hill and run like a madman to the header's upper opening to await some action. This is tricky since a booted stone will send the muleys elsewhere fast. The other is to gather up a small pile of stones from your concealed ridgetop hiding-hole. Wait till none of the deer is looking your way, then toss a rock over their backs onto the far side of the gully. If you don't overdo it, they just may come slipping and slinking back your direction. Then comes the big ambush, when you playing the part of the steely-eyed Apache.

Laugh if you must, but an open dump anywhere removed from civilization rates an early morning look-see! For some reason unknown to the biologists (vitamin deficiency, iron-poor blood, simple curiosity, plain cussedness?), muleys are nearly always to be found at the town dump from 4:00 a.m. till sunup. This is also a dandy spot to happen across coyotes and regal mountain lions.

Rattlesnakes always seem to be a first-timer's bugaboo out here. Don't ruin your trip with needless worry. The burning sun is death to Mr. No-Shoulders, and he'll stay under a rock all day. At night he roams, hunting, so use a light. It's good sense to never poke hands and feet where you can't see, but apart from this, just slip along quietly and keep your eyes peeled. Carry a good snakebite kit and know how to use it. Should an accident occur near camp, ice is the best medicine, followed by a calm but quick trip to a doctor. For what it's worth, I've been whacked by four poisonous reptiles—yet never in the desert!

Slightly more of a hazard are scorpions, so shake out your boots and bedroll before donning either. Carry sunscreen ointment and plenty of water. Unless it's a ranch-lease deal with attached guide, know how to use a map and compass. It could save your life.

Since desert sunlight is bright and harsh, a good layer of burnt cork or bowhunter's warpaint is a great idea. Nose, chin and sweat-shiny cheekbones are pure poison on a muley jaunt. Clothing need not be camouflage—dun or drab work clothes will work—but why tempt the fates? Bow camo and drab-painted quivers on bow or hip are a must. You'll find short magnum or take-down tackle a help in brush or when you have to crawl. And crawl you will.

With the petroleum pinch temporarily in hand, you should be able to buy gas throughout the Southwest. But keep in mind the unchanging fact that filling stations are few and *very* far between out here. Without accessory saddle tanks, your pickup may not hold enough fuel for cruising across the desert. Carry a minimum of 10 gallons extra in strong jerry cans. While we all love the simple joy of on-the-ground tent camping, the pickup-mounted RV is your best bet. Desert terrain has a cute way of impressing itself upon your spine.

Locate your camp on a smooth sandy spot with good drainage. Piles of rock or brush can mean unwanted vermin around the old campground.

Many ranchers offer jeeps and guide service. If you're going it alone on public land, include a four-wheel-drive rig as part of your gear. Standard pickups will do fine if equipped with heavy rubber and high clearance.

The desert has the reputation of being a blast furnace, and I've seen midsummer temperatures peak above 120 degrees. But from September on, noon heat shouldn't top 90°, dropping at night to a chilly 45°. Along comes a blistering blue norther and the mercury may plummet 50° in an hour! You can have chilblains and sunburn all in one day.

Lightweight goosedown jackets favored by backpackers are wonderfully handy since they can be rolled up and tucked under your belt when the day warms. Insulated long johns (thermal cotton) are a must. Insulated boots are needless. Strong, cleat-soled shoes are absolutely necessary on rocky slopes, while crepe-soled deer boots are fine in noisy brush.

If you've done your homework and can manage both odd-spotting and slow stalking, the payoff will be a 30-yard shot. But be prepared to whack your buck running at 45 paces, especially up in the rocky draws. Your broadheads will take a beating in the rocks, so carry a file or stone.

You'll be taking some potshots at stumps and jackrabbits. Jacks alone are nearly worth the trip! A miss in the rocks means a shattered shaft if you're toting fiberglass or wood, while aluminum will straighten only so many times before developing soft spots. With aluminum running in the three dollar range and fiberglass hard to find or buy, Port Orford cedar is coming back into vogue for jack shooting.

When logic lets you down, start to think muley. Look for rainsign in illogical places. Watch for browsed vegetation and hunt it out, even if it looks like a lousy spot for deer. Read the weather signs, check the town dump, hunt where no one goes, climb a lonesome windmill. Stop at every roadside culvert and check the hoofprint census. Call a coyote, and watch for curious buck muleys over your shoulder. Toss a rock into a brush header.

Comical in appearance, maddening to hunt, fabulous trophies at hunt's end—the muleys are out there waiting for someone who can think like a desert muley.

MOMENT OF TRUTH

The many hours of arduous effort and sacrifice have come to this—a decision which requires, at most, just a few fleeting seconds: the so-called moment of truth.

More bowhunters fail here than at any other time during the chase.

The decision is this: Just when is that precise moment when the deer is in bow range, has its guard down, and you stand the best chance of penetrating its defense with an arrow?

If you flunk, there go your hopes. There seldom is the luxury of a second try at the same deer.

Take what happened to me just last deer season, for example.

I was sitting in the high fork of a live oak tree, watching a track-littered trail which serpentined through the central Texas brush to a stock tank (farm pond, if you prefer). The better part of two days had been spent on the uncomfortable stand, and my patience was wearing thin. It was nearing sundown, and I was about ready to concede the hunt had been a washout when, lo and behold, a deer appeared—a nice eight-point buck that rounded a curve in the trail and walked directly toward my stand.

The buck obviously was unsuspecting of my presence. He was on edge, all right, as all whitetails are, but his ears were in a relaxed droop and he seemed intent on getting to the waterhole without worrying about any threat of danger. Probably he had traveled this trail countless times, and it wasn't a place he associated with trouble.

Suddenly he was in range and I had to make my decision. When I commenced raising my bow I realized my mistake. But it was too late.

I should have let the buck walk completely past the tree, not making my move until he was going away from me. But I didn't stifle my impatience. The buck snorted in alarm and jumped back, his ears cocked forward, listening and looking, his muscles tensed.

Hurriedly I brought the bow on up, drawing the arrow simultaneously. But by the time I had the nock anchored against my face, the buck had wheeled and was bounding up the trail, his white tail waving.

Compare my blunder to the success story of Mel Johnson when he bagged his record buck—the largest whitetail ever taken by fair chase—near Peoria, Illinois, in 1965. He was on stand in a soybean field when he sighted the huge buck coming toward him.

"My cover wasn't any too good, and I was sure he'd spot me; but

I remembered that a hunter dressed in a camouflage suit is almost invisible to game if he remains still,'' Johnson recalled. ''I froze. On came the buck. I saw that he was going to pass much too close for me to get off an effective shot: as soon as I would move he'd see me. There was only one thing to do. I let him pass me, and as soon as his head was turned away, I got to my feet and got off a shot—all in one continuous motion.''

Johnson, if you noted, did two important things to bowhunting success: he waited until the deer's head was turned, so it was less likely to detect the ambush; he remained absolutely motionless until he decided to act.

There also was another critical factor. When he made up his mind to shoot, he followed through positively with no hesitation. Even if the deer had detected the hunter at this moment, it would have required a split-second for the critter to regain his wits, find what had frightened him, and take evasive action. This almost imperceptible hesitation often is fatal. By the time the animal reacts, the arrow has arrived and it is too late.

At the moment of this crucial decision of when to shoot, you have many things working against you. For one thing, your quarry must be close, and this makes the human more susceptive to detection. For another, the very nature of your weapon demands revealing movement—raising the bow and drawing an arrow. The challenge is to get the deer close and make this move and defy the odds and kill the animal. That's what bowhunting is all about.

You can hedge on this ''moment of truth'' by being prepared. The location and preparation of your stand is a vital factor. So is your ingenuity and ability to negate the deer's defenses of smell, sight and hearing. An unsuspecting animal is much easier fooled than is the vigilant deer who is edgy and senses danger.

I personally prefer a tree stand which puts me above a deer's normal line of sight, making detection less likely. But sometimes no suitable tree is convenient, and this means waiting on the ground.

The foremost concern is to eliminate the human's telltale outline. That is the reason for camouflage clothing either behind or in front of greenery where it will blend in. Cover the face with a headnet or paint, wear camouflage or dull green gloves and even camouflage the bow. You can't be too careful. A seemingly insignificant detail might be the difference between success and failure.

Whether you get behind or forward of vegetation to wait depends primarily on your personal desires. Sitting in front of a bush in the open requires more concentration and alertness, seeing the deer before it detects you, then staying absolutely motionless until it is close enough for a shot. But one advantage of this stand is that there is less likelihood of a deer coming up from behind—your blind side—seeing you and snorting and alarming other deer nearby.

In a clump of trees growing close together you can improvise a very effective blind either by filling in the gaps with native brush or by wrapping a length of camouflage cloth around a triangle of trees and crouching inside. With this blind you can sit, and only your shoulders and head will show; you can move a cramped leg to relax muscles without much danger of a deer sighting you. But in such a stand you'll have to raise up and shoot, and that is just extra movement to give you away.

I also like to sprinkle scent liberally around my stand. On a calm day the air tends to suspend human scent and spread it about in ever-creeping concentric circles. Without the aid of artificial scent, the deer might come within bow range, get just enough whiff of human to become suspicious, and even if the animal doesn't actually spook and run, the odds of your getting a shot at it without it detecting the ambush are much reduced.

A deer's sensitive nose is its first-line defense. It perhaps will not become frightened by something unnatural it sees or hears, but the dread smell of a human is one danger signal that no crafty whitetail ignores. For this reason many bowmen dislike hunting when there is any prevailing breeze; they feel this is too much of a handicap.

Personally I'd rather hunt in a wind, especially a steady breeze from one direction. This eliminates those capricious gusts which some-times swirl in the woods, spreading your scent in a direction you don't want it to go. With a conventional wind you can locate your stand downwind from the direction you expect to see deer. The breeze is swaying branches and creating noise which aids you in going unde-tected. Touch a limb with your bow on a windy day and you might escape the error, but even this slight noise in a calm probably will alarm deer. The lifting of a bow into shooting position also might appear to be just a wind-blown branch to the deer—until it is too late.

A predictable air current, however, isn't a cure-all. This is just one more minuscule "plus" to your advantage. The studious bow-

Note the alert stance, taut muscles, forward-positioned ears and tucked-in tail of this deer about to vacate the area. If it's looking at you, you should already be at full draw, ready to release.

This whitetail is as relaxed as a deer can be. Note that muscles are not showing, ears are back, eyes appear half shut, and the tail is in normal position. If you're well camouflaged, you should get a good shot.

hunter, one who can successfully penetrate the deer's formidable defense, strings many such plusses together into a workable plan. He thrives on detail—such as getting his bow up and his arrow drawn and released with no noise and negligible movement.

When you get settled on the stand—whether it be a tree or on the ground—look about before you start serious hunting and see if you can maneuver your bow with impunity, eliminating the worry of carelessly striking a branch or bush, and that you can perform the act with a minimum of motion. A hunter who must raise his hands high to swing a bow over a limb or around a bush before bringing it into firing position is only unnecessarily handicapping himself.

More than anything else, that crucial decision of when to make your play depends on concentration—remaining statue-like and watching the deer's every move and trying to calculate that exact moment when the odds swing from the deer's advantage to the human's.

Try for this: a close side or quartering shot from the rear at an unalarmed game animal. Your arrow will reach vital organs with less bone protection.

Concentration also means you are alert to everything going on about you, seeing a deer before it sights you. Maybe you will actually hear the deer approaching and be ready when it comes into sight. Remaining acutely aware of what is happening at all times, sometimes two or more hours at a stretch on the stand, requires mental discipline and determination. Just keep reminding yourself that it could occur at any time, that magic drama when a deer appears. It can—and usually does—happen suddenly and unexpectedly. The successful bowhunter is one who is always anticipating. He thinks positively.

Once the quarry is in sight, every error is then magnified, for few mistakes of the human will go undetected. I prefer to get my bow up and ready the first chance I get, if the deer turns its head. Now all I must do is draw and release, which demands only a minimal amount of time and motion. I'm always holding my bow when hunting. Should your bow be laid aside, and a deer comes on the scene, you might never get the chance to pick it up without the animal knowing it. Anyway, that is just one more motion to contend with—another handicap.

This is where the suspense and excitement can get to you, when the deer is close and that time of decision is approaching. Eye the deer without moving your head, and try to detect a mistake which will give you a chance. You can tell immediately whether the deer is relaxed, is feeling relatively secure or is nervous. Should the deer drop its head, then abruptly bring it up, looking around, its ears forward alertly, don't become alarmed that you've been revealed. This is typical whitetail behavior. Just remain motionless. If the deer sees or hears nothing suspicious, it will switch its tail back and forth, lower its head and resume what it was doing. But if the tail slowly raises, standing out, the animal is edgy, sensing something is amiss. A deliberate stomping of a forefoot is also another sign of nervousness. A snort means the deer knows something is wrong, and if you plan on taking a shot, you'd better hurry. That critter won't be around for long.

A logical question is: When should you take a shot—as the deer is approaching, going away, or moving at an angle to your stand?

There is no ready answer, of course. It depends solely on the circumstance. A good rule of thumb is to take the first "reasonable" shot you get. Suppose the deer is walking and its head passes behind a bush and for just a moment now you can probably get the bow up and release an arrow. If it turns its head to look back, this might give you a chance; or maybe you will have to allow it to completely pass your stand and be going and looking in the opposite direction. But stifle your impatience and don't let the deer pressure you into a hurried and haphazard shot. If the deer throws up its head, is infinitely watchful and its ears are pushed forward to gather any sound, this doesn't mean it has detected your presence. Perhaps it is just a normal defensive reaction. Freeze and wait to see what it is going to do. Now would be the worst time to attempt a shot. The alert deer will quickly detect anything out of the ordinary. The inexperienced hunter tends to panic and to take a shot before opportunity presents itself. A hurried, forced shot is an unnecessary gamble, and it only encourages crippled game.

Attempting to outwit a single deer is challenge enough, but what if two animals arrive together—or maybe three? That compounds the dilemma, for there is scant chance that you will catch all unaware simultaneously. So if opportunity beckons, no matter how brief, take it and be grateful. This opportunity will most often come from letting the deer pass you and then shooting at the last deer in line as it passes or is past you. You'll be bucking odds, but after all, that's the name of the game when you hunt with bow and arrow.

Undoubtedly you will blunder or miss more times than you'll connect. A majority of bowhunters do, and welcome to the crowd. But don't dwell on your mistakes and let them psych you. Profit by what you did wrong and don't repeat the mistake. Trial and error—that is the way you become a better deer hunter.

WHERE TO AIM

Bowhunting is a sport of inches. Sometimes just a couple of inches will be the difference between a hit or miss, and even a fraction of an inch might determine a quick kill or just a crippled animal. Yet shooting a bow and arrow is such a tough procedure that error usually is measured in inches rather than fractions thereof. So the bowhunter "hedges" on his return by reducing this mistake factor to its lowest possible denominator.

This is accomplished in several ways: Having the proper equipment which is prepared correctly is perhaps the foremost consideration. Being a skilled hunter and getting the very best shot with the least margin of error is another. And, of course, knowing where to place the arrow for optimum results.

A fast-propelled arrow striking an animal's vital organs should accomplish two rudimentary assignments: creating intense hemorrhaging for bringing quick and humane death; encouraging sufficient external bleeding to leave an easily followed blood trail.

Simple mathematics tells us that a heavy object traveling at a rapid rate of speed will create the most damage upon impact, and this is true even of an arrow which kills by hemorrhage rather than shock. The more penetration an arrow gets, the better are the chances of getting massive damage to internal organs. And the farther a sharp broadhead tunnels through the animal's body cavity, the more opportunity it has to come in contact with organs and disrupt their functioning.

Bob Lee, veteran bowhunter and president of Wing Archery Company, says the draw weight of a hunting bow "should be as heavy as a person can adequately handle—and I mean *handle* and not merely shoot."

The basic theory behind this, of course, is that the heavier bow will cast heavier arrows at a faster velocity, and this results in better penetration.

"But be sure the bow and arrows are matched," Lee adds. "This is a common mistake among many bowhunters—having mismatched tackle—and a person can't get the needed accuracy with such equipment."

By proper conditioning and training of the muscles, the hunter can learn to handle (there's that key word again) a bow of heavier draw than he is now using.

But even driving an arrow completely through an animal is of questionable value unless the broadhead severs organs to induce bleeding. The bowhunter can greatly improve his odds for success simply by having his broadheads honed sharp. A dull head tends to roll flesh and organs aside, while a razor-like head cuts cleanly.

As a person practices with his equipment, he becomes aware of his limitations and capabilities. For example, if you find that at ranges beyond 25 yards your aim is erratic and arrows scatter, then work for shots at less than this distance. Whether you shoot instinctively or use a sight isn't important; what is imperative is that you put the arrow where you want it.

Now we come to that moment of truth when you are drawing on a big game animal. Where should you aim to get the quickest kill?

If the critter had a bull's eye painted on it, this would be a simple matter. But the hunter usually has just a brief time to size up the situation and determine where his point of aim should be. No two shots are exactly alike. Maybe the animal is standing broadside, quartering away or facing you.

The arrow kills a critter by disrupting either of its most vital life-sustaining functions: the nervous system or the movement of blood. The most surefire is to stop all or part of its nervous system. One deer I killed was trotting by my tree stand. I led the animal too much, so instead of hitting behind the shoulder, where I intended it to go, the arrow struck the buck's neck and completely severed the spinal cord. The deer fell there.

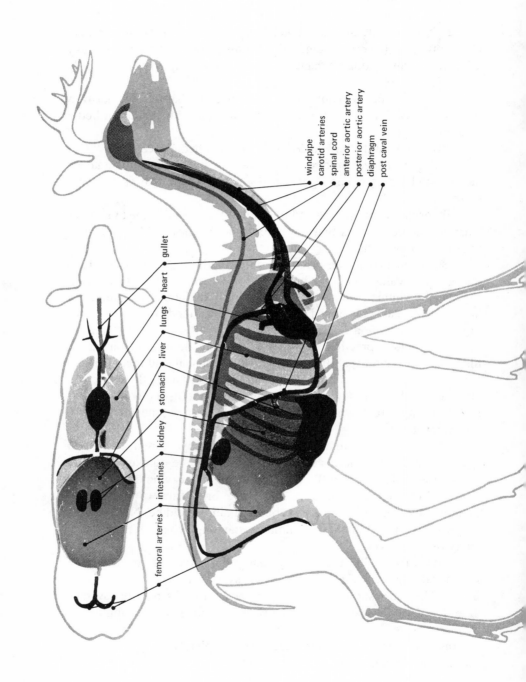

windpipe
carotid arteries
spinal cord
anterior aortic artery
posterior aortic artery
diaphragm
post caval vein

gullet
heart
lungs
liver
stomach
kidney
intestines
femoral arteries

ANATOMY OF A DEER

BOWHUNTING MINI-CLINIC

The drawings above give you the vital organs of a deer. But first, here are facts about deer (basically whitetail) to keep in mind.

Speed

Walking speed is about seven miles per hour, which means you'll have to lead them slightly. Top speed in short burst is 45-60 mph. Acceleration to full burst in a single leap, can be 25 feet or more.

Senses

EYES — Although color blind, vision is keyed to movement, unnatural reflections, contrasting tones or outlines. Keenly aware of unfamiliar structures and shapes, like new blinds in their natural habitat.

NOSE — Relies on it heavily for defense. Will believe nose above all other senses. Works upwind to identify intruders. Will often travel and bed down so can see ahead and wind will bring any warning from behind.

Commercial scents are an asset; they camouflage hunter's scent and the musk or natural deer scents will attract bucks during rutting season.

EARS — Always alert, even while eating. When ears find a suspicious sound, all other senses focus on that point. Necessitates quiet arrow rest,

silencers on string, soft clothing that doesn't make noise, and sitting silently on stand.

Characteristics

Adapt to practically any environment — wilderness, rural, suburban — which is why their populations are sound.

Very habitual — run rigid pattern if undisturbed.

Vulnerabilities

Extremely curious — stop after reaching cover, circle alarming objects and suspected areas, don't always take immediate flight.

During rut, bucks are moving throughout day, easily decoyed by musk scents, find them near ground scrapes, less wary during daylight hours.

They don't look up, so well positioned tree blind can be effective.

Habitual movement and time schedule under natural habitat conditions, unless disrupted by weather changes or extreme hunting pressure. You know where they'll be.

Warning Postures

FRONT FOOT STOMP — Indication that deer has spotted something worrisome, seems to be an attempt to provoke action. Hunter must sit without moving. Deer often resumes normal activity.

HEAD BOB — Head drops to feed, suddenly rises again, catching you in

mid-draw unless you have not moved. Raising head usually preceded by nervous twitching of tail. (However, casual movement of tail while feeding means deer is completely relaxed.)

SNEEZE — Generally with short whistle at end. Usually final warning before deer runs.

TAIL UP, STIFF-LEGGED WALK — Deer is on the launching pad, so shoot if you're going to.

Habitat

Need three main areas — cover, feed and play. Lush feeding available in fringe areas of forest and fields, cover usually in dense woods or brush, play areas in open fields.

Focus hunting efforts on fringe areas — fields near dense woods, brushy areas. Check for well-worn deer paths funneling into open fields. Best hunting is in late afternoon.

Hit Zones

HEART/LUNGS — largest area, generally any hit here brings deer down quickly. Frothy, pinkish blood indicates lung hit. Wait half an hour before trailing. Deer will travel short distance, then lay down. Long, medium brown hollow hair.

Drawings illustrate wide distribution of arterial and vein system, indicating that, though the heart/lung area is obviously the main vital region, almost any area can be vitally hit *and should be*

treated as such after any arrow hit.

NECK — Large artery and windpipe, will often down a deer in a short distance. But is not adviseable to aim at neck because of small target area. If hit here, wait at least one hour before tracking. Dark red, heavy blood trail indicates caroid artery wound. Short brown hair from vital area.

SPINAL CORD — Quick kill, generally knocks deer down on impact.

FEMORAL ARTERY — One of largest arteries in body, runs down rump and just inside hind leg bone. Produces heavy blood trail. If hit here, trail immediately so deer can't lie down and wound remains open. Dark red blood, in spurts. Long white or long brown hair.

PAUNCH AREA — Any shot behind diaphragm in stomach, kidneys, liver or vein under backbone. Liver and kidney shots give dark blood; wait at least one hour, preferably longer, so deer lies down and hemorrhages. Kidney and liver shots characterized by internal bleeding, sporadic blood trails, tough to follow; good shots in a generally bad area, must be handled properly.

Stomach shot in evidence by partially digested food particles on arrow, blood mixed with intestinal fluids, blood trail may start late and end soon. Wait at least four hours because deer is capable of running long distance with minor blood trail. Short, white hair from lower belly area; short, light brown hair higher up on animal's side.

But trying for a spine hit is too much of a gamble—unless maybe you are in a tree stand and the animal is walking directly beneath you. Even if you are off just an inch or so to either side, the broadhead still will bury into the body and find blood-carrying vessels.

An animal's body is a network of arteries and veins which all originate at the heart. Hit the heart or any major artery and you will get profuse bleeding; smaller vessels will give progressively less. I once shot at a buck which "jumped the string." The arrow caught him in the ham, striking the femoral artery. The resulting blood trail looked as though it had been poured from a bucket. The deer traveled less than 35 yards before going down.

The ideal spot to induce the most bleeding, it would seem, is the heart. It is, but the heart of any animal lies very low in the thorax between the front legs when the animal is viewed from the side. Here the forelegs, brisket bone and muscle give the heart quite a bit of protection.

If the arrow is forward too much—just an inch or so—it likely will strike the foreleg and perhaps just ricochet. A couple of inches low and the projectile will pass beneath the animal—a miss. Too far back, and it is in the body cavity where it must hit an artery or vein leading to and from the heart to get the desired results. About the only margin for error is above the heart, where there is a cluster of organs.

All big game animals are basically the same. You'll find the same vital organs in the same places. But the overall picture is different. A white-tailed deer, for instance, has long legs, while the javelina is squat, built close to the ground. An elk is a much larger animal with tougher skin and bones, and although its heart is correspondingly larger, it is much better protected against even a sharp arrow. The archer shooting from above—a tree stand, perhaps—stands a much better chance of angling an arrow into the heart region than does the hunter aiming from the ground, on the same level as his target.

To reach this area some bowhunters prefer the flat, two-bladed broadhead, reasoning that with the less resistance it will knife completely through the animal, severing everything in its path. Bill Clements, perhaps Arkansas' most successful bowhunter, is a great believer in this type head. As for me, I prefer the multi-blade head —either three or four cutting edges, preferably four. This type of head leaves a jagged hole which really pours out blood. Also, should the head remain buried inside the animal, it will jiggle back and forth,

The moose is a gigantic animal, but with an adequate draw-weight bow that will send an arrow through heavy ribs, it can become a fine trophy. Because of the heavy bone structure, your shot must be well placed. Don't try to drive an arrow through the shoulder; aim for the vital area low behind the shoulder.

continuing to cut as the critter runs. But neither type is of much value unless it is sharp.

The bowhunter's best shot, I'm convinced, is in the so-called high lung area, just behind the shoulder. A hit here might not give as much blood as a heart shot, but it will be sufficient—and in this area there is a bit more leeway for human error. If your shot sails slightly high, you are apt to hit the spinal column; should it be low, you'll be probing the heart and large-artery region. The arrow even can be too far back by an inch or two, and you will have a pretty solid hit. But get too far forward, and the shoulder bone is in the way. If this bone is hit just right, the arrow might penetrate; but usually it simply slides to the side or bounces back.

As the bowhunter becomes more experienced, he will learn how to aim to compensate for his own personal tendencies. With me, shots less than 25 yards tend to rise, while farther out the arrow is more

A fine double-shoveled caribou will provide years of memories for this bowhunter.

likely to drop. So if an animal is close, I aim low in the body. Should the arrow be on target, I'm in the heart region; even if it should rise slightly, I've got a fatal hit. On longer shots just the reverse is true: I aim high, for the lungs, so even if the arrow does drop, it will connect with vital organs.

Most bowhunters think of the classic broadside as the ideal position for a shot. Since one-dimensional drawings are usually sketched this way, the hunter has a vivid mental picture of where all the animal's organs are placed. This position comes closest to simulating target shooting. But if the animal senses something wrong and moves before the arrow arrives, then the projectile likely will hit the critter's midsection. A high shot will pass through the body without causing any extensive damage; a low shot will find the gut region, and that is one you want to avoid. While this might indeed be a fatal hit, there usually isn't much external bleeding, making the animal difficult to trail; and a gut-shot creature is apt to travel for long distances before going down.

Much better than the broadside is the quartering shot. The rear-quartering shot is preferred. Although the silhouette is not as large, more of what you see is vulnerable tissue. There is less chance of a bone deflecting the arrow, and it furrows more lengthwise through the body. Common sense tells us that the farther an arrow moves through an animal, the better are its chances of hitting vital organs. Should the arrow pass through the chest cavity, there is a possibility it might come in contact with all three vital organs—heart, liver and lungs.

From the rear, blind-side, of the animal like this, the hunter can put his arrow into a vital area without being detected. The head-on and front-quartering shots are less desirable, one reason being that the alert animal is more apt to detect danger—and from the front, body bones are a greater obstacle.

But if you do get a head-on shot, aim for the so-called "sticking spot" on the neck. Place an arrow solidly here and you have a dead animal. The broadhead carves directly into the body between the forelegs and above the tough brisket.

A temptation is to aim for the head. But most big game animals have small and well-protected brains. You are more likely to get just a glancing lick than you are a kill.

For the front-quartering shot, aim just behind the shoulder. While the heart, liver and lungs are fairly well protected from this angle, the network of arteries and veins just beyond are vulnerable. If the arrow angles across the animal, you probably will find a blood-carrying vessel. I once watched my hunting buddy Winston Burnham shoot a javelina that was trotting down a trail toward his stand. While the arrow hit a mite too far back, it traveled almost the entire length of the body, exiting just forward of a ham. An autopsy revealed that the broadhead hit a rib, forcing the arrow upwards where it traveled just beneath the spine, severing several arteries and veins. The javelina wheeled around wildly once or twice, then made just two or three jumps before falling.

AFTER YOU'VE HIT YOUR BUCK

Some successfully arrowed deer run only a few yards after they are shot, but are not found. Others travel several hundred yards—even a mile or more—leaving a clear blood trail, but still are not found. Some deer are trailed part way, then the search is given up. Some deer are found after they have been shot and trailed, but then are lost again when the hunter leaves to go for help in carrying his trophy back to camp. Somewhat ironically, the hunter himself occasionally gets lost while searching for his deer.

What does all this boil down to for the bowhunter? Very simply, it means getting an arrow into a deer is only *part* of successful deer hunting and that, after hitting his deer, the bowhunter often faces a considerably more difficult task—that of trailing and finding his wounded deer.

How do hunters make the mistake of losing their well-hit deer? Nearly always, it's because they don't know how to systematically go about trailing and finding a deer once they've hit it. Often, deer are lost because of simple mistakes—like not searching carefully enough for an arrow. A basic, unchanging rule: *always* assume you've hit your deer unless you know, positively, you haven't. If you can't find your arrow, assume it's in the deer—whether or not you see any blood at the spot the deer was standing when you shot.

How do you avoid losing your deer? Actually, it can be an easy job—if you will follow a few simple rules and practices. The main thing is to have a system worked out before you need it, and you'll make no mistakes.

The first thing you need to do—as soon as your deer is hit—is immediately make a mental note of where it was standing when you released. Not an "over-there-somewhere" spot, but an exact place. Pick an in-line object of some prominence on the far side of the deer. A straight line between where you were standing and that object should intersect with the spot where your trophy took the arrow. If you can, find some kind of distance marker, something that is nearly *on* the spot itself; a rock, stump or clump of grass will do fine.

Much of this may seem unnecessary, but it's not; more than once I have seen archers hit a deer, then in their excitement not be able to walk to where the deer was standing when they shot it. If you'll practice marking the spot this way, it will become a beneficial habit.

Also, watch the deer as it flees, noting the exact direction it's taking. Sometimes a wounded deer will immediately circle and come back to you; if you catch this change in direction, you might save yourself a lot of searching later on. Try to see if your arrow is still in the deer. Sometimes part of the shaft will protrude, and it's always helpful to know where you've hit your deer. Watch him as far as you can see him, making a note of the last place you caught a glimpse of him.

Watch *how* he runs. Often a deer's actions will tell you where he is hit, even if you can't see the arrow. If he hunches up like a high-backed Halloween cat, chances are you paunch-shot him. If so, get ready for a long, hard trailing job. Paunch-hit deer will usually (but not always) run a few yards with their tails down. Does your deer stagger, fall or favor a leg as he runs? If so, you've probably hit a leg or hit him very low in the shoulder or the hams. Again, this kind of hit can often mean a long, difficult tracking job, one that may net you nothing. (Long trailing jobs resulting from such poor hits can usually be avoided by passing up these questionable shots.) A good chest shot into the heart or lungs will often result in your deer jumping or bounding high into the air before he takes off—and such behavior nearly always means a solid hit of some kind. Of course, some wounded deer may exhibit none of these characteristics and still be badly wounded. So don't assume you missed if your deer runs off without showing any signs of being hit.

After you've hit your deer, marked the spot well, and watched him as far as you can see him, what then? *Wait.* You should not only not rush after your wounded deer, but also not even move out of your stand. An arrowed deer that's badly wounded may run only a few yards before stopping. I have even seen badly wounded deer actually stop and lie down within sight of the hunter's stand. I know of documented cases where the wounded deer even returned to within bow range to see what had happened, thus giving the archer a second chance to shoot. But a deer will never do any of these things if you give away your presence by hurriedly leaving your stand.

How long should you wait? Most veteran hunters agree that you should wait at least 30 to 45 minutes. Others say that two hours is not too much. Some hunters recommend waiting six to eight hours before trailing paunch-shot deer. Most deer will die within an hour if well hit, but others take longer. If you don't push them, often they will go no farther than 200-300 yards before they lie down. But if you push them by following immediately, they might go for miles.

If you push a deer into heavy cover while he's still strong, you might end up losing him altogether. The first big buck I arrowed I followed immediately. I knew I'd hit him well, and his blood trail was so heavy I was sure he wouldn't go far. I hardly gave the buck 15 minutes before I went after him. The result? I pushed him nearly a mile—into a water-filled swamp where it was impossible to trail any longer. I hunted that buck a full day and a half and never found him.

This points out another thing—wounded deer will frequently head toward water.

The one exception to waiting a considerable amount of time before you begin trailing is when the weather dictates that you must begin immediately. If there is heavy rain or snow, you really have little choice but to begin trailing as quickly as you can. Otherwise, all sign of blood or tracks will almost certainly be lost within minutes. Sometimes, too, if you hit your deer near the end of shooting hours, it's advisable to start trailing immediately, at least for a short distance. Most of the time you'll find your deer—if he's really hit hard. Sometimes, of course, you won't; if I don't find my deer within a few hundred yards, I quit pushing the trail until morning. If the weather forecast warns of snow or rain, however, I usually continue trailing after dark with a light. Early season hunting, with its warm days, often dictates that you must follow immediately rather than picking up the trail in the morning; a dead, ungutted deer can spoil quickly if left all night, especially in some of the southern states where seasons are rather warm.

After you've waited in your stand a sufficient amount of time, get down and check the spot where the deer was standing when you shot. Look for blood, hair and, of course, your arrow. If you can't find your arrow, assume automatically that you hit your deer. Usually there will be blood at or near where the deer was hit, and you should be paying attention to what kind of blood it is. Lots of bright red blood usually means a deeply-penetrating flesh wound in the shoulder or hams. If the blood has a pink frothy appearance, a lung shot is almost a certainty. Very dark blood often indicates a paunch shot, especially if you find small particles of stomach contents mixed with the blood. Dark red blood with the food particles often means a hit in the liver. If you have not pushed your deer, these are good indications that your deer will not be too far along the trail.

If there is no blood at the spot where the deer was standing, begin searching in sweeping arcs back and forth in the direction the deer fled, moving from where the deer was standing to where you saw him last. Usually you'll pick up the trail. Sometimes (in fact, most of the time), wounded deer will make several leaps before they actually start bleeding, so be prepared to look around some before you find blood. When you do, start trailing your deer, moving slowly so you won't miss any sign. If there is a clear blood trail, you should have little difficulty following it. If the blood trail starts out heavy, then reduces to a faint trickle or seems to play out completely, don't give up.

Place a stick or handkerchief at the last spot of blood you've found. Then start searching for more by swinging back and forth again in arcs that intersect the line of travel the deer was following. When you find another spot of blood, place another stick by it, then continue this leapfrog method of following until you find another. If you do happen to lose the trail altogether, you can always go back to the last marker and start over. Trailing this way is often slow and tedious, but for me it has often meant the difference between finding and losing my trophy. Unfortunately, it's at this stage of trailing that most hunters either lose the trail altogether or give up, thinking the deer they hit was not seriously wounded.   ·

Don't just look for blood on the ground. Often a deer will be leaving telltale splotches of blood on bushes and limbs several feet off the ground as he brushes them (a badly wounded deer often bumps into trees). Keep a sharp eye peeled for those splotches, especially if you shot directly down at your quarry. If your arrow did not completely penetrate the deer, chances are he'll do a lot of bleeding internally —and most of the blood you'll find will be high up, where he brushes the entry wound against limbs and vegetation.

Sometimes, of course, a deer will not bleed externally at all; if this happens, you've got trouble, and your best bet is to try to track the deer by following the prints his hooves have made in the soil. If you are lucky, maybe there will be snow on the ground to assist you. If the terrain you are hunting prevents this kind of trailing over a considerable distance, however, you're still not completely out of options. If the law allows it in your hunting area, another way of finding such non-bleeding deer is to put a dog on the track. In some parts of the world, this is a common practice; it prevents the loss of plenty of deer. Better check local game laws, however, before you try to find your deer this way, since it's illegal in some areas.

As a last resort, you can simply start checking the most likely spots in your area where a wounded deer *might* go. How do you do this? By remembering two things. First: a wounded deer will almost invariably follow the line of least topographical resistance as it flees, especially if it's hard hit. This means it will almost never climb and will usually try to stay on level as much as possible or run downhill (but rarely down steep hills). Second: remember that a wounded deer is going to be trying to reach dense cover or water as quickly as possible. Remembering these two things, it becomes a relatively simple matter to predict where your wounded deer might be—if you know your hunting area reasonably well.

If you don't know the area particularly well, it's a good idea to carry topographical maps. Such maps provide an excellent means of locating likely spots a deer might be, and it's surprising how accurate a guess you can make by using them. If your deer starts bleeding again, such maps will often help you pick up the trail again so you can trail in a more conventional manner. The main thing to remember is that you should exhaust *every* possibility.

Wounded deer will invariably head for heavy cover to lie down, so how you approach them is important. If the blood trail you are following turns into heavy cover, it's sometimes wise—especially if you think the deer is still capable of fleeing farther—to circle the cover and come in from the opposite side. A wounded deer, if still alert, will be watching its back trail. And if you come into the thicket slowly, chances are good you'll get a finishing shot before the deer gets up again. If you don't circle the cover, but instead approach directly, guard against becoming so preoccupied with the trail itself that you forget to look ahead for the deer. I once did this and ended up following a badly wounded spike buck for an unnecessary mile. If I'd been watching, I would have had a perfect finishing shot at 20 yards. As it turned out, the deer staggered away, and it took another two hours of trailing to finish the job.

When you do find your deer, mark its position well if you are going to have to go for help to carry it out. More than one hunter has misplaced his gutted trophy so thoroughly he is unable to return to it. You can avoid this if you will chart your progress, while trailing, on your topo map. On the map—with the help of a compass and visible landmarks—you can note your trailing progress, as well as the *exact* location of your fallen trophy.

If you don't want to bother with maps or a compass, carry a roll of inexpensive white ribbon, tying a short length of it to limbs and brush as you follow the trail. Using maps or ribbons to chart your path will not only leave an easy-to-follow trail back to where the deer is, but also eliminate the common problem of finding your own way out of the woods after a deer has led you a merry, confusing chase. It's a bit embarrassing to have your hunting buddies out all night looking for you.

So be prepared when you deer hunt to adequately take care of the hunting job that often remains *after* your deer is hit. The best way to accomplish this is to plan what you may need to do before the need arises. Keep in mind those things which you can do to increase your chances of finding your trophy: Make a mental note of where your deer was standing when you shot; watch it as it flees to see if you can spot a protruding shaft; watch *how* it runs and in what direction; stay in your stand for at least 45 minutes before you begin trailing (if weather permits); sweep the area with 180° arcs until you pick up the blood trail; if you lose the trail, employ the leapfrog technique of trailing; chart your trailing progress on a map or with white ribbon; approach wounded deer carefully for a finishing shot.

Finding your deer after you have wounded it is the humane, sportsmanlike thing to do, and it avoids the terrible waste of one of the choicest meats in the world. Never abandon a trail until you have exhausted every possible means or alternative. To do less is unpardonable. In a time when anti-hunting groups are massing forces against all kinds of hunters, it is especially important that everybody take a hand in the fight to preserve the right to hunt and intelligently harvest our wild game. Making sure you bring home all the game you hit is a good place to start.

BUGLING THEM IN

The Eastern bowhunter who yearns for an opportunity to hunt some species of big game other than whitetail, and still plans such prospects within a limited budget, would do well to consider an elk bowhunt.

This king-sized deer is just about the toughest trophy to come by with the bow. Wapiti's spooky nature can put the craftiest whitetail buck to shame. I might also add that if you're successful, the reward will be twofold—a coveted trophy plus some of the most tasty game meat anywhere!

There are many western areas with elk hunting potential. Unfortunately, the most highly publicized areas pose two problems: extreme hunting pressures and high rates. In addition, few feature a special archery season. This means competing with the rifle hunters for game that is doubly spooked and alert.

Colorado has a special archery season which usually opens in mid-August for mule deer and elk. This offers the bonus of a combined hunt, while keeping the cost within reach. Hunting pressures are nil and the elk population is ample.

There are many reliable and highly competent outfitter/guides in Colorado. My experiences have been confined to the services of Jack Peters, who operates the Tru Sport Lodge at Meeker. Jack is a bowhunter. This places the outfit on a more attractive basis, for he knows what the bowhunter encounters and tailors his hunts accordingly.

Tree hunting is legal in Colorado. Being well-aware that the hunter/success ratio finds the best results by this method, Peters has over 65 tree blinds located throughout the hunting country. This gives him the flexibility to move his bowhunters around without crowding anyone, as well as to pick blinds that will fit your experience and physical limitations.

Hunting from tree blinds offers the most shooting at both deer and elk. However, this method of bowhunting requires patience and a good degree of optimism. Many find this steady diet impossible. That bowhunter can vary his hunting by stalking for muleys. If elk are your hopes, you can try one of the most exciting means of bowhunting you may ever experience—bugling the bulls.

Bugling begins when the rutting season begins. This is when the bulls round up their harems of cows and like other antlered species acquire a rather reckless and belligerent attitude.

A call is used. The idea is to sound like a challenging bull elk on the prowl for cows. If the rut is on and a bull is within hearing distance, chances are you will get an answer.

Now the fun begins. If you sound like a smaller bull, you may get the answering bull to come toward you. That is, if you have located a bull of fairly good size, in a fighting mood and with few, if any, cows in his harem.

As mentioned before, here is an animal of extreme spookiness and unpredictable actions. No two bulls will react in the same way, and the times that a bowhunter will be caught flat-footed will far outweigh the chances to connect.

A big animal, about 800 pounds on the hoof, the mature elk will carry from five to seven points on one side of his massive beams.

To have one of these big fellows step into sight, within less than 20 yards, without making a sound, can shake you up with thrills that defy description!

When elk are rutting, skillful bugling on your part will draw in a trophy like this fine bull.

Let's suppose you are going to give this method a try. All hunting is done on foot. Good elk country is at the higher altitudes—7,500 feet and higher. Elk frequent the dark timber during most of the day. This is rough terrain with many canyons, ravines, steep sides and hundreds of windfalls. Even if you're hunting on horseback, you will sometimes spend more time leading your horse than riding.

When you bugle and get an answer, the bull may be a good distance away. Move at once, working in the general direction of your reply. Remember that you are imitating a bull that is roaming in search of cows—so you must play the part. If you keep bugling from the same spot you will either sound like a big bull that already has a harem or sound suspicious enough to send the answering bull the other way!

Assuming that you keep getting an answer as you move along, keep a sharp lookout for cows as you close in. If they spot you first, they will usually spook the entire harem, and your bull will be gone.

You finally get within 100 yards or so of the answering bull which you now can hear plainly as he grunts and brays and becomes excited. You realize that you have reached the maximum distance you may close in and now must position yourself within about 20 yards of the elk trail you are near while your guide drops back a good 50 yards or more.

Conceal yourself to some degree, but leave an opening to shoot toward the elk trail, nock an arrow and wait.

If the bull sounds like he is still hesitant to close in, the guide gives another final call. This many times allows the bull to pinpoint what he thinks is the position of his supposed opponent, and he will come in fighting mad!

Here's where you must keep your head and let the bull pass your position before trying to shoot. If you shoot before the bull has passed, the bull will spot the movement and whirl and spook before you can get the arrow off.

Add to all this the fact that when the bull is past you the shot must be placed in the vital heart-lung section. If this is done you can expect to find a dead bull within 100 yards or less.

This is the way things happen if all goes well, but there are a few little things that can spoil the entire show. Wind direction must remain in your favor. If the bull winds you, he will leave the area—fast! If the bull sees you, he will break. If either you or your guide make too much noise getting into position, chances are that the bull may spook. Then there is also the chance that the bull may chicken out at the last moment and leave you sitting.

Picture the dense cover of jackpine and imagine yourself posted and waiting for a bull that just bugled within shooting range. You move your head slowly to keep as much area in view as possible —carefully, for the turning motion of your head can easily be spotted by the bull. The bull trots into sight, passing within 30 yards of where you are posted—and you are looking the other way. You get only a fast glimpse of the bull as it passes with hardly a sound. Caught flat-footed, you don't have time to draw before the bull has disappeared into the timber!

This is by no means a constant pattern of behavior. The next bull may run his cows around a point where he thinks he might have them concealed, turn and come back without making another sound, after having answered the first bugle on your part—10 minutes ago! Some bulls will run their cows smack into the waiting bowhunter while bringing up the rear.

One young bull carrying three on a side had only one cow with him when we tried a bugle along the side of a canyon of dark timber. We got an answer from a bull about a mile across on the other side, and before I could nock an arrow, the young bull—who had never let out a sound—came running in with a cow in front of him. The cow swerved within 20 feet of me and cut down over the side, while the bull stopped about 20 yards behind. By the time I spotted the bull he was running down the side. I had no shot!

Another bull who had led us on a merry chase for several miles of hard climbing finally quit answering, so we gave up and started back. We were within a short distance of our "four-by" when we were stopped in our tracks by a loud bugle within a couple hundred yards. That bull had been following us for over a half hour. We worked toward the bull who to all indications intended to fight. The sound of hooves within 75 yards revealed where the bull spooked, and the slight breeze on the back of our necks told us why—the bull had scented us.

There are other hazards you confront in this method of hunting. We worked one bull for several miles, getting good answers each time we bugled. Finally we could hear the bull turning our way. We had to skirt a beaver pond to avoid crossing an open park where the bull might have spotted us. A big old beaver that was swimming around slapped the water with its broad tail as it dove. That danger signal was all the bull needed, and he was gone!

Young bulls are not capable of bugling until they reach three years or older. Spikes will emit a shrill, squeaky bugle—no comparison to the slow buildup of the mature bull. The real bugle reaches a high-pitched, piercing whistle, then drops to a low tremolo usually followed by a grunt or two.

We had one bull work himself into a frenzy as he kept running his harem of more than 20 cows back and forth in the dark timber no more than 100 yards away from us. We positioned ourselves, challenging and being answered, and finally turned the bull. As the bull started our way, a spike nearby evidently decided to move in and steal a few cows while these two bulls were having a fight. The spike almost walked into Peters. Crashing off through the timber, the young bull spooked every elk within earshot!

This method of bowhunting offers so much in comparison to the waiting type of hunting. Although I did not shoot an arrow at a bull, I found the hunt satisfying and highly educational.

Bowhunting equipment for elk does not have to be in the super-heavy class, but it cannot be light either. A bow of 50 pounds or more will suffice, for the shots will be within fairly close range. Rely more on sharp hunting heads for utmost penetration, and place the arrow in the lung area.

Normal weather conditions require no more than the ordinary outer clothes worn back East when you're after whitetails. Remember that you will be covering a lot of country on foot, and this activity will keep you warm. Camo clothes are ideal, and hunting shoes with a good sole for footing are a big help. You will probably need binoculars for preliminary scouting, but in thick timber you can't see the elk until they are within close range so you won't need binocs there. A bow quiver seems most ideal for this type of stalking for it minimizes noise as you work through the heavy cover.

A bit of conditioning prior to the hunt will prove helpful. Build up the legs and lung power. The high altitudes make breathing more difficult, and the steep climbs and ascents will take their toll on unconditioned legs.

Jogging is a fine conditioner for both lungs and legs. A flight of stairs can be put into good use to strengthen your legs. If nearby country or some local hill is convenient, you can exercise there and possibly include some stump shooting practice. Many archery courses have targets on sidehills; practice on them as much as possible.

BEAR HUNT THAT GOT MY GOAT

Although this is admittedly an isolated instance, it did happen. And it could happen to some of you if you're not fully prepared.

With more leisure time available, more disposable income, ease of travel and growing interest in bowhunting, more and more outfitters and resort operators everywhere are becoming aware of the opportunities to host bowhunters. Most of the problems arise when a genial host fails to realize the specialized needs of a bowhunter—and when the bowhunter fails to fully check out all conditions and requirements for his planned hunt.

Don't let this instance scare you away. There are plenty of responsible, knowledgeable outfitters in the U.S. and the Canadian provinces who want to help you make your hunt a success. And any time you cross a governmental border—local, state or national—you can expect variances in regulations. So go adequately prepared, keep your eyes open and your broadheads sharp and you should have a good hunt.

"I'm leaving!"

"Me, too."

"This sure ain't no bear hunt."

"He's not getting any more money out of me."

"Me either. That's $50 down the drain."

And so the conversation went among the seven discouraged bowhunters spending their second day at a lodge in northern Ontario. We had come up here to hunt bear. The outfitter had obligated himself to furnishing food, housing, hunting guides, prebaited areas, blinds and other assistance. Yes, he had provided housing—but little else.

And so the group disbanded. Why?

From the time we hit the town closest to the lodge, our problems mounted. First of all, the radio-telephone to the camp was dead and had been all day, according to the telephone operator. After waiting for what seemed an interminable number of hours on the predetermined boat dock, the lodge owner/outfitter finally showed up with two boats and one of his Indian guides. While the owner went into town to get a new generator, the Indian guide was to take us back across the lake. But there was no way we were going to get across the lake with all of our gear in two boats. And by now the water showed three-foot whitecaps. To reduce the load, two guys decided to stay on the dock and send their gear with us.

It's a good thing they did. We got out about a mile and a half when the tow rope broke. I had decided to ride the second boat, and it's a good thing I did. It's the only thing that saved our equipment. I was able to keep the boat in line with the breakers until the guide got the motor started and spliced the tow line.

When we finally got to the lodge, the fellow who organized the whole thing met us at the dock. He immediately apologized—because nothing was ready.

Nine hunters were sent on to Timmins. Four who had not traveled so far went home, and seven experienced hunters stayed on and tried to form a hunt. But the lodge had not prebaited for bear. Friday night we scouted the area looking for logical bear areas, only to learn that the lodge was located on a peninsula, and this meant very little chance of seeing bear in the vicinity. There was only one trail which led to another lake.

Before long, we also learned that the two Indian guides were really fishermen and didn't know their way out of camp. We spent all Friday night trying to decide what to do. We decided to give the owner two days to put something together. He finally agreed to get another Indian guide who was a trapper and also to go into town for fresh bait.

Friday morning while he was in town, we used the boats and scouted the area again. We came for dinner at 1:00 p.m. only to find that the cooks refused to serve us—we were late, dinner was served at 12:00 sharp.. After much persistence, they finally served us—and then quit.

The owner finally showed with a guide and two small boxes of meat for bait—not nearly enough. He convinced the cooks to stay on. He spent the afternoon calming down the fishermen who were upset because we had apparently taken their fishing boats that morning. The guide seemed to vanish from sight. That left us with no guide, little bait and no boats. We started to pack.

The owner learned that we were packing. He took one boat from the fishermen and rounded up the Indian guide. He then insisted that we hunt the garbage dump 22 miles away. Although this is against the law in Canada, anything was better to us than being stuck on that peninsula. We boated across the lake and loaded into an old blue truck. The road to the dump was unreal. We walked part of the way because the truck could not make it up the hills.

The owner pulled up to the dump, parked at the edge and promptly went to sleep. Our faithful guide went to the railroad tracks at the other edge of the dump to watch for trains. The hunters spread out, and I climbed on top of a railroad car to get above the mosquitoes and flies. No bears showed. We left at sundown—which was 10:00 p.m. Enough of this hassle; we all decided to leave the next day.

The news traveled. The only boat left in camp the next morning had a broken motor. We all were tired of playing games. We pushed the outfitter: "If you don't have a boat for us by noon, you'll swim our gear out."

The motor was functional by noon. Dale and I got the first boat out.

When we got back to town, Dale and I went to the restaurant and related our experiences to the owner, who then offered to take us bear hunting. Off we went, way off into the bush. But this fellow knew what he was doing. He took us to an area where the moose tracks were so big you had to worry about falling in. Half a mile from the truck, the black flies came at us for the first time. Since we hadn't encountered them before, we were not carrying any protection. We split to cover several trails. The flies were all over us. In about an hour I noticed a couple of blood spots on my wrist. When I rolled up my sleeve to clean off the blood, the whole arm was bloody. I decided to get out of there and headed for the truck. By the time I got there, Dale and Herman were both inside with the windows up and spraying 6-12 to kill the thousands of black flies inside. That evening the owner's wife doctored my arms with antibiotic cream.

The first night in bed was not bad, and the swelling had not started by the time we got up at 5:00 a.m., so we decided to go it again. We didn't get out of the cafe until 8:00 a.m. due to the local traffic who "wanted to see the bowhunters." That day Herman said he would take us where people didn't go but bears did. He was right. We went 45 miles back into the bush. The first 25 were okay. Then we crossed a bridge that required Dale and me to get out and guide Herman across. We crossed two more, in worse condition, then the trail ended.

On we went. Finally we stopped in the middle of nowhere and selected our bait site. We had Cutters with us this time. We put on the repellent and opened the windows to test it. The stuff really worked! For the most part, the flies wouldn't even land on us. I stepped out of the truck and tucked my shirttail in—and came up with a handful of blood. They had already found the unsprayed area. I plastered Cutters on my waist and legs, and never got another bite. But I had already had enough.

We put out the bait and built the blinds. Herman watched and learned. When we got through, the three of us went down the trail to do some looking. We separated, with plans to return to the truck at noon. I don't think I ever found the right fork. Somewhere I jumped a moose and had to back track to stay away from him. Rather than have a confrontation, I chose to back up the trail. Just as I came around the bend, I saw Dale 50 yards ahead of me. He was doing a lot of looking and not moving. He, too, had come face-to-face with a bull moose and wasn't sure what to do. Noon came, and no Herman. Dale stayed at the truck while I went on stand at my bait. Dale went into his blind at 3:00 p.m. At 4:00 p.m. I left my blind because the black flies were so thick I couldn't open my mouth to breathe. Every time I did, I inhaled flies.

Herman was not back yet. I started to worry. I put on more Cutters, and went to sleep beside the truck. By 6:00 p.m. the flies were so thick their noise was driving me crazy. I went back to the blind. When I came in at 7:00 p.m., Herman was conked out, asleep in the truck. Dale came in 30 minutes later looking like a wild man. He said he was losing his mind from the flies. We both agreed that a man could not keep his sanity if he were lost in this bush for three days.

Even Herman, who lived up there, hadn't experienced anything like this before. He had walked 4½ miles into the next township, and the farther he went, the better the bear sign looked. He finally found a place where the brush was torn up for 40 yards around. He couldn't figure this out because it looked like a bear had done the damage. He climbed a tree to wait. After two hours, a 250-pound bear came into view. The bear looked around, then threw himself on the ground and rolled. The bear found some low brush and dragged himself through it. Then he lay on his belly and pushed himself through the brush on his hind legs. The flies were driving the bear mad.

Herman watched this for 25 minutes, but the bear never got close enough for a shot. When the bear left, so did Herman.

We got back to Foleyet and Herman's place at 1:00 a.m. We sat and talked about the hunt till 4:00 a.m. The black fly bites were getting to me. My arms were so swollen, I didn't know where to put them. Dale and I decided to get out of there, and without sleeping we headed south—for home.

There are three main reasons for joining a group expedition rather than embarking on a Canadian hunt alone. First, hunting by yourself in the millions of acres of unfamiliar Canadian brush is impossible. Without a guide you would become hopelessly lost in no time, regardless of your previous experience—and there is always the possibility of injury. Second, with no previous knowledge of the area and insufficient time to research it to locate game, your chances of finding animals are almost nil. If you wanted to go alone, you couldn't do it without a guide. And, third, hiring a guide for one person can be prohibitively expensive.

But hunting in groups or joining expeditions can be successful, fun and relatively inexpensive if the proper selection of outfitter and planning is done beforehand.

Some hunting groups come back with super enthusiasm to return again and again, always having a great hunting vacation. Here are some of the things to check so you'll have a good hunt:

Outfitter/Guide: Does he have all the facilities? What's his previous track record? Talk to previous hunters. You can rely on their recommendation for a guide or outfitter. Some outfitters advertise a guaranteed hunt. This normally means guarantee of visual contact with the animals. It is assumed that the archer has the hunting skill to make the hunt successful. Too many fishing or camping outfitters portray themselves as hunting outfitters. Be wary.

Hunting Area: Are the facilities accessible to the hunting area? If not, do they require transportation? What method of transportation? If boats are required, verify ahead that one is assigned to you, that you don't have to share it with 20 fishermen. Are safety flotation devices furnished in the boat? Don't assume they are there just because the brochure says so. If the outfitter is located on a nonworkable location like an island or peninsula, he's not going to be able to produce bear in the immediate vicinity. Under no circumstances pay more than a small deposit until the facilities can be checked out.

When in a boat on Canadian lake waters, don't wear full camouflage suit and boots laced to the knees. In Canada, storms often come up suddenly and without warning, and you need to be ready for a tipover.

Guide Assistance: Is the area virgin? If it is, you definitely need a guide who is familiar with the terrain and the game. In essence, don't accept a guide who just reported to camp and doesn't know where he is. A good guide can find the bear sign, keep you both out of trouble and generally dedicate himself to a successful hunt.

If the area is not virgin and has some semblance of mining and timber trails—and you have successful past experience in similar woods and know how to read area maps with the use of a compass (and you have a helluva lot of confidence in yourself)—you can probably get along without a guide.

Normally the timber and mining roads will have grown over with brush as the natural resources were depleted. Compass deviation can vary considerably with metal deposits, and you should assume you will wind up lost. The map will be of little use due to the fact that there are a great many lakes in the area and they all have a tendency to look alike from the ground.

Camp Food Facilities: These are the first clues—if meals are served at predetermined hours (such as 7, 12 and 6)—that you're at a fishing camp. Hunters do not work on a schedule. Any outfitter who doesn't realize this isn't a hunter.

Hunting Licenses: In Ontario, which bears the brunt of most of the hunting pressure, a valid hunting license from any previous time or location in Ontario is acceptable proof of proficiency to obtain a permit. Failure to produce a previous, or your home state, license requires the hunter to pass a written and verbal hunting and firearms test. (This test exists only in Ontario and Quebec.) The test includes safety practices, game laws, courtesy rules and firearms handling. The total test is firearms-oriented.

It can be a tough test for a U.S. hunter without previous study or coaching because Canadian game hunting, firearms handling and storage laws are somewhat different from ours. If you wish to get manuals in advance for study—and you should—write to the Department of Natural Resources (Toronto, Ontario, Canada). The Department will send you a list of provincial field offices, and you can write to whichever field office you choose for the proper manuals, hunting regulations, license costs, and so forth.

The test was begun a few years ago, when their hunting safety statistics showed that they were having too many accidents among non-resident hunters. The test is short and not that difficult, but it has helped them weed out the non-serious types who are up there on a lark.

Entry to Canada: Items banned from Canadian entry include bear bait, fresh fruit, cigarettes in volume, alcoholic beverages.

Take plenty of hunting gear—such as bows and arrows and bow strings—but do not take so much that it can be construed as moving commercial products across the border for resale. Anything bearing a Canadian seal going into the territory may be challenged on the way out as an export.

If you are driving, have with you your valid driver's license and car registration.

Returning to the U.S.: If the hunt is successful, there is a trophy fee for the animal coming out. If you have made any purchases in Canada, limit them to $100 to avoid payment of duty. You can bring out one U.S. quart of alcoholic beverages and one carton of cigarettes.

The ideal way to salvage a trophy animal for mounting purposes is to fly it from the nearest airport direct to a taxidermist in the United States, following his instructions in preserving it.

Preservation in the Wilds: Be prepared for extreme weather changes—from snow storms one day to 90° weather the next. The most prevalent insect pests are black flies and mosquitoes. The most deterrent type sprays for mosquitoes appear to work the same. An occasional mosquito bite will cause irritation, but there is no serious concern. Counter methods for black flies are not so successful. Only one product tested by this group worked—Cutters. The black fly is approximately twice the size of a gnat with teeth approximating a shark's. Their bites simulate a razor cut, leaving a badly wounded individual who doesn't realize he is injured. Exposed surfaces of skin rarely are attacked. The fly crawls under the clothing around the collar, wrists, ankles and belt areas. The hunter doesn't realize he's one bloody mess until he moves a portion of his clothing. (There are a few lucky people who are not susceptible.) One archer in the group had as many as 13 bleeding cuts on one square inch under his sleeve.

PRONGHORN CHALLENGE

Dancing waves of heat shimmered from the parched, white prairie crust and faded into the dry air just above three-foot high clumps of sage. They were out there all right—waiting for me to make one bad move.

I picked the sinuous ribs of sage stems apart just enough to see the gang of them standing there. How bold they were, I thought. Brazen animals—challenging me to stand like a man and fight in the open. They knew I was there, even though my camouflaged form blended well into the wall of sagebrush that surrounded me.

Maybe they could hear me breathing? I wouldn't put it past these super creatures. This was their home and they knew well the bodies and shapes of Wyoming sage that surrounded their water hole. A blind built too high, too low, too thick or too thin warned them of danger.

Two of the lead does took several cautious steps toward my blind. Then they came to a halt, arched their necks and stared. One of them let out a snort similar to the danger signal a whitetail deer makes.

With the signal, the three bucks in the herd began pacing back and forth behind the does and fawns. One of them was a magnificent specimen. The prongs on his heart-shaped, black horns looked like they would measure at least four inches or more. His horns extended more than halfway above the tips of his ears. Both were indications that the antelope was a better-than-average buck. One like this would score high on the Pope and Young chart.

The herd was about 80 yards out. It was a long shot—made even more difficult by a gusty, Wyoming plains wind. Making allowances for the wind at that distance would be difficult and risky. I was trying for a buck. Hoping to direct an arrow through a maze of does and fawns into a vital area of one of those bucks would be like wishing for the wind to quit blowing in Cheyenne.

Kneeling, I nocked an arrow, took a deep breath and slowly maneuvered myself into shooting form. The bucks had not moved. The big one was standing broadside. I drew on him, allowing for the wind.

My release was smooth, causing only a muffled thud as the bow popped back to its natural shape. For a second the arrow was on target, but it also took just a second for all three bucks to react to the ''twangless'' release. The pronghorns were ten yards away by the time my arrow reached the spot where the trophy buck had stood.

Since then I have had many more good bow shots at pronghorn antelope. Without exaggerating, the number of releases under 80 yards totals about 40. I have yet to bag a pronghorn with bow and arrow, yet I feel well qualified to relate to you the techniques for hunting them.

Antelope hunting is not a ''kill 'em and hang 'em high'' sport. It is a tough, frustrating, challenging sport—a sport that I love. Anyone who must bag an antelope with the bow to feel enjoyment will soon quit. But to most dedicated archery antelope-hunters, the challenge of hunting these spooky beasts is enough to keep us coming back year after frustrating year.

This prairie smoker does not run like any other big game animal in our country. Call the creature a broken field runner if you like. In shiftiness, the animal resembles a cottontail; in speed he resembles Bob Hayes. The antelope is smart as a prairie fox and gutty as a six-point bull elk. So how do you hunt the pronghorn?

There is very little similarity between hunting antelope with a rifle and with a bow. Getting close to pronghorns—under 100 yards—is as tough as breaking the goal-line stand on the football field.

Ground comes slowly when stalking or waiting for antelope. Patience and picking the right "moves" are the keys to good shots.

Some bowhunters have been lucky enough to stalk the pronghorn to within shooting distance. These occasions, I believe, are the exceptions rather than the rule, because stalking antelope is like trying to sneak up on a flock of wary honkers in an open cornfield.

There are a few exceptions to the toughness of stalking, however, and I'm sure that a few bowmen can vouch for that. In rough, broken country it is sometimes possible to take antelope by surprise —especially if they are feeding or drinking.

A guard animal is usually posted near the herd, and it takes an extremely quiet, careful sneak to get off a shot. Many times I would get within 60 yards of some antelope without the aid of a blind. But when I raised my bow or arm to shoot, the animals were off in a blaze of speed and dust.

The best method for producing shots and chances of bagging an animal is to hunt from a blind. You get more standing shots and can take your time to get better shots. The selection of your hiding place is the most important move you can make. If you are a nonresident hunter, chances are you will let a guide do the picking for you. Most likely he will choose an area near a well-used water hole with plenty of cover for a blind.

I pick an area near a road or highway that is well traveled. Contrary to many opinions, the animals near such routes of traffic are not as spooky as those isolated from men and vehicles.

In the summer and early fall pronghorn water at least twice a day. Like clockwork, bands of animals filter to the water spot shortly after sunrise and around 2:00 in the afternoon.

Besides depending on this supply of water, the animals in the area have become conditioned to the sights and sounds of man and his machinery. The little bit of confidence that antelope gain by seeing and hearing man turns out to be an advantage during hunting season.

There are many such areas in Wyoming and other antelope-hunting states. They are easy to find because they are well traveled and are often overlooked by rifle hunters because of their proximity to the highway.

Maybe now you have a tender spot for the antelope; after all, I suggested taking advantage of the animal's need for water and his faith in man. Unfair? Not in the least. The time and effort you take to choose an area for a blind is only the beginning of the preparations needed for shots at pronghorn. Antelope will always have the edge on you. As a bowhunter, you just try to narrow the gap a bit.

When you camouflage for antelope hunting, you blend yourself into the terrain and vegetation to the best of your ability. There are no shortcuts or minor allowances for the sake of comfort or looking good. Face, neck, hands (if gloves are not worn) and all exposed parts should be painted with camo cream. You are dealing not with a whitetail or a mule deer, but with animals that depend on *sight*, speed and hearing for survival. Only the best camouflage job is acceptable. Hat, shirt and trousers can be of standard camo design and coloration. Be careful that white tee-shirts do not ruin an otherwise good job of blending in with vegetation. Bow should be camouflaged either with a cover or paint. Take care to cover the white limb tips common on hunting bows.

A friend of mine is a firm believer in masking human odor by using a commercially prepared deer scent when antelope hunting. The main thing to remember is to avoid sprays, hair tonics and perfumed soaps that can give you away.

Observe the travel pattern of antelope in a specific area for two or three prime moving hours before setting up a blind. The time spent watching will prevent time being wasted in moving the blind along a game trail.

Antelope use game trails. Several of them will lead to and from the water hole. Unless spooked, the pronghorns I observed followed the same trail to and from the water hole. When spooked, they weren't particular if they were on a trail or not.

Construct a blind at least 20 yards off the trail. Many times you can position the blind between two separate trails so two traffic lanes can be covered at once.

If at all possible, pick a clump of sagebrush, grass or rocks already natural to the area and use the covering as the blind or the foundation for one. You will find that too high a blind will cause a lot of suspicion if it is not natural to the area. A blind too low may not adequately conceal you.

The blind should be as high as the top of your head when you're kneeling. Since a lot of time is required in the blind, you would get uncomfortable in a long crouch without being able to stretch. In the kneeling pose, you should be able to stretch high enough to shoot over the walls with just your head, bow and arms visible.

Rather than stack too much vegetation or rocks on a blind site, I have found it better to dig a shallow pit instead. An army entrenching tool (translated into civilian: a small, collapsible shovel) fits the bill nicely.

There are few instances when you will have the time or chance to stand for a shot, so practice accordingly. Antelope are blessed with excellent peripheral vision. Unless they are walking or running directly away, they will spot you before you have a chance to draw. This knowledge comes after many attempts to stand, draw and get off a shot. A pronghorn gains about 30 yards on you while you're getting him in your sights.

The blind should be enclosed. More than once antelope have surprised me from behind. Often, after they have been scattered, there is no set direction of their travel to and from water.

Scattered openings near the top of the blind sometimes enable a bowhunter to shoot through the blind. These openings must be high enough to shoot from a sitting or kneeling position. If a pronghorn stops directly in front of the opening, you have an excellent chance of sticking him. The running shot—difficult at any time—is especially difficult through the "peep hole" since you can't follow-through with a lead.

When animals are approaching the blind, they can detect movement inside it from nearly 100 yards away. Stay perfectly still.

It will be up to your judgment and ability as a shooter to determine the best time to shoot. I have let antelope come within 20 yards of my blind hoping they would turn away or broadside. My first attempt at drawing the bow would send them bursting for daylight because all their senses are functioning at the 100 percent mark that close in. (Your senses, if you are like most bowhunters, will be somewhat obscured by a thumping heart and trembling arms. Antelope are just not ordinary beasts.)

That's what makes the pronghorn a tough bow challenge.

CHAPTER FIVE

VARMINTS, BIRDS, SMALL GAME
●
LET THE GAME HUNT YOU

Bowhunting and predator calling are sports tailor-made for each other. Armed with bow and arrow, the hunter needs his quarry close—the closer the better—and the challenge of calling is to lure a wary predator within eyeball-to-eyeball confrontation before the critter realizes it has been duped.

It is rudimentary in fact, but complex in reality. A predator is a super-sly animal that doesn't make many mistakes. It takes a skilled caller to inveigle one into an unsuspected ambush. And once the animal arrives on the scene, the hunter must raise his weapon, draw an arrow and get off a shot without the critter detecting his presence.

In calling, unlike bowhunting, mastering the "weapon" is the easiest step of all. A common mistake is for someone to purchase a call, spend considerable time trying to learn the proper tone and pitch, then head for the woods and try it briefly a few times. If nothing immediately shows, he swears and be-damns that the thing won't work.

I carried the same hangup at first. Then a veteran caller gave me some sensible advice. "No two rabbits sound alike," he said.

After much calling and observing, I've learned the sagacity of what he preached. A California friend who came to hunt with me played a weird-sounding tune on his predator call—nothing resembling the pitious cries of a crippled cottontail rabbit. Yet he got results.

Anyway, an alternative is to use some type of electronic player with records or tapes of authentic animals in distress. If you believe this to be unsporting, you haven't tried predator calling. (But don't try electronic or record calls in states where that equipment is not legal.) Luring the animal within range is just the beginning of the game, one which the predator usually wins.

All kinds of varmints will respond to the proper call. The most widespread and plentiful are bobcats, foxes, coyotes and raccoons. The conventional dying-rabbit sound will attract predators no matter where you might live. A bird-in-distress call also is very effective. It is particularly alluring to raccoons.

But there are many sounds which can be used to exploit a predator's most basic weakness: its need for food. I remember a calling trip that Murry and Winston Burnham, the game-calling brothers, and I took to southern Texas. We were miles from the nearest house on an eerie, dark, moonless night. After getting set for action, Murry switched on the cartridge tape player. I couldn't believe my ears! From the speaker came the throaty clucks of a contented Plymouth Rock hen. And surprisingly, within minutes a curious coyote came running.

"I don't know why you were surprised," Murry told me later. "Shucks, all predators like chicken."

The neophyte caller usually is guilty of several common mistakes, but probably the primary one is that he does not show proper respect for his quarry. A predator is a crafty, wary and sly critter. Despite the pressures man has put on it, using everything from trained dogs and poisons to traps in an attempt to eradicate it, the predator not only has survived, it actually has thrived and multiplied and expanded its range—which should tell you something. A predator didn't accomplish this feat against great odds by being dumb and careless. So when calling predators, pay attention to every detail, using your ingenuity to counteract an animal's defenses of smell, sight and hearing. Proper preparation is the key.

The foremost consideration is calling in territory where predators roam. You would be amazed by the number of persons who head into a convenient locale to call without knowing whether there is anything present to call. Even if the caller hasn't done his homework—being reasonably assured there were predators where he was hunting—he should move around and try many different places, relying on the law of averages to find a spot where an animal will be within hearing range of the call.

There are varied ways of locating likely calling territory. Visual

Varmint calling and hunting is excellent year-round sport in many areas, often providing close shots.

sightings perhaps are the best. If you should sight a fox scampering across the road, for example, then this area would be worth a try. Predators generally are creatures of fairly limited range; should you see one, you can almost assume that it lives somewhere close by.

Another method is to search for telltale sign: tracks and droppings along country roads and well-traveled trails and around waterholes. Study predators and their habits. Learn what type terrain each prefers and its food preference. The more you know about your quarry, the better are your chances.

Once you pinpoint likely country and start calling, there are a couple of other mistakes to avoid. Don't spend too much time in one spot, and be familiar with the countryside so you won't travel in a circle and broadcast your call over the same terrain again and again. When critters like the fox, coyote and coon are going to answer, they come in a hurry—usually less than 10 minutes. The bobcat is more deliberate and requires more patience and time—up to 30 minutes.

A call will carry maybe a half-mile in calm weather, which means you should move at least this far between stops. A coarse, deep-pitched call, imitating a jack rabbit in distress, will reach farther than will the higher cottontail voice.

Any prevailing breeze tends to muffle the call, so you need not move as far between stops. A wind also is a disadvantage in that it send the sounds farthest in the direction you don't want it to go —downwind where any approaching predator will be spooked by human scent. For this reason the optimum calling condition is calm or with a very negligible breeze. If the wind is strong enough to shake heavy tree branches, you might as well stay at home. The odds definitely are against your luring anything within bow range.

There is another minus effect of calling in a high wind. You "wise up" predators in the area. Perhaps one will answer, but get a whiff of human scent before approaching within bow range. Instinct tells it there is some relationship between the sound and the dreaded human, so it becomes suspicious, much more difficult to fool. Since access to productive hunting territory is becoming increasingly more difficult, it is smart to try and beguile predators when you figure the advantage is yours.

One way to improve the advantage is to call at the right time. Of all the daylight hours, I like the very first one best—from dawn until sunup—when the weather is cool and usually there is an absence of wind. The last hour—from sundown to dusk—is almost as good. And if your state law permits, consider night calling. Predators are primarily nocturnal, and when they are prowling, searching for food, they are most susceptible to a call. Predators come most readily to a call during the dark of a moon. If when you can get away is the wrong time of month, arrange your schedule to hunt before the moon rises or after it sets. Maybe the moon will disappear around midnight, so in this situation sleep early in the night, hunt later.

Once you are in the woods, preparing to call, take a few minutes and be sure you have everything right. Check the breeze, no matter how slight, and put it into your face—away from the direction you are watching and where you expect an animal to show. Use scent liberally, sprinkling the liquid both around your stand and on your clothing. Rabbit scent will help attract predators.

Once you negate the critter's ability to *smell* danger (its primary defense), concentrate on the other two senses—sight and hearing. (A bobcat, unlike the fox or coyote, depends more on its eyesight than smell.) You can best avoid a predator's eyes by getting above its normal line of sight, just as you climb a tree to ambush deer. But leave the call on the ground; the animal will be drawn to the sound and will be less likely to detect you above. If you are using an electronic play, this is simple. Just switch it on and get in the tree. But should you have a mouth-blown call, have a companion hide on the ground, well concealed, and blow on it while you crouch in a low fork of limbs; and be prepared to shoot with a minimum of commotion. Of course you want to sit motionless until you are ready to make your play.

Wear camouflage clothing, and if you hunt on the ground, either construct a quick and crude blind by stacking a few limbs and logs or push back in a green bush where your camouflage will blend with the surroundings. If a predator shows, watch its eyes and don't attempt to get a shot while they are trained in your direction. The element of complete surprise is another advantage.

And lastly, don't become discouraged and give up without giving the sport a fair shake. It is just a matter of being in the right spot at the right time. There can be many reasons why a predator might not respond to a call. A common one is that maybe another caller has been in the area recently. A predator once fooled by a call isn't going to be suckered again—not for a long time. It profits from mistakes.

That, too, should tell you something.

THE MANY STEPS OF VARMINT STALKING

The marmot had been playing hide and seek with me for 10, maybe 15 minutes. Obviously there was a labyrinth of tunnels beneath the rough-rock talus along the mountain slope, for one moment the critter would pop into view on my right, then shortly appear at my left. It was a guessing game just where it would appear next.

The rockchuck's radar system had an accurate fix on my position, and since there was no place to hide, I only could hope that it would get careless, make a mistake and give me a shot.

But whenever I'd see the wily critter and move my bow that way, it promptly would vanish underground again. The marmot didn't seem particularly frightened, but it was suspicious. My mistake had been that I'd gotten careless and let the animal detect my presence before I was within range for a shot. Should the archer get his chance before the animal becomes wise to what is happening—while it is unsuspecting with its guard down—then the odds are in the human's favor; but once the hunted detects even the slightest hint of danger, the odds swing abruptly. A suspicious wild animal throws up a defense screen that is formidable.

I finally gave up on this marmot in the Beartooth Mountains of southern Montana. Frustration simply got the best of me. I think it is the wise man who recognizes when he is stymied.

But frustration is almost synonymous with stalking varmints. To me, the ultimate challenge is stalking and eventually bagging with bow and arrow a wily creature like the woodchuck. You're matching wits with the critter on its home territory with all the odds on its side. About the only thing going for you, the hunter, is intelligence.

Look at it this way: When waiting on a stand or using some type of call, the animal comes to you. By remaining motionless, you minimize the chances of detection. But to stalk you must create movement, and that makes you susceptible to immediate detection. An animal is alert to what goes on around it. Survival demands awareness.

Yet animals, like humans, get careless. A woodchuck, for example, knows its den is nearby. Should it receive a danger signal, it can quickly disappear into its burrow. That innocuous-looking hole is its security blanket.

A jack rabbit depends on its legs, well knowing that if need should beckon, it simply can outrun danger. That is why nature blessed it with speed.

These, then, are the two extremes—the fairly slow and awkward animal which never strays far from its protective den and the speedy critter that roams freely. But in either case, the animal becomes too confident of its unique survival trait. Because the woodchuck knows its den is there, it relaxes its guard and isn't quite as aware as it should be. When that happens, the critter is vulnerable. The hunter's only chance is to exploit this defensive lapse.

But such lapses usually are just momentary. The hunter must learn when he can advance and when he must imitate a statue. Most small animals depend basically on their eyesight. A critter's eyes are conditioned to movement and it can be fooled by something which does not move. The most crucial point of the stalk comes when the bowhunter is within range and is ready to make his move. Movement is mandatory in bowhunting; the hunter must raise his weapon and draw the arrow. His only hope is to complete this maneuver while the animal isn't looking his way—or simply pull and shoot rapidly and gamble that the animal doesn't take evasive action.

A varmint, by my definition, is any animal which can be hunted year-round. The word derives from vermin which, according to the dictionary, means "noxious, troublesome, or objectionable animals collectively." But I don't consider them such. Any animal which can provide hunting pleasure can't be all bad.

What can be hunted year-round will, of course, vary from region to region. In my central Texas bailiwick, for instance, a popular quarry is the so-called rock squirrel—which does resemble a squirrel in appearance but in fact is a rodent that lives in ground burrows or rock crevices. The list might include such critters as the woodchuck, rockchuck (marmot), jack rabbit or even the diminutive ground squirrel.

The most popular varmints, however, are primarily diurnal—the hunter wants them up and about during the day—and they are creatures of limited range. You don't want to initiate a stalk only to see your intended quarry go trotting over a distant hilltop. You want to be reasonably sure that he will be right where you sighted him, or at least close by, when you arrive on the scene.

The obvious first step is to locate game. Pinpoint a varmint in your area and then learn where it is available in huntable numbers. If it is the woodchuck, for example, get in your automobile some afternoon, drive to various farms and stop and ask each landowner if he has woodchucks on his place and if you can hunt them. In this respect, being armed with bow and arrow has its advantage. Many farmers will allow bowhunters, but not riflemen.

Hunt when game is most active. During a warm winter spell, this might be any time of day, particularly just after a severe storm. But usually, you'll see more varmints early and late in the day, when they are feeding. A foraging animal is more vulnerable to the stalk than is one that simply is sitting and looking.

Get on high ground, and if you can see a long way, use binoculars. Just sit and search diligently. This serves a two-fold purpose: you see the game before it sights you and you can study the terrain to determine the best approach for making your stalk.

Try to get some object between you and the animal. The closer the object—a tree, perhaps, or a boulder—is to your quarry, the better.

Despite its uncanny eyesight, no varmint is capable of seeing through a solid object.

The main concern now is to move quietly. Avoid snapping a twig or kicking a rock or doing anything that might forewarn the animal of your presence. Wear soft footwear if you can.

Once you reach the object, you can prepare to shoot if you are within range. When you take the shot is your decision—you know your capabilities. If you are reasonably accurate at 30 yards, make your play when you approach that close. But all things considered, the closer you get, the better are your chances—both of hitting the animal and of being detected, which is the problem.

Probably once you reach the object which let you cat-foot close with impunity, you will have to continue forward without this advantage. This is the test which separates the skillful from the haphazard.

You should be wearing camouflage clothing. It helps to streak your face with paint or cover it with a headnet.

Watch the animal intently. As it lowers its head to feed or turns it the other way, move forward. When the head turns or comes up, make like a statue. Any successful stalk is built on patience. Go after each animal as if this is the *only* stalk you'll get to make the entire day. Haste invites premature detection.

Instead of stalking directly toward the animal, circle it, angling closer as you move forward. For some inexplicable reason, a varmint is less likely to become alarmed by this approach than it is the straight-on stalk.

When you do move, take light, quick steps. There really is no advantage to crawling. It is too slow, and you're unable to rise up and shoot once you approach close.

Never watch the entire animal; concentrate on its head. Move only when you believe its eyes are trained in another direction.

An animal is easily confused for a split second. If you can get its head turned in the opposite direction and you have the time to raise the bow, draw and aim deliberately; then how sweet it is! But usually you'll get only a snap shot.

Suppose, however, that you are about 35 yards from your quarry when it suddenly spooks and jumps for the safety of its burrow. Quickly slip close, avoiding heavy footsteps that might create ground vibrations. Any wild animal is curious. Most likely it will stick its head out briefly to find what alarmed it. If you are ready, you'll get a shot.

Your ordinary deer-hunting outfit is fine for varmint hunting, or you can use a light bow if you prefer. The arrow can be tipped with a broadhead, blunt or judo point. But if you are using a lightweight bow—35 pounds or less—I'd recommend a sharp broadhead. An animal the size of a woodchuck or jack rabbit is tougher than you think.

If you miss your shot, don't worry about it. Varmints are plentiful. Go looking for another likely target. That's one bonus of this off-season sport.

JAVELINA "HOW TO"

Not the faintest breeze stirred. A January chill hung over a remote, corrugated ridge in southeastern Arizona. Charlie Ash hunkered against a boulder on the ridge, glassing for javelinas as the sun crawled over the horizon like a reluctant sleeper emerging from beneath warm blankets. At five minutes before eight, Ash spotted a band of five of the collared peccaries on a broken-rock slope a quarter-mile away. At four in the afternoon, eight hours later, he still tenaciously concentrated on making his javelina bowhunt a success.

Call if what you may—javelina, collared peccary, desert pig—in Arizona it is the archer's favorite game species. In part, such top honors stem from the fact the peccary is much easier to score on than deer, antelope and other larger—and generally spookier—game animals. What's more, he exists in abundant numbers. Rarely weighing more than 50 pounds—state record is 54 pounds—he has been described as an oversized head on four legs. I like to think of this little desert dweller as having a head *and* a body, just no neck.

The javelina's range is broad, from the Southwest into Argentina in South America. In Arizona he prefers a habitat of sunny hillsides in desert chaparral and pinion-juniper country. Specific herds have specific home ranges of several square miles, and they may eke out their entire lives within that particular area. Nature has provided them with a salt-and-pepper coloring that blends in with their chosen landscape. This protective coloring is aided by keen senses of smell and hearing. Their eyesight has been rated from poor to fair. All of these factors must be considered by the serious javelina bowhunter.

Like Charlie Ash. In 1957, Charlie plunged into archery after reading an outdoor article by Fred Bear. In 1960 Ash became fascinated with the idea of taking javelina with the bow. After five frustrating years in pursuit of the little desert pig, he had yet to score.

"There is a great deal of difference," says Ash, "between shooting at paper targets or inanimate objects and at live game wearing fur or feathers. I felt this increased stress every time I drew on javelina—if I managed to get in range. Which was rare. Or if I got lucky enough in my amateurish way to spot pigs."

The lack of success inspired Ash's determination rather than detracted from it. He re-evaluated the javelina and his methods of hunting it. He studied the animal like a dedicated biologist. He made pre-season stalks; he pinpointed pig hotspots. Did it pay off? The following season Ash downed his first javelina—and with unerring accuracy has repeated his performance consistently for the past seven years!

"I believe the most important single factor for a successful javelina bowhunt," he says, "is critical glassing of good pig country. Ninety percent of the javelinas I've seen in the past seven years I would have overlooked without binoculars. I do plenty of pre-season scouting, preferring to hunt rugged country with ridges and hills instead of flat country. Probably the finest pig country in Arizona is near Florence; but because of its flatness, it is extremely hard to score. There are no high vantage points from which to spot pigs. You have to depend on cutting their sign and taking a chance you'll see them before they see you. I believe the odds are more in favor of an archer who hunts country with high ground, even though it has a smaller population of javelina."

During the Arizona archery season, which is generally held in January, javelina feed primarily during the day. In the blistering-hot summer months they forage nocturnally to escape the intense sun. They like mast (acorns), large amounts of roots, bulbs, mesquite beans, agave, some grass and numerous other plants. One of their favorites on the desert flora menu is prickly pear cactus.

"Javelinas will knock pads off the prickly pear cactus plants, then kick them around to break off the sharp spine points," says Ash. "They're not exactly known for their table manners. Archers can find clues to the whereabouts of javelina by checking for 'crumbs' of plants dropped while they are dining, or where they've been digging for roots and bulbs."

Ash learned that on cold days javelinas tend to stay bedded down until after sunup. Once they rout out, they may feed until about a half hour before noon, knock off for a snooze, then resume eating until dark.

"I have actually located unseen javelinas because of their noisy eating habits," Ash says.

Because of their excellent camouflage, bedded-down pigs are especially hard to locate. An archer may scrutinize the land in what he believes to be minute detail, only to start to move to another stand and suddenly find pigs scattering all around him in hasty retreat. Under these conditions an arrow rarely gets nocked before they are gone. Ash attributes his poor luck in the early years of his javelina bowhunting partly to not being able to recognize a bedded-down animal while looking directly at it.

"You'd be surprised how often a bedded-down pig looks like a barrel cactus or a rock," he says.

"How close can a careful bowman get to a javelina under good conditions?"

"Would you believe two or three feet?" he said. "I cannot say I'm an archer with exceptional shooting skill—only that I have learned to stalk into easy arrow range. A steady breeze on the face is highly desirable—providing, of course, the wind is from the pigs. Even though they have reputedly poor eyesight, they are capable of distinguishing movement up to 75 yards, and some care must be exercised that the archer isn't seen. If an archer uses the same cautious stalking methods he uses on deer, he is practically guaranteed to get in easy arrow range."

Ted Knipe, former regional supervisor for the Arizona Game and Fish Department, has skillfully slipped into javelina herds and grabbed their squealing young. The adults made no attempt to defend the young, but instead frantically retreated to save their own skins. However, this is not to say javelinas will not bite. When this writer worked for the Arizona Game and Fish Department several years ago, a wildlife caretaker stepped into a cage with a "tame" adult javelina. This normally docile animal ripped one of the man's legs so savagely it took a couple of dozen stitches to close the wound.

"Once several of us were contemplating how to get a wounded pig out of a cave when it decided to come out on its own. It looked like all of us were attempting to set records for climbing thin air," Ash said.

"Incidentally," I asked, "what is the best method for getting a wounded javelina out of a cave?"

"If you can get some light into the cave, maybe with a mirror if

Careful stalking will get you within close range of javelina, sometimes closer than you really want.

you don't have a flashlight," he said, "finish it off while it's in the cave. Otherwise, it's a hazardous job; one I don't want. If a bowman places an arrow in the chest cavity more than 50 yards away from a cave, more than likely the animal will keel over before it can hole up."

Ash believes the intelligence of a javelina is highly overrated. But he still gives the animal credit for being wary. He says that one time a herd of javelinas will stand, stupidly staring at an archer as he sends arrow after arrow into the herd trying to down a pig. The next ten times the herd will scatter in a dozen directions before an archer can even reveal himself. Back on that chilly ridge in southeastern Arizona that January morning was a classic illustration of javelina unpredictability. It also demonstrated Ash's dedication to pig hunting with the bow.

Without a breeze to aid him on his stalk, Ash inched to within about 100 yards of where the five peccaries foraged on the rocky hillside. He settled down in a wash where he could still observe the pigs while he waited for a wind to come up. About an hour later, a mature adult ambled down the wash to root under a mesquite tree less than 10 yards from Ash. He congratulated himself on his good luck and released an arrow. It missed; the pig moved just as he let the arrow fly. Alarmed, the pig woofed and raced up the hill—right through the middle of his feeding brethren—and disappeared. Remarkably, the foursome took little notice of the panicked pig.

Ash settled down in the wash again. At 11 o'clock a good stalking wind did come up, and he closed in on the feeders for a payoff. But he stopped cold when another member of the band drifted down the hill toward him. It was a large boar with very black bristles. It started to bed down under a buckthorn bush just 10 feet from Ash. Ash drew, but before he could release, the boar sensed him and woofed loudly up the hillside. This time the lunch party went with him.

At 2:00 p.m. Ash ate his lunch, then returned to glassing the slope. It almost startled him to find that three of the original band had returned and bedded down in the shade.

It took him two hours to cover the 100 yards that would put him in easy arrow range. Within 10 yards of one javelina, he placed a shot in its abdomen. A slight miscalculation. Pandemonium reigned. The arrowed pig went up the hill; normally wounded animals run down. The other two bolted into the brush. A loud "woof." A pig ran out the other side of the brush, sans arrow. Behind the brush lay a small cave. The mystery was solved. Ash's pig lay finished at the mouth of the cave. The pig that had run out was evidently the one Ash had shot at earlier in the day.

The hunt success for javelina archers runs about 11 to 12 percent. The firearms hunters' score has been as low as 18 percent. Rarely do hunt figures run this close between gun buffs and archers. Ash feels that were riflemen as cautious as archers, their scores would at least double. He also feels that if archers took more time to stalk in close before releasing their arrows, they might better the smoke-polers. Whatever you do, it'll pay you to hunt like expert Charlie Ash and be sure to bring home the desert pork chop.

BUSHYTAILS, THE BIG LITTLE CHALLENGE

There are many animals to hunt, and there are nearly as many ways to hunt them; but there isn't a more difficult matching of method and animal than hunting squirrels with a bow. They offer the bowhunter the most easily trodden hunting path to near-insanity and sheer frustration.

I lose, break, bend, mutilate and hang arrow after arrow on squirrels. Understandably, I've not kept a record, but I would conservatively estimate that I've lost or ruined the better part of a gross of good arrows on squirrels over the past several years—not counting the culls I've futilely propelled at them.

On other animals, I do fine. With squirrels, though, I'm jinxed. Exactly why I keep after them, I'm not always sure. Once I almost wrapped my bow around a tree and quit hunting them, but then I killed my first bushytail. Since then I've scored with more regularity, and I've picked up along the way a number of tricks and tips that will greatly increase the archer's chances of scoring on the smallest, quickest, most sharp-eyed, elusive small game animal in the woods.

If you'll systematically employ a few of these tricks, you're certain to get more squirrels. But don't plan on keeping a family of 12 in fresh meat if you're going to bowhunt bushytails; the kids might get a little hungry.

First, do your best to locate concentrations of squirrels, spending some time in the woods prior to season's opening to locate squirrel sign. Hunt where there are heavy stands of nut trees—hickory, oak and black walnut, for example. In the early spring, watch for mulberry trees; squirrels can't resist the juicy fruit while it lasts. Keep an eye peeled for nests, and if you don't see at least several, you might as well look for another place to hunt. If you are hunting an area where there are wooded lots and open pastures, look for spots where livestock is fed. If the farmer is feeding grain, squirrels will often stay nearby to get their share. Also, if there are corn fields adjoining your woods, these are nearly always hotspots, especially in late summer and fall. Just station yourself near a fence and get set. You may not get a whole sackful, but you're bound to get some shooting as the squirrels cross the fence into the field.

Once you've located what seems to be a good hunting area, concentrate on actually seeing bushytails. This may seem excessively fundamental, but a surprising number of hunters fail to see most of the squirrels in the woods—mainly because they don't look for them properly. Sometimes, of course, you will see a squirrel exposed in a tree fork, on a limb or jumping in plain view. Spotting these is easy.

But much more frequently only *part* of a squirrel will be visible. If you will train your eyes to be sensitive to these parts, you'll be able to sort the outline of a squirrel from a mass of limbs and foliage where otherwise you might have missed seeing him. Binoculars help.

What parts do you look for? Watch for a bit of his tail hanging off a limb; its shape, color and texture will give away a concealed squirrel quicker than anything else. His ears, too, will often protrude above the edge of a limb, and while they are rather small, you can spot them if you're really looking. His nose will sometimes stick above the edge of a limb, and it makes a sharp protrusion that often appears decidedly out of place in its inanimate surroundings. The same is true of a squirrel's eye, which is shiny, black and reflective—contrasting sharply with everything else on the squirrel and all trees as well. That shiny black dot often provides a highly efficient means of locating him. Remember, if you venture forth looking only for *whole* squirrels, you're going to miss seeing most of them. But if you train your eyes to watch for *parts* of squirrels, you'll start seeing squirrels where you didn't think any existed.

You also need to listen for squirrels even when you can't see them. If there is no wind blowing, you can nearly always hear claws scrape on bark or hear the sound of a squirrel working a nut. Listen also for squirrels to bark and scold. And watch for falling cuttings; by tracing their path you can gradually isolate, even in thick foliage, the exact whereabouts of a bushytail. When you do, just wait for him to finish his nut and go for another one. That's when you have a chance to shoot.

How should you be hunting in order to consistently spot bushytails and get shots? For the bowhunter, one word answers the question: *slowly*. The self-imposed limitations of the archer's weapon are brought into sharper focus by squirrels than by any other animal. This quickly becomes evident when you start hunting them. You'll have to pass up shots the gun hunter wouldn't think twice about taking. And if you don't compensate for this by hunting slowly, you'll come home empty-handed more often than not. By hunting slowly, your chances of getting shots *before* the squirrels realize you are around are greatly increased; this is the edge you need.

I'm convinced your best approach is a combination of still-hunting and standing. Locate potential standing spots—places where you've noted heavy stands of nut trees, nests or other squirrel sign —then slowly hunt from one such spot to the next. Stay about 20 or 30 minutes at each spot, remaining quiet and motionless; if nothing happens, slowly move on to another likely spot. I've found this technique produces more squirrels than any other method.

The time you hunt will to some extent govern how you hunt. In the spring when there is heavy cover, you'll stand a much greater chance of being hidden from your quarry as you stalk and try to get in close. You can move more quietly in the spring, too. At the same time, however, clear, open shots are less frequent because of heavy foliage. In late autumn and winter fallen leaves open up the woods; you can shoot more easily, but stalking quietly is accordingly more difficult. In open woods, the squirrel can also see you coming much farther away, further complicating scoring.

Whatever method you follow, it's generally best to hunt from daylight until about 10:30 in the morning, then from about 4:00 until dusk. In spring and summer warmth squirrels will generally snooze during the middle of the day. In winter, they will often come out later in the morning after the sun is fully up, staying out and remaining active until midday.

It's also a good idea to learn to use a squirrel call—especially if you choose to stand most of the time, moving only when necessary.

The cottontail rabbit ranks number one among small game for bow-hunters. It provides excellent training for fast shooting. Many bow-hunters use their standard deer hunting gear so they become highly familiar with its feel and shooting characteristics.

Squirrels will respond to a call just as many other animals will; you will put more meat in the pot if you take advantage of this. Many good calls are available commercially, but I prefer to use one of my own making most of the time. It's a small hollow box about four inches long with a section of flat clip spring from a rifle magazine attached over one side of the sound hole. A knurled metal shaft is sharply drawn over the edge of the spring, and the sound produced is much like the coarse, husky bark of a squirrel—and often a real squirrel will come to investigate. With a little practice, you can successfully imitate most sounds a bushytail makes.

What equipment should you use on bushytails? I normally use a short hunting bow, often the same one I plan to use in the fall deer season. Most of the time I use cedar arrows with blunts or field points. Too many arrows are going to be ruined or lost to make it economically feasible to use glass or aluminum shafts. Blunts, with their increased shock power, are far superior to any other kind of point; for his size, a squirrel is surprisingly tough. If you'll use a blunt of the same weight broadhead you'll use for deer, bushytails will provide you with some good shooting practice. The same camo suit you use for deer hunting is also desirable for squirrel hunting. Bushytails are among the most keen-eyed small game animals in the world.

Regardless of your hunting methods or equipment, don't expect to set any records the first time you go after squirrels. If you're serious, you can score enough to keep things exciting. I can't think of better stalking and shooting practice for bigger game under real hunting conditions. Along the way, you'll gain a new respect for squirrels.

HIP-DEEP IN DUCKS

Orange feet hanging, the spoonie flapped her wings as she settled through the dead timber. Her eyes were glued on her kin in the tempting medium below. The frozen aerial target was easy pickings as I came back to my Apache (three fingers under) draw. The bodkin broadhead zipped home, and the hen plummeted to the shallows.

I had purposely placed my decoys in the deadfall of timber so the ducks would have to settle in slowly rather than glide into the water. My blocks were well painted and would even fool a duck hawk if it should happen by. As I retrieved my second shoveler, I thought this must surely be the grandest sport for any bowman. Yet I knew, too, that only centuries ago it was a way of life for many of my ancestors.

Though decoying is probably the easiest way to take ducks, there are certainly other enjoyable methods. When I first began to leave my scattergun at home in favor of my bow, sniping was my only successful venture. While a shotgunner would be kicked out of any decent duck club, there is certainly no reason to scorn the bowman for this same action. Hitting a four-inch body at 30 yards isn't a sure shot!

Short bows are a must for all waterfowling—something along the line of 56 inches, or even shorter if your height should dictate its use. I use two bows for my duck hunting—one is 58 inches and the other is a 52-inch model. The usefulness of these compact bows can readily be realized when the water is creeping ever higher on your waders. My stubby 52-inch Magnum works well in the deep-water ruddy sanctuary. The low flight profile of the spiketail makes him an insult to a shotgunner's ability, but makes him a bowman's dream. I like to try to get them when they taxi for a takeoff. I say *try*.

A good coating of silicone spray gives my fletching the waterproofing that not even a duck could provide for its own feathers.

Arrows break, nocks get busted and broadheads rust. A dozen expensive flu-flu broadheads last about as long as a box of high-priced magnum shells. For the whitetail convert, the challenge of the stalk and craftiness of deceit begins all over again.

My buddies and I use two types of arrows for waterfowling —regular fletched broadheads and the flu-flu. While I prefer six-feather fletching, one of my friends wouldn't nock anything less than an eight. His bow has a slightly heavier draw weight than mine, so they get about the same range. The flu-flu broadheads are for the flight shots and the standard broadheads are for long-range sniping.

One thing we unanimously agree on is that screw-in points are the best happening to bowhunting for waterfowl since the invention of the flu-flu. The broadheads on duck arrows will be knocked off, rusted and buried in gumbo mud time after time. If you can't afford the added expense of stainless blades, they will have to be given tender loving care after quiver-riding all day. The convertible system eliminates field sharpening. When one blade has been dulled past use, simply screw it out and replace it with a new broadhead. I prefer bodkins, with flat

Ducks are an elusive target for an arrow, but with practice, skill and some luck they can be taken.

broadheads coming in a close second. Whichever blade you select, it must be sharp and come to a good point.

I've settled on wood arrows for ducks. Glass costs more, and you do lose arrows when duck hunting. For some reason, in my experience wood arrows seem to withstand the punishing falls best when they connect. The arrows don't always zip through these birds. Basically, arrow selection is a personal choice.

While looking like an unconfident packhorse or his kin, I always have a large shoulder quiver bouncing along with me to my favorite decoy haunt. No noise is made with my shoulder quiver for it's too full of arrows. I drew a big laugh from a first-timer who accompanied me once. After 30 minutes, he was borrowing from me. Being a nice guy, I didn't poke any fun, I just let him do the retrieving.

A hip quiver didn't work out; the arrows were always dragging against the blind and falling out. I then decided that perhaps I should only use it when jump shooting. While this might work out in your locale, all of my jump shooting takes place while wading. The belt quiver always stayed wet. A bow quiver doesn't carry enough arrows.

Stalking ducks demands good camouflage. I use virtually all patterns—even plain marsh brown if it blends in best. I carry a few inflatable decoys in my game bag while stalking the puddlers such as teal. If you jump any in dense cover, toss the inflatables out quickly in an open spot. A few passes, and they will come back into the deeks.

After the shot related earlier, my bag stood at two shovelers and one teal. While this might sound like a good bag for bowhunting, I've always wanted to limit out with archery tackle.

I knew that if today I would get my 100 allowable points under the Texas point system, I had to get going. Sniping would perhaps get me some more ducks on a small mangrove pond. The short growth combined shrubs with live and dead grasses, so I voted to change camos before setting out after my elusive daily limit.

Indians may have lacked today's expensive camouflage gear, but they did not lack ingenuity. Their bows didn't shine, so a bow sock was never needed. Their sinew strings blended perfectly with the surrounding vegetation. All that was left for them to do was to take on animal forms and then stalk within reach.

While I enjoy wearing my comfortable camo jacket, I have not forgotten the initiative of the ancestors that gave birth to this fantastic sport. I steal my daughter's crayons regularly when making camouflage tape or better camo bow strings.

I was now at the edge of the pond and noticed that my hand was shining in the mid-morning sun, so I added a streaking of soft mud.

A few feet within the water of the pond I got my first shot at some jumping teal. I released the arrow at about 60° up. (I have my qualms about shooting an arrow at any greater angle than this.) The flu-flu hit dead center in a mesquite branch and the shaft split.

A mottled duck jumped at the far end of the pond. I began calling her with all the seductive tones I could muster. She turned and flew to a spot just 10 yards from my decoys.

The camo job had performed true!

I released the arrow a bit high in case she spotted the flu-flu.

Thud.

Though a bow could easily kill a duck at 200 yards, getting close is a must for scoring. Ducks can pick up the flight of an arrow easily and dart above or below to avoid its path. While I have connected on long shots, my misses far outnumber the dead ducks.

Use your imagination for camouflaging. No one can sit in a Louisiana marsh and tell you what would be best on your favorite stock pond in New Mexico. The best way to check camouflage is to look at yourself in a colored photograph.

Several years back, I had two guests shooting scatterguns over an old timber burn. Both gunners had similar shotgun abilities, but only one managed his limit. He had taken me up on my advice of black pants and a black windbreaker. The other hunter was 30 yards down the bank and was getting shots at marginal ranges. He was wearing jungle pattern.

Just as extreme, I wore the only matching pair of cattail fatigues I have ever seen. The design was sprayed on with flat paints. Add a few other leaves around and stand in the open for bluebills. This has worked time after time for this less intelligent fowl.

Take notice all winter what the ducks are and are not wary of and then find camos the same color.

I can imagine that most bowmen are reading this with more than a bit of skepticism. Shotgunners always prepare themselves before opening duck day by spending hour after hour on the trap range. The more respectable nimrods even shoot hand trap from the exact blinds where they will be gunning on that first dim morning. If gunners do this and bowhunters know that bowhunting is far more difficult than scatter-gunning, then why shouldn't the duck-hunting bowman be out on the range!

I don't mean out on the trap range. I mean on the Frisbee range.

A child's toy, yes, but the best darn flying target for archery practice I've ever seen.

With practice, this flying saucer can be made to fly just about any conceivable pattern a duck could. With practice, you can make the Frisbee return like a boomerang. All of these tosses are easy to learn.

The throws are done underhanded, regardless of the dipsy-doodle you wish to present for your fellow bowmen. The boomerang, which saves a lot of footwork, is thrown at an incline into the prevailing wind. The slower the wind is blowing, the higher the Frisbee must be thrown. The result is a stall at the peak of the climb. I use this antic when trying to duplicate decoying birds.

The other decoying Frisbee (or duck) is the floater. This is again a stalling throw, but this time the throw is made from some distant spot. The Frisbee (duck) then settles in with pinpoint accuracy. If mallards are in your area, then by all means practice this shot intensely. Only a greenhead hunter can appreciate this graceful landing.

Though pass shooting usually seems almost foolhardy, this flight pattern can be duplicated by thowing the Frisbee extremely hard with the wind. If the saucer gets on top of the wind current, it'll fly for a hundred yards or more.

So much for the aerial stunts. As I said earlier, I see no reason why a bowman should be embarrassed about taking ducks by sniping. I use a full-bodied expanded-foam decoy for sniping practice. A decoy made from expanded foam will last longer than your arrows will. I work out over land and in shallow water in order to duplicate both of my field-hunting actions.

Whether I'm practicing for deer or ducks, I always try to dress and shoot as I would when hunting. It's fine to hit paper targets, but you'll get very duck hungry if this is the only practicing you do. Shoot target rounds with your camos on, practice while wearing waders, but by all means practice with both flu-flus and standard arrows.

While I'm practicing sniping, I use old broadheads which are no longer fit for hunting. If I'm Frisbee shooting, I use a converta arrow with a bludgeon tip.

I have long been an advocate of field-dressing game birds; this especially includes birds taken with a bow. The enzymes are released freely when the broadhead cuts digestive organs. Dress them within 30 minutes.

Today I finished far short of my daily limit of 100 points, and yet I had enjoyed every moment of the day. On just such a day as this the original Americans had made their hunts.

TURKEY, THE BIG GAME BIRD

I was sitting by a large oak tree watching a deer trail about 30 yards away when three wild turkeys appeared, walking at a fairly rapid pace as though fleeing from danger, but still looking ahead and on all sides. They were alarmed, but not panic-stricken. I moved my head slightly to get a better look, and the turkeys quickened their pace as if they had seen that slight movement. They soon disappeared in the thick brush.

Less than 15 minutes later a trio of whitetail deer came down the same trail. I was able to draw my bow, get off a shot and bag one of the deer before the other spooked.

This incident demonstrates the fact that one of the greatest challenges faced by a bowhunter is bagging a wild turkey. Compared to the whitetail deer, the turkey is much more wary. It is less abundant and prefers more secluded habitat. Its eyesight is superior to that of the deer. While a man might fool a deer by remaining perfectly still, the turkey will spot him instantly unless he is completely camouflaged. The turkey will flee immediately when he catches sight of man.

How do you go about bagging one of these elusive birds with a bow and arrow? It is a difficult task that relatively few archers attempt. However, the challenge involved is increasing the number who do attempt it.

Basically there are two types of turkey hunting: fall hunting and spring hunting. In the fall the hunter is likely to find mixed flocks of hens and young gobblers; in the spring flocks will be dispersed, and the turkeys will be intent upon mating.

First, let's discuss hunting these birds in the fall. At this time of year a number of turkeys are taken by deer hunters who happen to spot this wily game bird more or less by accident. In Florida an archer is allowed to take both hens and gobblers, so the chances of success would be much greater there than in an area where only gobblers are legal game. A hunter on an elevated tree stand has a much greater chance of drawing his bow and shooting at a turkey without being seen than does a ground-based hunter.

Turkeys are creatures of habit. They leave plenty of sign—such as tracks, droppings and marks on the ground where they have dug up acorns, insects and other food. The hunter who can scout out such an area and locate a path traveled by the turkeys could set up a blind or tree stand within shooting range of this trail and have a very good chance of getting a shot.

He would also have to be very careful to avoid spooking the turkeys while scouting out the area. The turkey will change its habits whenever it comes in contact with man. In fact, it is not found at the edges of civilization as deer and other wild animals are.

The turkey prefers dense woodlands and swamp far off the beaten track where it does not have any contact with man. Frequent hunting or frequent encounters with man will drive the big birds even deeper into the wilderness. If the hunter should scatter a flock during the fall, he can sometimes use a caller effectively to lure some of the birds back within shooting range. Scattering flocks in this manner and then calling the birds back is a practice that has been used by hunters for many years.

To give you some idea of how difficult it is to bag a wild turkey with bow and arrow, let me quote you a few figures. On Blackbeard Island National Wildlife Refuge, off the coast of Georgia, the turkey season was open for eight years during the same time that bow hunts for deer were held on the island. Although several hundred deer were killed during that time, only three turkeys were bagged by archers. Steve Rambo and Arlie Collins of Atlanta were two of the successful bowhunters. The late Ben Franklin of Millen, Georgia, (an accomplished bowhunter who bagged more than 25 deer, a black bear, and a number of wild hogs and other game animals during his hunting career) was the only other archer to bag a turkey on Blackbeard Island.

John S. Lyon—Information Officer of the Land Between the Lakes, located in Tennessee and Kentucky—told me that 3,000 permits were issued during the 1971 bow season for deer and turkey. Not a single gobbler was bagged by archers. He states that there is a large turkey flock in Land Between the Lakes and it is one of the few native flocks of these birds in the eastern United States.

The archer must not only be up to the task of hunting the turkey, but also have adequate bowhunting tackle. Bob Lee, president of Wing Archery Company, recommends the same tackle that the archer would use for hunting deer. He stresses that no point other than a sharp hunting broadhead should be used for turkey hunting. A number of archers prefer simple two-edged broadheads to multi-bladed broadheads for turkey hunting. They believe that they will get better penetration through the feathers with this arrangement. Ben Pearson developed his famous Deadhead for turkey hunting. There is a possibility, especially with a lighter weight bow, that multi-bladed heads will not penetrate as deeply. This would probably not be a factor if the hunter used a 55-pound or heavier bow and made his shots from close range.

"Spring gobbler hunting is where you separate all the real turkey hunters from all the rest," says Hubert Handy, Chief of Game Management for the Game and Fish Division of the Georgia Department of

Natural Resources. "The birds are no longer in flocks, and in this state only the gobblers will be legal game. Anyone who calls and kills a mature turkey gobbler can figure that he earns his trophy."

I might add that the hunter who uses a bow and arrow rather than a shotgun to bag his turkey has *really* earned his game. The spring hunts in most states are scheduled to coincide with the latter part of the breeding season. By this time most of the hens have been bred and have already taken to the nest, and the gobblers will come more readily to the call. For the most part, the hens are incubating fertile eggs and are out of the hunter's way. Besides being an ideal time to call turkeys, it assures that some of the older gobblers can be harvested without hurting the total turkey population.

There are two basic types of turkey calls—those held in the hand and those held in the mouth. Perhaps the most popular is the box-type call manufactured by M.L. Lynch and others. The hunter operates this call by scraping the long-handled lid of the box over the top of the sides. Rubbing it on one side produces the mating call of the hen; rubbing it on the other side produces the call of the gobbler. Another hand-held caller is the slate which is rubbed with a hardened stick to produce an imitation of a hen.

The mouth call is a small rubber disk placed inside the mouth. If you can use this call effectively, you will have both hands free to shoot and won't have to worry about the additional motions or noise of laying aside other callers.

To gain the required skill with a turkey caller, you should practice in the presence of an experienced turkey hunter if possible. The next best thing is to obtain a record of turkey-calling techniques, then study the recording and practice until you can successfully imitate it.

Find a roosting tree being used by a large gobbler. One of the best ways to do this is with an owl call. Toms will answer an owl even in the darkness. Position yourself before daylight and begin to lure the gobbler into range as soon as it is legal to do so.

Although using the mating call to lure a wild turkey into shooting range may sound unsporting to the person who has never tried it, it is really quite challenging. The turkey comes to the call with every sense alert. He can be spooked by the first foul note or mistake made by the caller. His mating urge is strong, but not stronger than his innate cunning and will to survive. The hunter who calls too frequently will rarely, if ever, deceive a wise old gobbler.

The instant the turkey suspects something is wrong, it will flee. You must spot the bird first, make as little motion as possible drawing your bow, then shoot quickly and accurately at a small target before the gobbler spots you and leaves.

J.K. (Mac) McLain, Jr., former president of the Florida Bow-hunters' Council, Inc., is an avid turkey hunter. When I last talked to Mac, he told me he had called in 16 gobblers in one year and had one just about in position for a shot when a fox spooked it.

"I have called several in for other fellows," Mac says, "but so far, a tail feather is all I have to show for my efforts. My arrow clipped the feather out of a big gobbler when he flew over my tree stand. Needless to say, if I had hit that tom in the air I would have been pretty proud."

A team of bowhunters could gang up on a gobbler by having one man do the calling while the other waits in a tree stand or blind a short distance away. By taking turns at calling or standing, each member of the hunting party could have an equal chance at shooting a gobbler.

The importance of camouflage in turkey hunting cannot be stressed too strongly. The use of camouflage makeup for the hands and face is strongly advised. A wild turkey has one of the sharpest pair of eyes in the forest—and a keen sense of hearing as well.

The gobbler can be distinguished from the hen primarily by the whisker-like growth called a beard which dangles from the center of his chest. He is larger than the hen and his feathers have a metallic green-black sheen that makes him almost black compared to the dull brown color of the hen. In areas where hens are protected, you must be particularly careful to distinguish the sex of the bird before shooting.

In most southern states, a turkey is considered big game. It may be odd to think of a bird as big game, but there are reasons for this classification. An obvious one is the turkey's size. It may weigh 20 pounds or more. It is our largest game bird. In addition to size, hunting the turkey requires methods similar to those required for bagging whitetail deer, elk or moose. Small game tactics or tackle are not sufficient to bring down this fine game bird. The bowhunter who desires to pit his skill against the wild turkey will rarely bring home the makings of a big meal, but he will find challenge galore in the deep oak forests.

A good turkey hunting guide book is *Hunting the Wild Turkey* by Tom Turpin. It's an old book re-issued, and with a special introduction by Roger Latham, one of Pennsylvania's and the country's top turkey hunters. Cost is $1.70 from Penn's Woods Products, Inc. (19 W. Pittsburgh St., Delmont, Pa. 15626).

Turkey Hunting Tips

- Find the highest turkey-population areas
- Position yourself properly
- Call sparingly
- Check periods of peak gobbling activity (affected by weather)
- Be in position before daylight
- Choose listening spots near high, less dense areas
- Stay far enough from other hunters so they won't spook birds
- Stay alert; don't move too early
- Wear good camouflage clothing
- Turkeys are often active on rainy days

CHAPTER SIX

BOWFISHING

●

CARP HUNTING, A TO Z

When the spring sun breaks through again and the streams rise, there is a type of hunting that offers pleasant hours of shooting, much game —usually—and is one of the best methods I know to introduce a beginner to the fun of bowhunting. But it's still different enough from game-animal hunting to be exciting in its own way.

Carp shooting might be classified as hunting—you must find carp, and after you find them, you still have to approach with caution. Cast a shadow on the water, and all you will see is a swirl of muddy water.

The best places to find carp year-round or in the off-spawning times, particularly in my area of the West, are in the irrigation ditches, sloughs, backwaters and tulle areas of lakes. If there is deep water, the carp will come to the shore edge; but at first shot they will dive to deeper water.

A few scouting trips will pay off. "Know of any carp areas at this time of year?" I recently asked Steve White of San Diego, California. White hunts and fishes all the time, except when working—and he thinks about it then.

"There's a slough over on the Colorado River that has more carp than you can shoot in a week. Want to go?"

"Maybe I'd better warn you that I'm the number one jinx in good areas," I said. "I have gone into fabulous areas and found nothing. But that's part of the sport."

Also part of the sport is a license. California requires a fishing license to shoot carp with a bow. It's best to check your state fishing laws before going into the field, too.

The river was low, more like a big stream. You could walk across in many places. We ambled along the banks searching the water for carp. They like the cattail and brushy sections.

"There's one!" And plop went White's arrow. He had fouled on the reel and broken the line; the shaft hit the carp sideways. My jinx was working.

I moved along the bank while he retrieved his arrow. White was wearing hip boots; I prefer a pair of old rubber shoes. I once became waterlogged in a pair of hip boots with water up to the waist. I get wet now instead. Footgear is up to the individual. Some prefer hip boots; others use waders. Some fish barefooted in a swim suit or a pair of old pants. Tennis shoes protect your feet from broken glass and also prevent stone bruises.

As I peered into the glare from the easterly sun, I wished I had remembered to buy the pair of polaroid glasses I had promised myself for this trip. A hat of some type to help shield the eyes, a pair of polaroid glasses to see under the water, maybe a towel draped under your cap so the ends hang down on each side and block out sunlight —these all help you see more fish. Regular sun glasses help reduce eyestrain and glare, but don't help you see into the water as well as the polaroid glasses will. I had tried my yellow lenses, but they didn't give enough penetration.

I thought I saw a fin moving—and there lay my first carp of the day. I came to full draw on my 55-pound bow, held below the fish in the shallow water and plopped him right through the spine.

We proceeded slowly, fishing the banks to the spillway of Laguna Dam. My jinx held—they were pouring cement spillways and had the water turned off completely.

The equipment needed for carp shooting is a bit different from regular tackle, but not completely different. The bow that works best is your regular hunting bow—or an old one if you don't want to get water all over your good bow. You may want to stick with a recurve bow; a compound seems to offer too many opportunities to hang up the fish line in the cables or wheels. But make your own decision. If your wife and kids want to join in the shooting, they could use lighter tackle; 30-

to 35-pound bows will bag carp—if you hit them right, if they aren't too deep, if they aren't too far from the shooter, if the arrow isn't too heavy and a few other variables.

You can get fish arrows at your local archery shop. They are usually made of solid fiberglass and weigh 800 to 1,000 grains. This, compared to your regular hunting arrow in the 500 grain range, means the accuracy range of this heavy arrow is short. The usual shot at carp is under 20 yards, and the heavy arrow is needed for minimum deflection and maximum penetration into water—and hopefully into carp.

This arrow may or may not have a rubber type of fletch. Carp shooters will often argue about the value of a fletch of this type on a fish arrow. The basic reason is for guidance, but the argument arises from the fact that the fish line is attached to the nock end of the shaft and also guides the arrow as it comes from the bow. The line unreels from a special solid-mount stationary reel attached to the bow, and this drag on the shaft holds it straight.

Barbed fish points have many variations. The best heads have strong points to withstand rock hits. They will often have wire or other flanges projecting from the sides of the head. Many heads have a threaded point that can be unscrewed with finger pressure. Remove the barbs, and the fish slides off easily. If the barb doesn't detach, you will have to cut or yank the arrow out.

Some barbed heads have a keeper or ring that holds the barbs in line with the point. When the point goes into or through the carp, the ring is pushed back, releasing the barb and holding the fish.

Fish reels come in a variety of styles. There are small circular-type reels that tape onto the bow just below the handle. Tape the two flat sections to the handle riser below the hand, tie one end of your fish line to the reel and you're ready for fishing. Or modify the tape-on style—which fits any bow—by attaching a bar across the back of the reel with two screws and welding it to a bolt that is threaded on the end. This screws into the stabilizer insert many bows have today. And more circular-type reels are being made with screw-in attachments.

Another style of reel is the shoot-through variety. There are several on the market, but Mac's is one we have used with success. This tapes onto the bow. It is a large circular metal device that you place above and below the sight window of your bow. You shoot *through* the reel. This reel is big enough to stay out of your sight picture, doesn't bother the hand when shooting, but does snag at times in bushy areas. The main thing is that it works very well.

A variety of fish points.

Some archers have tried attaching a regular spinning reel to the lower limb of the bow. This may be a workable rig, but you would have to try it first before taking it into the field.

With any reel, take a few minutes in the backyard for a quick test. Attach a line to a regular arrow and shoot into the bales to see if a new reel design or idea will be practical and whether the line comes off well.

Bowfishing line is usually 50- to 90-pound test braided nylon. Carp can weigh over fifty pounds. I haven't seen one that big, but twenty pounds isn't uncommon. The main reason for the heavy line is that you will be shooting into water—and maybe roots, rocks, deep mud or who knows what in the bottom. If the fish arrow sticks in a submerged log, you might be able to pull it out with a heavy line.

Be sure the line is braided, not twisted. Nylon is good, but the braided line won't twist and kink as much when wrapped on the reel. Twisted line snarls and kinks easily, and you soon have a tangled mess on your reel. You can usually buy the braided line in fishing outlet stores.

There are usually two holes in a fish arrow—one just below the nock end and the other on the barbed head. You don't have to attach the head to the shaft unless you want to.

Run the loose end of the line through the hole at the nock end of the shaft. Many prefer to take a couple of half hitches below the hole with the line, then proceed down to the hole in the head. If the fish pulls the head off the shaft, you still have the fish because he's impaled on the barbed head. The shaft will come back, since you have the line attached to it, too.

Another method, if you like, would be to fasten the head to the shaft with a pin or Ferr-L Tite cement. Tie the line to the nock end and let it go at that. A hard ricochet hit off a rock may loosen the head, but this won't happen often.

If you fasten the line to the head or barbed point only and don't run it through the hole at the nock end, the mass weight of the arrow will pull the shaft to the side. The arrow will hit the water—and possibly the fish—sideways due to the drag of the line fastened directly to the point.

When you shoot into the water from an angle, allow for the depth of the carp in the water. A rule of thumb would be to aim one foot low for each foot the carp lies under water. This is where the fun comes in. You see a big carp across the slough not more than two feet under water, hold below him, fire—and then find that he was deeper than you thought. The arrow goes over the carp's back. On the next shot you overcompensate and shoot under it. It is much fun and great shooting—and even better when you connect.

The reason you must hold under the image you see is the downward refraction of light in water. If you hold directly on the carp, you will shoot over it by quite a margin. How much to hold under, how big the fish, how deep the carp, how far you are shooting that heavy fish arrow, how heavy a bow you are using, what angle you are shooting —these are a few of the variables involved in bowfishing. Once you get the feel of it, you will begin connecting regularly.

Regular hunting camouflage sleeves on the bow limbs help prevent the shine from regular limbs—the reflection can spook fish.

A regular camo shirt wouldn't hurt. Wear anything but bright or white colors. Carp may not see definite colors, but they certainly spotted the red polo shirt I was wearing faster than the khaki shirt White wore.

Bowfishing is like any other hunting with the bow—the targets are where you find them. Get a good location, rig your bow for bowfishing and go gig a fish.

CARP IN THE DARK

The night was dark, and thunderheads were building in the west. The air held the cool, damp feel of an impending storm. Bullfrogs in the marsh seemed to resent our intrusion as we made our way toward the open water of Saginaw Bay—a favorite spawning ground for Michigan carp.

Ron Carlton and his daughter Margaret of Flint, Michigan, had invited me along on what Ron described as the most fascinating way to hunt carp with a bow and arrow. He described the numbers and size of spawning carp in Saginaw Bay as being beyond belief.

As we sloshed out through the marsh and into the edge of the bay, it became apparent that Ron knew what he was talking about. Everywhere we looked, spawning carp were rolling on the surface or working their way up into six to twelve inches of water.

Margaret pointed with the Coleman lantern that we were using for a light. "Here comes a big one, Dad!" The light apparently wasn't bothering the fish a bit because it kept coming.

Ron tracked the oncoming fish, and when it turned broadside about 10 yards out, he came to full draw—and the arrow buried into the side of the carp. Water flew in all directions as the carp worked the water to a lather. Ron grabbed the line just as the carp took off on a subdued run. All he got for his troubles was a line burn on his fingers. Finally the carp slowed, and Ron worked it back hand over hand.

The fish, a rotund female full of eggs, allowed Margaret to pick it

These two carp hunters anchored in shallow reeds and waited for carp to come to them. Note the towel under the cap of the hunter on the left; it shades out sidelight and makes aiming easier.

up, remove the arrow and place it on a stringer. We've found that often there will be someone on shore who wants the fish, so we take the fish we shoot back to shore. It's good conservation.

We moved down the shoreline slowly, moving cautiously so we wouldn't trip over clumps of vegetation on the bottom. Muskrat houses or runaways along the bottom are two frequent causes of archers getting wet after dark.

The drycell miner's light on Ron's head was probing into all the shallow water like a one-eyed monster. Soon he turned up what had to be the mother lode of carp; literally thousands of carp were piled on top of each other in a shallow drainage ditch and adjacent field. Everywhere we looked for a two-block area, we saw carp. The odd thing was they were almost all the same size—15-pounders on the average, with a smattering of larger 20- to 25-pounders.

Margaret stood between us with the lantern while Ron and I shot. We'd arrow one fish, and others within 20 yards would scatter; but soon they'd be back. The water started to get muddy from the activity when I suddenly saw a huge carp, at least a 30-pounder, swimming toward me through the shallow water. Dozens of other tempting targets flitted by in front of the biggest one, but I had the arrow nocked and waited patiently for it to cruise within shooting distance.

The wait was as intensely interesting as waiting out a buck in a blind. Twice the fish acted like it was going to move away, then back it came.

Slowly the carp closed the distance. I came to full draw, tracked the fish briefly and made a smooth release. The arrow slashed into the water and barely creased the fish's skull. That carp went absolutely berserk; it tried twice to jump in the shallow water and then went barreling through the water with its back out. The water hissed spray as it worked toward deeper water.

Ron meanwhile had shot an impressive number of carp in the foot-deep water. As I turned around to bemoan my luck at misjudging the light refraction after dark, Ron made an excellent shot and collected a fine double. This isn't too hard a shot, providing you can line up two fish close enough together to enable the arrow to go through one and into the second.

We finished out the evening just one jump ahead of a rainstorm with probably two dozen carp, which were all we cared to drag out of the marsh.

Bowhunting for carp at night is a fascinating way to hunt these trash fish. But before you head out for a try, consult your local game laws. Some states prohibit the sport. Michigan laws are more lenient than most; they allow night hunting for nongame species like carp, suckers, garpike and dogfish.

In Michigan carp usually spawn in the shallows in mid-May.

Night shooting for carp isn't legal in some states; but where it is, bowfishermen score often and big.

When dandelions are in full bloom on the lawns or when flowering crab and quince trees are blooming, this is the time to grab your bow and head for your favorite carp spawning grounds.

Illumination of the surroundings is a major factor when night bowhunting for carp. A two-cell flashlight isn't the answer. We used three types of lighting when we hunted—a six-cell flashlight, a drycell miner's head lantern, and a Coleman two-mantle lantern. The Coleman lantern provided the greatest amount of light, although it seemed to fade a bit around the edges—where you need the most light.

The six-cell flashlight pinpointed the fish very adequately, but it didn't cover a large enough area. And you couldn't hold the light and shoot—which is a definite handicap.

Actually, the miner's head lantern might be the ticket if the unit provided a bit more light. One thing about this rig though is that it takes a bit of getting used to. You must remember that the light beam shines off the top of your head. If you're not careful, you'll shoot over the top of every fish. Learn to compensate for this factor, and you'll have a great time.

Two methods of hunting pay off—wading and stalking the fish or sneaking up on them in a canoe or small flat bottomed boat.

I prefer wading because you can often sneak to within five feet of the fish, something you usually can't do with a boat. For wading, chest-high waders are the ticket. Hip boots are out because you'll often need to cross slightly deeper areas to get to shallows.

We used a few techniques that should work anywhere carp are found in shallow water spawning. One trick was to carry a six-foot stepladder. We found that if someone stood near the top with the lantern, it would illuminate a much wider area of water. The man with the bow could then climb up two or three rungs and shoot from that elevated position. We were quite surprised at how this tactic increased our chances.

Carp do quite a bit of cruising when they spawn, so another trick is to locate a lane of migrating fish and just stand still. Often these migration lanes will be openings between clumps of cattails or other emergent aquatic growth. Position yourself, and let the fish come to you.

When rough fish are in extremely shallow water with their backs exposed, they become super spooky. A splash twenty yards away will send them scooting for deep water in a boil of muddy water.

When it's necessary to wade and search for fish, a cautious step-by-step movement is in order to keep from tripping or spooking the fish. Most dunkings come about when you try to wade like you'd walk down the street. Develop the stream wading technique of keeping one foot planted securely until the other foot finds firm bottom.

A canoe with a gas lantern mounted on the bow will give added dimension to carp hunting at night. A good man on the stern can silently work the archer in the bow into close shooting range, providing someone doesn't bang the side of the canoe with a paddle or make other noise.

Canoe bowhunters can usually take advantage of a light breeze and drift downward as silently as a hunting owl. Often all you'll need is just a bit of steering to keep you drifting along close to shore where the biggest carp are.

Shooting from a moving canoe can add to the challenge of hitting a moving carp. It's not as easy as it looks. And the problem of light refraction seems to be increased after dark due to the weak light of the lantern.

Bowhunting for carp at night isn't for everyone; it's hard work sloshing around in a dark marsh.

But where it is legal and for those who are willing to expend a little energy, it offers an exciting new avenue for archers anywhere carp can be found.

SHOOTING AT UNDERWATER SHADOWS

"You fellows find what you're looking for?"

As a matter of fact, we hadn't. Three of us looked up somewhat disconsolately from the boat we had rented at Tom's Cove on Chincoteague Island, near Virginia's eastern extremity. We told him the stingrays that we had come to shoot with our bows and arrows had thus far eluded us.

"I thought maybe that's what you were looking for," the stranger said. "I'm Bob Umphlett. This is my wife, Nancy," he added with a nod toward his most attractive boatmate. "I've been watching you and thought that's what you were hunting."

Bob and Nancy had eased their boat next to ours as we sat glumly trying to figure out why the stingrays we had come to shoot had so far seemed non-existent. The tide had gradually covered the flats where we expected to find them, and we were wondering where to go next. Bob had the answer.

"There isn't much time, but I can run you up the bay where I think we can find some rays. Big ones."

We didn't need much more urging to tie our craft to a stake in the bay and transfer to Bob's spotless boat. The three of us consisted of Guy Ekler of Highspire, Pennsylvania, Frank Youngfleish from nearby Hershey, and me. I live a hundred miles from Guy up Pennsylvania's Susquehanna River at Berwick. Guy engineered the trip, since he had previously hunted with much success at the same spot on Virginia's east coast.

As we sped north, Bob told how he speared stingrays for the sport, but was unfamiliar with the bow and arrow. He appeared quite interested in our rigs. We were using conventional solid-fiberglass fish arrows with regular bow reels taped to our hunting bows. However, to the back end of the 80-pound test shooting line, we had attached the line from a light saltwater fishing rod. Consequently—if everything went right—once a ray was impaled by an arrow, the line would pay off the bow reel, and the fight would then be transferred to the fishing rod.

There was a good reason for the rig. A big ray could rip an arrow out even if the heavy shooting line held. Anyway, we were looking for the maximum in sport, and this setup seemed to offer the greatest potential. I had yet to see it work, although chances were improving. Bob cut his motor as he headed into the shallows along some weed beds. He unslung a heavy push pole and then moved to the stern.

Within a short distance there was a sudden cloud of mud and a dark shape sped away from the boat. Then another ray sailed away, a telltale cloud obscuring the bottom where the boneless creature had just been.

"They're tough to see," I said.

Guy laughed. "Sometimes they nearly cover themselves with mud. They appear chocolate brown in this water."

No more rays showed for some distance. Then I thought I detected a brown spot through the somewhat murky water. I drew quickly and slammed an arrow at the object.

The shallow water exploded in a froth of mud and blood as my shooting line quickly flipped from my bow reel. There was an ominous clattering of my fishing rod as it started after the line—I had forgotten to open the bail of the spinning reel! I grabbed quickly and flipped the bail as the 30-pound test line stripped out rapidly. Finally, the ray slowed, and I engaged the drag. For a few moments the stingray continued as though nothing had happened, the click of the reel screaming its protest. Then I leaned against the rod with all my weight and felt the big creature turn.

It looked as though it was going to be a long fight as the ray and I alternately gained line. But gradually I worked it in to the edge of the boat. It was then we discovered that we had left our gaff in our own boat. We had trouble!

The stingray, especially one this size, is a formidable creature. The two-edged barbed stingers are extremely dangerous. Not only are the slime and dirt on the stinger a perfect setup for gangrene, but also the poison released by the ray can prove fatal. Anyone hit with the barb should get heat on the wound fast, because heat deactivates the poison. Then he should see a doctor. In effect, I had won the match. But the ray was still game, although failing to take more than very short runs against the drag.

"Go ahead, Guy. Give him another one. This could take all day."

Guy grinned back at me and took aim. His shaft dug deep into the vitals of the flapping creature. Now we had two lines on it. Carefully we again worked the ray in to the edge of the boat where Bob waited with a length of rope in his hand.

While we held the creature steady, Bob slipped the rope through its gills. He flipped it over so that the potentially lethal stinger could not be used effectively, and then he pulled the ray over the side. With one foot on its tail, Bob took his knife to remove the stinger located about a third of the way from the tip of the tail on the top side. It was then we discovered that my ray had a double stinger. After they were removed, there was no further danger.

I estimated this stingray at a conservative 60 pounds, although others thought it would weigh substantially more. Since we had no scale to weigh it, I am only sure that it was extremely heavy—since it took most of my strength to hold it up for photos.

Water and blood made a mess of the bottom of the spotless boat. Nancy Umphlett looked woeful, but she graciously said nothing. We found no more rays as the moving tide churned the bottom. On the way

Saltwater bowfishermen find sharks and rays offer exciting bow shooting opportunities.

back it was obvious that Bob was getting hooked on this bow and arrow bit.

After a night in Guy's camper we were on deck early to give them another try near some clam beds Bob said should be good. We went in his boat. Guy was especially anxious for the opportunity to try out some experimental arrowheads he had made and to test the efficiency of some detergent-bottle floats he had brought along.

We cruised along the fences erected to keep the rays from the commercial clam beds. Mollusks make up much of the stingray's diet.

There is no protection given rays to my knowledge, since they are generally considered pests by commercial netters and clammers.

It was some time before we finally located a patch of seaweed which had a population of stingrays. Frank scored first on a smallish ray that gave quite a tussle when the arrow caught the edge of its "wing." This time, however, we had the gaff aboard. Guy made sure it worked on the ray when Frank got it alongside after recovering the detergent-bottle float.

Then Guy shot his experimental point into a ray, and he tossed the empty detergent bottle overboard. We watched the bottle take off across the mud flat, knowing that it probably wouldn't go out of sight. We looked for more of the rays that kept flipping out from the front and sides of the boat. Then I got into a medium-sized stingray of perhaps 40 pounds and gave it the bottle. This one took off toward a small reef and lay quiet. We continued on, searching the shallows.

Then Guy spotted a big one! Only this time he went back to the fishing rod after the hit. He immediately had his hands full. There was no need to rush, and Guy wanted to handle this one himself, despite our offers of assistance. Several times he brought the big ray in close, only to lose line as it made another charge for open ocean. At last it was alongside. Guy put the gaff to it. It was a good try, but the stingray was too much for one hand. Off it went again—with the gaff. Fortunately, the arrow held, and Guy worked the ray back in until Frank could reach the gaff handle. This one, too, covered a good section of the boat bottom.

The tide was rising, so we turned back to gather up our detergent bottles. Mine produced a fair-sized stingray. Guy's was a smaller ray and appeared to be giving little trouble as he lifted it toward the boat. Again, the experimental point pulled through, and the ray slipped back into the water and took off for parts unknown.

Except for the disappointment produced by the experimental fish head which simply wouldn't hold under the tremendous pressure of a stingray, we counted our trip a complete success.

Although the stingray is probably best known, there are about 400 species in the group made up of rays, skates, sawfishes, guitar fishes, electric rays, eagle rays and mantas.

We found the stingray tough enough to test our bows and rods.

When venturing over salt water for bow targets, it is well to go prepared for big game. Some stingrays go well over 200 pounds, and there is always a chance at a shark. Consequently, solid-glass arrows and heavy, *sharp* fish heads are in order. A bit of advance knowledge of the type of game anticipated should be obtained, since there are dangers lurking in salt water for the unwary.

The most important thing to remember about stingrays is that they must strike upward to inflict damage. They can sink their barbed spear heads deep into flesh, so bring them in over the boat side inverted until they are helpless. Then immediately cut the stinger, or stingers, from the tail.

Choice of rods for such bowfishing is a matter of personal preference. The lighter the rod, the more sport is available. Wrap the line on the bow reel in the conventional manner, leaving enough end when you start so that it can be tied to the fish line. Or skip the bow reel altogether, and tie the fish line directly to the arrow. This does involve a risk if you forget to keep the spinning reel bail open, since the quarry may take your rod and reel over the side before you can grab it.

Although larger plastic jugs may be used as bobbers, it is much handier to use the smaller bottles which can be taped lightly to the bow so they can easily be pulled loose if a hit is made. It provides greater mobility for the archer. Strength of line is optional, but it doesn't pay to go too light where large rays may be found. Somewhat heavier line—50 pounds or more—is recommended, since bringing the fish in hand over hand will not provide the same leeway permitted by rod and reel.

For off-season hunting excitement, there is little that can match the commotion when a big ray is impaled by an arrow. They are tough, strong, available. And you do a service to commercial fishermen and clam diggers when you make a kill. A photo and the fleshed-out stinger make a memorable trophy of your experience.

Gar of all sizes provide top sport for bowfishermen in southern and south-central areas of the country. This alligator gar weighed 84 pounds.

CHAPTER SEVEN

TROPHIES AND FOOD–THE FINAL REWARDS
●

FIELD DRESSING BIG GAME

There's no sanctified method of field dressing a big game animal. There's a logical order, of course, in the steps you take. But most people have slight variations on these steps. The things that everyone agree upon, however, are these: common sense, care, cleanliness, a decent knowledge of the animal's anatomy and a sharp knife. These will result in a field-dressed animal of top quality.

Since the insuring of fine steaks and roasts begins the minute you have your game animal, here are a logical series of steps to take when dressing the animal. These steps refer to the dressing of a deer; if your trophy is a bear, elk, moose, or other big game, you will have to adjust accordingly—but the steps will be similar.

Now before you hang your bow in a nearby tree and haul out the knife, there are two mighty important steps you must take: (1) Make sure the animal is dead. It's totally senseless to wade right in without checking and suddenly be slashed with a flailing hoof or tossing antlers. Poke the animal in the eye with your bow tip. If there's no reaction, you're almost ready to begin. (2) Tag the trophy, then begin field dressing.

● 1. Position the carcass with the head slightly downhill, causing the internal organs and fluids to gravitate away from the area of your first incision. Use rocks or small logs to prop the carcass upright on its back; spread the hind legs and tie one to a tree, rock, or whatever to keep the carcass positioned. On a buck, begin by cutting around the penis sheath and testicles back toward the pelvic area and anal vent. Cut carefully around the genitals on both sides, and cut deep enough to free the organs at the point where they attach to the body.

● 2. To free the anal vent and colon, use a very sharp knife and cautiously cut around the vent so the blade scrapes the inside of the pelvic bone wall. This cut releases the colon from the body. At this stage many hunters pull the lower intestine out far enough to tie it off with heavy cord or knot it, preventing spillage of excrement as the dressing process continues. Do not pull the colon loose from the internal organs, however.

● 3. Open the body cavity with a shallow *cut through the skin only,* starting either in the pelvic area and moving forward or at the rib juncture and backward. (If you begin at the rib juncture, place the carcass with the head uphill so the internal organs will gravitate away from the point of incision.) Pull up loose skin to begin the cut, and use the fingers of your free hand to guide the knife blade while also pushing the stomach muscles covering body organs out of the way. Have the knife between skin and belly muscles; this will allow you to cut the skin cleanly without cutting hair. Near the pelvic area, avoid puncturing the bladder. Belly skin will put back, exposing the stomach muscles. Make a shallow, careful cut through them so the intestines will be exposed. Insert your free-hand fingers into the cut and pull the muscles up. Use your free hand to hold the muscles up and keep the body organs away from the knife blade as you continue the cut.

● 4. When the cut is completely through the stomach wall, loosen and roll out the paunch. Save the liver and put it in a plastic bag. Roll the carcass onto its back again and split the pelvic or aitch bone to remove the colon and sex organs. (This step may also be done before opening the body cavity.) Slice through the meat to the pelvic bone and locate the bone suture. With the edge of a heavy knife or axe blade, plus a couple taps with a rock, open the bone suture and carefully split the pelvic bone. Remove all the remaining organs at this end.

Some people begin field dressing with steps 3 and 4 outlined here, then go to step 1. Again, this is a matter of personal preference.

● 5. With a small knife, slice around the perimeter of the diaphragm, the thin fleshy wall between the intestinal cavity and the heart-lung cavity. If you are not saving your deer as a trophy, you may

BIG GAME FIELD CARE

There's no sanctified method of field dressing a big game animal. There's a logical order, of course, in the steps you take. But most people even have slight variations on these steps. The things that everyone agree upon, however, are these — common sense, care, cleanliness, a decent knowledge of the animal's anatomy and a sharp knife will result in a field dressed animal of top quality.

Since the insuring of fine steaks and roasts begins the minute you have your game animal, on this poster are a logical series of steps to take when dressing the animal. These steps refer to the dressing of a deer; if your trophy is a bear, elk, moose or other big game, you will have to adjust accordingly.

Now . . . before you hang your bow in a nearby tree and haul out the knife, there are two mighty important steps you must take:

1) Make sure the animal is dead. It's totally senseless to wade right in without checking, and suddenly be slashed with a flailing hoof or tossing antlers. Poke the animal in the eye with your bow tip. If there's no reaction, you're almost ready to begin.

2) Tag the trophy, then begin field dressing.

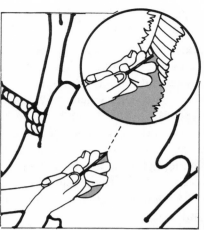

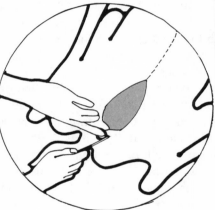

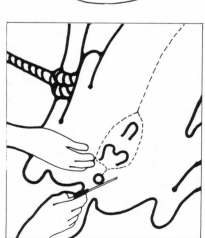

1 Position the carcass with head slightly downhill, causing internal organs and fluids to gravitate away from the area of your first incision. Use rocks or small logs to prop carcass upright on its back; spread hind legs and tie one to a tree, rock, etc. to keep carcass postioned. On a buck, begin by cutting around penis sheath and testicles back toward pelvic area and the anal vent. Cut carefully around the genitals on both sides, deep enough to free the organs at the

2 To free the anal vent and colon, use a very sharp knife and cautiously cut around the vent so the blade scrapes the inside of the pelvic bone wall. This cut releases the colon from the body. At this stage, many hunters pull the lower intestine out far enough to tie it off with heavy cord or by knotting it, preventing spillage of excrement as the dressing process continues. Do not pull the colon loose from internal

3 Open the body cavity with a shallow cut, starting either in the pelvic area and moving forward, or backward from the rib juncture. Pull up loose skin to begin cut, and use fingers of your free hand to guide the knife blade while pushing body organs out of the way. Near pelvic area, avoid puncturing the bladder. Belly skin will pull back, exposing stomach muscles. Make shallow, careful cut through them so intestines will be exposed. Insert free hand

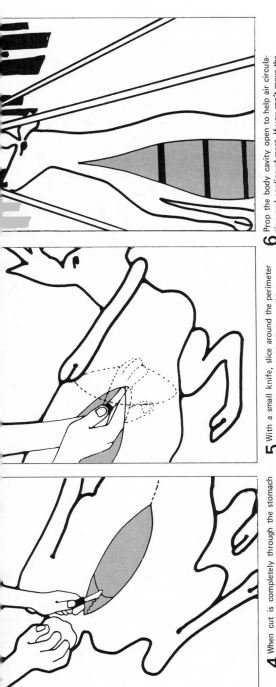

4 When cut is completely through the stomach wall, turn the carcass so it now rests with head uphill. Loosen and roll out paunch. Save the liver and put in a plastic bag. Roll the carcass onto its back again and split the pelvic or aitch bone to remove colon and sex organs (this step may also be done before opening the body cavity). Slice through meat to pelvic bone and locate the bone suture. With the edge of a heavy knife or axe blade, plus a couple taps with a rock, open the bone suture and carefully split the pelvic bone. Remove all remaining organs at this end.

5 With a small knife, slice around the perimeter of the diaphragm, the thin fleshy wall between the intestinal cavity and the heart-lung cavity. If you are not saving your deer as a trophy, you may want to continue the body-length cut. Use a heavy knife or saw to more easily cut ribs away from breastbone. At the base of the neck inside the body, sever windpipe and gullet. Pull out heart, lungs, windpipe and gullet. Save the heart in your plastic bag.

6 Prop the body cavity open to help air circulation and cooling of meat. If you can't move the carcass out of the field by yourself, prop it up to enhance draining of any remaining blood or body fluids. If possible, hang it from a tree or tripod of poles by its front legs or antlers. If you can't manage that, drape it over a log or pile of rocks. Skinning in the field is a controversial subject. If it's extremely warm, skinning should be completed as soon as possible. Otherwise, wait until you return to camp, using the hide as insulation and to keep the meat clean until you get there.

want to continue the body-length cut. Use a heavy knife or saw to more easily cut the ribs away from the breastbone. At the base of the neck —inside the body—sever the windpipe and gullet. Pull out the heart, lungs, windpipe and gullet. Put the heart in your plastic bag.

• 6. Prop the body cavity open to help air circulation and cooling of meat. If you can't move the carcass out of the field by yourself, prop it up to enhance the draining of any remaining blood or body fluids. If possible, hang it from a tree or tripod of poles by its front legs or antlers. If you can't manage that, drape it over a log or pile of rocks. Skinning in the field is a controversial subject. If it's extremely warm, skinning should be completed as soon as possible. Otherwise, wait until you return to camp, using the hide to insulate and keep the meat clean until you get there.

Tips to properly field dress and cool your trophy.

The most important objective once your game is down is to save the meat. Here are some tips in reaching that goal:

.Take the necessary tools into the woods each day. The main tool is a sharp knife. A pocket knife with a blade two-and-a-half to four inches long is the handiest. It carries easily and is easiest to use. A short-bladed "hunting" knife is okay, too. You won't need a big sheath knife unless you'll be skinning the trophy (when you'll probably go to a particular skinning blade style)—or if you need a heavy knife to cut the pelvic (or "aitch") bone and leg bones. If you have a daypack or fanny pack, it's easier to carry the big knife there than on your belt. A big knife, of course, is also handy for cutting branches for a blind. You'll need a small file or stone to keep the knife sharp.

.Take some small, strong rope; nylon is good. Five to ten feet will be plenty. You'll need this to tie one leg while you're dressing the animal or to hoist it into a tree or Spanish windlass so the carcass will cool quickly. (Two poles tied together near the tops, with the trophy's head also tied there, can be pushed up with another pole, also tied near the top, for a jury-rigged triangular hanging unit.) Some elk hunters take a small block-and-tackle for this purpose.

.You'll need a cloth bag to encase the carcass if you're in warm climates where flies and other insects can get at it. If you save the heart and liver, you'll need a couple of plastic bags to protect them. A few people take a box of ground black pepper which they rub over the carcass to help keep flies off the meat; it also helps form a protective glaze.

.Some hunters carry a small hand-axe to cut branches for blinds and to split the pelvic bone. Many veteran hunters carry a folding saw either in a belt sheath with a knife and file or in their backpack. The saw is considered less work to split the pelvic bone, less dangerous than pushing on a blade that might slip, and is better to cut through ribs or quarter the carcass (which you'll be doing if you field dress an elk or moose or have to pack out any animal).

As you begin field dressing the animal, be alert for the broadhead and insert, if you used a broadhead with insert. You could cut yourself.

.Some hunters believe in removing the big metatarsal glands on the outside of the hind legs near the "knee"; some don't. If you're careful while you field dress the animal and don't rub your hands or knife over them, you won't have any trouble keeping the meat clean. Removing them is generally a guarantee of getting the musk on yourself.

As you split the pelvic bone (for better cooling of the hams and for easier field dressing), be careful not to cut the rectal tube, urinary tract or bladder. If you should accidentally do so, wash off the meat the urine has touched and then rub it dry.

.Be careful not to puncture any of the stomachs (this type of animal has four stomachs). Use a shortbladed knife and guide it with your index finger. Some hunters prefer to have a blade slightly shorter than their index finger so they can reach just past the point and feel the area to be cut before the knife reaches it. If you do accidentally make a wrong cut—or the broadhead has punctured any of the stomachs or intestines—wash the meat the digestive juices have touched as quickly as possible. Use plenty of water or snow because the juices will spoil the meat quickly. Then rub the meat as dry as possible.

With the animal completely field dressed, trim away as much internal fat as possible (fat turns rancid and helps create the "gamey" taste which people often refer to). Then wash or rub out the blood with a cloth, leaves or grass.

Some hunters prefer to split the rib cage to the brisket for additional cooling. If you have a real trophy that you intend to have mounted, be sure you don't cut too far. If you have a deer in warm country, it's best to open it up as much as possible. Do the same with elk, moose, and so on; it's amazing how much area there is to contain body heat. Prop open the body cavity with sticks.

.In warm country or early in the season, some hunters prefer to skin the animal on the spot for additional cooling, then either quarter and bag the meat or bone it out and bag it.

.Get the carcass off the ground as quickly as possible. Air can thus circle and cool the entire carcass. The time it takes to drag a deer to camp and hang it up is not critical, providing you do this as soon as you find the animal. If you drag it out of the field, you may wish to use some cloth or rope and tie the body cavity shut—if you'll be dragging it over open or dusty ground. For regular brush country areas this isn't necessary, unless you've split the animal clear to the brisket. Common sense and a look at the terrain will tell you what to do better than will a host of pronouncements here. Don't worry about bruising the meat, for an arrow-killed deer should have most or all of the blood drained from the meat, and without blood it will bruise little, if any.

If you want to carry out the animal instead of dragging it, tie the legs together at the knees or slit the skin on the rear legs between the main bone and the cartilage and run the front legs through this slit. Tie the front legs near the hooves, and you have a type of T-bar for carrying. Be sure to cover the hide with a red cloth for safety.

Carrying them out on a pole looks romantic, but you'll need two guys with a lot of patience and nerve. If you insist on carrying it out this way, tie the animal's body close to the pole so it won't swing. This is generally the least practical way to transport a deer.

If you're in an area where the nights are cool but the days are warm, and you won't be able to get the carcass to a processing plant or your own cooler for a while, keep the carcass shaded and covered —even if you have to use a sleeping bag or a couple of jackets and move them a couple of times during the day to keep them out of the sun.

.Get a bag over a skinned carcass if you're going to have to leave it in the field for a while. A big muslin bag will permit good air passage, and with a couple of sticks inside the bag it will be free of the carcass all the way around. This will aid air flow and keep flies away from the meat. (If the bag is in contact with the meat, flies can lay their eggs right through the muslin.)

.With an elk, moose or big mule deer, you may need to go get additional help and leave the carcass behind. If you leave the carcass whole and unskinned, get it to a shady area, turn it on its belly and cover the body cavity openings with brush (pine boughs work well) to restrict flies and birds but permit cooling. Skinning, quartering, bagging and then hanging it in a shady area is better, of course. Whichever you choose, move the meat away from the intestines and organs so the birds and insects will not be attracted to the meat.

When you're transporting any big game animal home, don't tie it over a front fender next to the hood of your car; engine heat will thaw it if it's frozen and spoil it if it's just chilled. Tie the trophy on top of your vehicle, over a rear fender or in the trunk. (Be careful here; some states require that part of the animal be visible). If you carry it on a rear fender or on top, a tarp or piece of heavy plastic wrapped and tied around it will give additional protection from snow, rain and road dirt.

TROPHY CARE FOR TAXIDERMY

Any hunter fortunate enough to fulfill his big game dream will likely want to preserve the trophy in the form of a mounted head for the wall or, in some cases, as a full-sized rug.

Preparation of an animal for mounting is a touchy matter, but not as mysterious as some taxidermists make it seem—as long as you follow certain steps.

What usually happens is a hunter will ruin the head in the process of removing it from the carcass, either by cutting the neck skin a foot too short, or by sawing the antlers off right at the base (which renders them useless to a taxidermist), or by making careless cuts through the skin which the taxidermist can't hide.

Sometimes, even after the hunter has taken the proper steps to save his trophy hide, he'll let it spoil.

All animals, regardless of size, start to decompose and spoil very shortly after death. If this spoilage goes unchecked, the hair will begin to slip and fall out of the skin. If you can't get your whole animal to a taxidermist quickly (within 12 hours) and the weather is warm, the animal must be skinned and the skin treated to stop spoiling and to hold the hair in place.

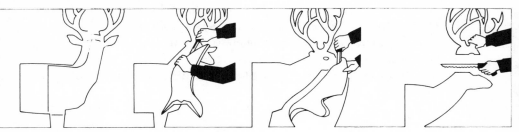

Let's look at the proper method for saving an antlered specimen.

First, it's a good idea to at least partly remove the neck skin *before* the animal is bled. If you bleed an animal with a cut in the throat, you may ruin the appearance of a mounted head. Also, blood will stain light- or white-haired animals if it dries. Nearly all bowhunters feel sticking a deer in the neck with your knife is a waste of time; the deer has already bled to death from the arrow wound.

Now you're ready to remove the skin—remembering to always avoid making a cut through skin on any part of the head which will easily be seen after the mounting.

Start skinning with a series of outlining cuts across the front shoulders of the animal, down the side to the base of the legs and straight down across the brisket skin. Leave more skin than you think the taxidermist will need; he'll cut it to fit.

Never cut into the throat skin. Once you've outlined the cape, make a cut from between the shoulders along the back of the head to a point between the ears. From that point make a short diagonal cut to the base of each antler.

Now begin carefully peeling the skin off, pulling toward the head and leaving as little fat or meat as possible on the hide.

Take your time and use extra care in freeing the ears. Use a dull knife to free as much tissue as possible while loosening the skin, and then sever the cartilage of each ear at the base of the head to free it.

Work slowly around each antler, using the point of the knife or a screwdriver to release the skin.

Great care must be exercised to avoid cutting through the eyelids (also the lips and nostrils), or the finished mount will lose its realistic appearance.

Leave an inch or so of inner skin (or gum) around the mouth so the taxidermist will have less trouble modeling the face. Cut the nostrils free, but leave them attached to the skin.

Once the entire skin is free, you should scrape it as clean as possible with a dull knife, removing all the flesh and fat you can find. Be extra-careful not to break the skin.

Lay the skin over a smooth log where it will remain firmly in place while surplus tissue is pared off with a downward and forward scraping motion. When finished, the ears should be turned inside out and salted, and care should be taken to pack the inside of the lips well with salt.

Wash away all traces of blood and dirt, and rub ordinary salt

(Borax cleanser is another excellent preservative) into all other exposed areas of the skin. Roll up the skin, flesh inside, and after several hours repeat the salting procedure.

Salting and subsequent drying of the hide are critical for preservation, especially if you can't get the trophy shipped immediately. It can be dried in a shady, well-aired area. Never dry in the sun, close to a fire or where it sits folded.

Because most taxidermists now use ready-made papier-mache or plastic-foam forms for mounting heads, it isn't necessary to save the skull. It is important, however, to cut enough skull around the antlers to give the taxidermist a base to work with. Saw off a section of the frontal bone (to which the antlers are attached). It's better to cut too much bone than not enough. The same applies here if you want a simple antler or horn plaque mount.

If the skin is intended for a rug, some hunters saw out the teeth plates for added realism.

If the skull is wanted (and it must be saved if it's an antlerless trophy, like black bear, to be measured later for Pope and Young records), remove all flesh by carefully boiling the skull and then scraping off all spoilable flesh while it's still warm. Don't boil too long, or the bones will separate and the teeth may fall out. Enlarge the hole at the base of the skull with a chisel or hatchet to remove the brains.

You might want to also save the feet of hooved animals for any of a variety of novel ornaments—like inkwells, ashtrays, cigarette lighters, lamps or coatracks. Cut the legs off well above the ankle joint, peel the skin down and scrape away all meat. Don't remove the leg bones. Salt the flesh side and let dry.

Skins intended to be used for rugs or tanned for leather products also should be removed with caution. For rugs, start your cut from the corner of the mouth and then down the throat (not from the lip and down the middle of the lower jaw as some do). Extend the cut along the underside of each leg to the foot.

Once these cuts are made, the next step is to begin pulling the skin around the carcass. I prefer to skin the back end first and cut the hind feet off at the ankle joint to be skinned out later. Try to avoid any more cutting as this might cut the pelt; use your hands and thumbs whenever possible.

Leave the hooves or claws attached for full mounts or rugs. If you're skinning for leather, it isn't necessary to skin out legs. The extra leather from legs is minimal and seldom worth the work.

Most skins (bears in particular) must have the fat removed because it "burns" the hide and soon rots. Once removed, follow the salting procedure.

The cost of a trophy mount varies considerably, depending on locale, reputation of the taxidermist, the type of animal, whether it's a simple head or full-shoulder mount. Fee for tanning is by square foot and varies according to the type of leather wanted. Rugs also vary, depending on size and whether you want a full-head or half-head trophy. And you must remember taxidermy is an art requiring hours of tedious, painstaking work. You pay accordingly.

To comply with state game regulations in most places, the hunter's game tag should be attached to the antlers of a head being shipped. Roll the hide in a piece of canvas and ship it with the head, using rawhide or comparably strong cord to secure bundles. Avoid wire (it may rust or cut if too tight). Label perishable trophies as such and ship the fastest way possible (air express is used by many) to the taxidermist, alerting him of your shipment.

If you have specific instructions for your taxidermist, enclose them with the trophy. Or call him and let him know exactly what you want.

Mounted specimens, if executed by a competent taxidermist, should keep for years. Arsenic is used to treat scalps to avoid damage by moths or other insects. Trophies should be dusted frequently, and hides groomed occasionally with a damp rag dipped in kerosene. Antlers should never be varnished or polished. A natural finish can be maintained by simply washing with warm water and soap, then brushing with an equal mixture of linseed oil and turpentine (wipe off the excess).

Outdoor air isn't a tonic for mounts. If displayed outdoors during summer, store indoors during winter.

A bit of patience helps you get the trophy in the first place. A little more patience will insure that you have an admirable trophy for years to come.

PROCESSING BIG GAME

There probably are as many theories on skinning and butchering deer as there are successful deer hunters. Which means that if you get what you want, you've done the job right. Some people like more roasts than steaks, so they process the meat accordingly. Others like plenty of stew meat, so they don't grind as much for burgers.

There's no one way you should begin the process. Some hunters process the animal as soon as the meat is cool; others prefer to skin and hang the carcass to age for about a week; still others hang and age the carcass without skinning for two weeks to a month.

Our intention is simply to show you a basic method that will work. You can provide your own variations, if you want, as you gain experience and learn what works best for you.

Your decision will be governed by personal preference, time available and general weather conditions at the time of the kill.

If the weather is warm or the meat must be transported before it's thoroughly cooled, skin and quarter the carcass as soon after killing as practical. Wrap each quarter separately in clean canvas or cloth. During transportation, be sure air can circulate around the carcass quarters or it will spoil (i.e., don't close it in a car trunk or under another canvas covered with other hunting goodies).

If the carcass freezes, allow it to thaw slightly in just-above-freezing temperatures. This will make skinning much easier.

To skin the animal, first cut off the hind legs just below the hock (similar in position to our knee) and the front legs at the knee joint. Slit the skin on both hind legs between the main bone and the cartilage. Then run a stout pole or commercial gambrel through these slits, spread the hind legs as far as possible, attach a rope to the pole and around some overhead support and hoist the animal off the ground.

Slit the skin on the inside of each leg to the belly cut, up the brisket and neck and around the neck just below the head—assuming that you are not intending to have a trophy mount of the head and shoulders. If you intend to have a trophy mount, the skin must be slit up the top of the neck and shoulders, downward behind the shoulders around the chest and at the baseline of the chest on the front legs.

Pulling by hand and using the knife as sparingly as possible, begin peeling the skin down over the hams and body.

Pull the skin away from the meat far enough to let you slip your hand in between and carefully separate them. (One good way to loosen the hide without tearing the meat is to roll your fist into the crevice between meat and skin. This works extremely well in areas that don't skin out easily.)

PROCESSING BIG GAME

There probably are as many theories on skinning and butchering deer as there are successful deer hunters. Which means that if you get what you want, you've done the job right. Some people like more roasts than steaks, so they process the meat accordingly. Others like plenty of stew meat, so they don't grind as much for burgers.

And there's no one way you should begin the process. Some hunters process the animal as soon as the meat is cool; others prefer to skin and hang the carcass to age for about a week; still others hang and age the carcass without skinning for up to two weeks.

Our intention is simply to show you a basic method that will work. You can provide your own variations, if you want, as you gain experience, and learn what works best for you.

Your decision will be governed by personal preference, time available and general weather conditions at the time of kill.

If the weather is warm, or the meat must be transported before it's thoroughly cooled, skin and quarter the carcass as soon after killing as practical. Wrap each quarter separately in clean canvas or cloth. During transportation, be sure air can circulate around the carcass quarters or it will spoil (i.e., don't close it in a car trunk or under another canvas covered with other hunting goodies).

If the carcass freezes, allow it to thaw slightly in just-above-freezing temperatures. This will make skinning much easier.

To skin the animal, first cut off the hind legs just below the hock (similar in position to our knee) and the front legs at the knee joint. Slit the skin on both hind legs between the main bone and the cartilage. Then run a stout pole through these slits, spread the hind legs as far as possible, attach a rope to the pole and around some overhead support and hoist the animal off the ground.

Slit the skin on the inside of each leg to the belly cut, up the brisket and neck and around the neck just below the head, assuming that you are not intending to have a trophy mount of the head and shoulders. If you intend to have a trophy mount, the skin must be slit up the top of the neck and shoulders, downward behind the shoulders around the chest and at the baseline of the chest on the front legs. (For full trophy handling information, see "After

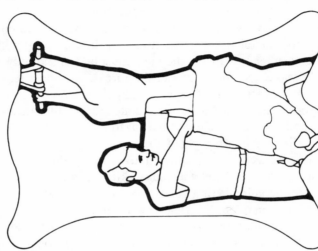

the Hunt," *Archery World*, Dec. 1972.)

Pulling by hand, and using the knife as sparingly as needed, begin peeling the skin down over the hams and body.

Pull the skin away from the meat far enough to let you slip your hand between and carefully separate them. (One good way to loosen the hide without tearing meat is to roll your fist into the crevice between meat and skin. This works extremely well in areas that don't skin out easily.)

Keep a steady tension on the loosened skin with your free hand at all times, and get someone else to pull on the hide where you really need to exert pressure. Don't try to go too fast.

Roll the hide evenly off the entire body as you progress toward the shoulders and neck. Keep loose hair off the meat.

Some people hang a deer by the head or antlers and skin from front to rear. This system works well, but you may need to tie a leg securely to keep the carcass from turning.

Another skinning method is to make a half-hitch with a rope around the loosened neck skin and pull the skin off in one fell swoop. To do this, you'll need plenty of space and two or three strong helpers.

After the carcass is skinned, use a damp cloth to remove hair, excess blood and dirt. Adding a little vinegar to the water makes it easier to pick up hairs and debris.

Aging is generally considered necessary to improve the flavor and tenderize the meat. It also gives the meat a firmer "set" which makes it easier to cut and handle.

Hang the meat in a clean, dry place at constant temperatures of 34-36 degrees F. for a week or 10 days.

If you have skinned your deer in the field, hang it 12 to 24 hours to cool before butchering. But if you're in hot weather, or don't have the time, start butchering right away.

You'll need a solid table or work bench (hopefully not more than 30 inches high, because you'll need leverage on some of the sawing); sharp meat saw; sharp, heavy butcher knife; smaller sharp knife, sharpening stone or steel; freezer paper; masking tape and felt tipped marker.

There are several ways of going about butchering. The most universally used method is to saw the carcass in half lengthwise, splitting the backbone cleanly if possible, and then cutting each half in two leaving two ribs on the hind quarter.

This is done because it's a nebulous area, with everyone basically making up his own mind where rib roasts end and steaks begin. And if you leave the last two ribs on the loin area, the meat cuts will retain a little better shape.

Once you've quartered the carcass, further cutting can basically be achieved by following the sectioning chart shown here. In the round steak area, cut them to whatever thickness you desire (an inch and a quarter is good). Cut loin-area steaks to whatever thickness you wish. The same goes for shoulder roasts or steaks; if you choose to make the shoulders into roasts, they'll be thicker than steaks.

To remove the ham, cut just forward of the pin bone (front part of the pelvis). Use the meat saw only for bone and cartilage, and the knife wherever else possible.

To free the shoulder, make a cut just to the rear of the shoulder blade and up and around close to the rib cage.

You can bone a ham by following with your knife between any of several easily separated muscles. Trim this entire chunk from the bone.

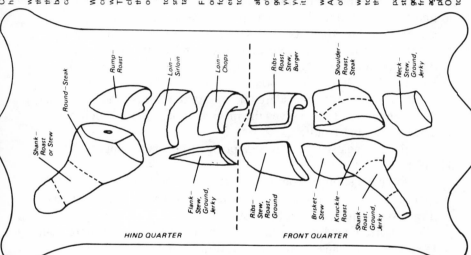

Shank— Roast or Stew

Round—Steak

Rump— Roast

Loin— Sirloin

Loin— Chops

Flank— Stew, Ground, Jerky

Ribs— Stew, Roast, Ground

Ribs— Roast, Stew, Burger

Shoulder— Roast, Steak

Brisket— Stew

Knuckle— Roast

Shank— Roast, Ground, Jerky

Neck— Stew, Ground, Jerky

HIND QUARTER   **FRONT QUARTER**

Cut this into boneless steaks; the top of the ham makes a good roast.

Instead of cutting the loin area into steaks with bone attached, you may wish to cut along the dorsal spines the length of the backbone, then along the ribs and lateral spines of the backbone. Now, with a little knife work, you can lift out the entire loin. Good steaks here.

Wrap the meat for freezing immediately after cutting. Use the proper freezing paper; double wrapping is advised for moisture retention. Trim as much fat as possible from the cuts and clean them of bone sawdust and scrap. Package the meats in amounts to suit your family's one-meal needs.

Pull the paper as tight to the meat as possible to force out air. Make packages firm and smooth for easier stacking. Seal with masking tape and label and date each package.

To wrap securely, use the "butcher" wrap. Fold one corner of the paper over the meat, roll once or twice toward the opposite corner, then fold in the sides of the paper so they will be enclosed as you continue rolling the package toward the last corner.

(Since venison is dry, it's suggested you add about 20 percent beef suet or whatever amount of beef or pork you wish. The amount can be governed by your personal taste preferences. If you use pork, you defeat your purpose because you have to cook the meat too well done, and it again becomes dry.)

Plastic bags, which can be sealed very tight, work well as the inside wrap for ground meat. After sealing the plastic bag, wrap it in a layer of freezer paper.

With steaks and chops, place two layers of wax paper between each cut. They won't freeze together and will be easier to handle when thawing for cooking.

For best results, send the entire batch of packages to a locker for fast freezing. Then store them in your home freezer. If you can't get a locker to do this for you, turn your freezer to its coldest setting, spread the packages as equally as possible over all shelves and place them as close to the walls as possible. Once they're frozen, turn the temperature back to 0 degrees F. for continued storage.

Keep a steady tension on the loosened skin with your free hand at all times, and get someone else to pull on the hide where you really need to exert pressure. Don't try to go too fast.

Roll the hide evenly off the entire body as you progress toward the shoulders and neck. Keep loose hair off the meat.

Some people hang a deer by the head or antlers and skin from front to rear. This system works well, but you may need to tie a leg securely to keep the carcass from turning.

Another skinning method is to make a half hitch with a rope around the loosened neck skin and pull the skin off in one fell swoop. To do this you'll need plenty of space and two or three strong helpers.

After the carcass is skinned, use a damp cloth to remove hair, excess blood and dirt. Adding a little vinegar to the water makes it easier to pick up hairs and debris.

Aging is generally considered necessary to improve the flavor and tenderize the meat. It also gives the meat a firmer ''set'' which makes it easier to cut and handle.

Hang the meat in a clean, dry place at constant temperatures of 34-36° F.

If you have skinned your deer in the field, hang it 12 to 24 hours to cool before butchering. But if you're in hot weather or don't have the time, start butchering right away.

You'll need a solid table or work bench (hopefully not more than 30 inches high, because you'll need leverage on some of the sawing); sharp meat saw; sharp, heavy butcher knife; smaller sharp knife; sharpening stone or steel; freezer paper; masking tape and felt tipped marker.

There are several ways of going about butchering. The most universally used method is to saw the carcass in half lengthwise, splitting the backbone cleanly if possible, and then cut each half in two, leaving two ribs on the hind quarter.

This is done because it's a nebulous area—with everyone basically making up his own mind where rib roasts end and steaks begin. And if you leave the last two ribs on the loin area, the meat cuts will retain a little better shape.

Once you've quartered the carcass, further cutting can basically be achieved by following the sectioning chart shown here. In the round steak area, cut to whatever thickness you desire (an inch and a quarter is good). Cut loin-area steaks to whatever thickness you wish. The same goes for shoulder roasts or steaks; if you choose to make the shoulders into roasts, they'll be thicker than steaks.

To remove the ham, cut just forward of the pin bone (front part of the pelvis). Use the meat saw only for bone and cartilage, and the knife wherever else possible.

To free the shoulder, make a cut just to the rear of the shoulder blade and up and around close to the rib cage.

You can bone a ham by following with your knife between any of several easily separated muscles. Trim this entire chunk from the bone. Cut this into boneless steaks; the top of the ham makes a good roast.

Instead of cutting the loin area into steaks with bone attached, you may wish to cut along the dorsal spines the length of the backbone, then along the ribs and lateral spines of the backbone. Now, with a little knife work, you can lift out the entire loin. Good steaks here.

Wrap the meat for freezing immediately after cutting. Use the proper freezing paper; double wrapping is advised for moisture retention. Trim as much fat as possible from the cuts and clean them of bone sawdust and scrap. Package the meats in amounts to suit your family's one-meal needs.

Pull the paper as tight to the meat as possible to force out air. Make packages firm and smooth for easier stacking. Seal with masking tape and label and date each package.

To wrap securely, use the "butcher" wrap. Fold one corner of the paper over the meat, roll once or twice toward the opposite corner, then fold in the sides of the paper so they will be enclosed as you continue rolling the package toward the last corner.

(Since venison is dry, it's suggested you add about 20 percent beef suet or whatever amount of beef or pork you wish. The amount can be governed by your personal taste preferences. If you use pork, you defeat your purpose because you have to cook the meat too long, and it again becomes dry.)

Plastic bags, which can be sealed very tight, work well as the inside wrap for ground meat. After sealing the plastic bag, wrap it in a layer of freezer paper.

With steaks and chops, place two layers of wax paper between each cut. They won't freeze together and will be easier to handle when thawing for cooking.

For best results, send the entire batch of packages to a locker for fast freezing. Then store them in your home freezer. If you can't get a locker to do this for you, turn your freezer to its coldest setting, spread the packages as equally as possible over all shelves and place them as close to the walls as possible. Once they're frozen, turn the temperature back to 0° F. for continued storage.

Use the same methods for cooking venison as for beef of similar grades. It's best to trim the outer layer of fat from the meat before cooking because it will have a stronger flavor than the meat.

In general, tender cuts of meat are cooked by dry heat; less tender ones by moist heat. Young bucks and does furnish the more tender meat. Strips of bacon over the outside of a roast will help to keep the meat from becoming too dry.

Tender cuts (such as rib and loin chops, round steak, leg roasts) can be pan-broiled, oven-broiled or roasted. Less tender cuts (such as neck, shanks, chuck and brisket) should be cooked with moist heat. These cuts may be ground for deerburgers or meatloaf.

Less tender cuts may be made more tender by marinating for 10 or 12 hours in French dressing or a spicy marinade. Many people, however, feel the entire flavor of venison is lost with a marinade and prefer simpler cooking. Rather than killing the original venison flavor with spices and herbs, use salt, freshly ground pepper, and monosodium glutamate which blend with but do not destroy the original flavor. Vegetable flavors (such as onions, garlic, tomatoes, chopped parsley and celery) are complementary and bring out the taste of the meat.

An excessively strong flavor indicates: improper handling of the meat; the meat was not bled properly; paunch juices leaked onto the meat and were not wiped off; the meat was not cleaned properly; the carcass was not kept cool during transport; or too much fat was left on the meat.

If you get a gamy taste, you haven't done your fieldwork or your homework. And that is a shame, because venison is food fit for kings.

CHAPTER EIGHT

THE FUTURE OF BOWHUNTING
●
THE BOWHUNTER AS A BIOLOGIST

Wild game can be its own worst enemy. It needs our help. But not total protection, as many pseudo-conservationists advocate. Nature's way is no longer the plausible plan for the perpetuation of game animals.

The oft-quoted checks and balances of nature aren't totally applicable in our modern society. Man has been the pivotal factor. He has altered the scheme—in the guise of progress or whatever—in such a way that wildlife has become dependent upon him.

But let us not bemoan this fact. Sure, man has made mistakes, but the pluses far outnumber the minuses. Thanks to our help, most wildlife not only has survived, but also has actually multiplied and greatly expanded its range.

For this the hunter can tip his hat.

While others have talked, the hunter has dug deep and paid dearly—more than $142 million in 1974—for the privilege of seeking these game animals he has helped conserve and perpetuate. And at the same time *he has been beneficial to non-game creatures*.

Consider the rare whooping crane, for example. Hunters have not only provided it with a winter home (the Aransas National Wildlife Refuge in Texas), but also paid for research projects to bring it back from near extinction. In some places there is no open hunting season on sandhill cranes because of the fear that a hunter might kill one of the migrating whoopers by mistake. Hunters have quietly accepted the ban.

We, as bowhunters, are just a small segment of the overall picture, but a vitally important part. The amount of game taken annually by bowhunters usually amounts to less than that killed by automobiles, so it's obvious that we collectively don't produce a dramatic effect on total game populations. We're simply one more part of the whole. Hunters are increasingly seeking higher quality recreation in which their hunting and archery skills are supremely challenged. But unless we stand up and be counted, we might find this privilege and recreation buried by the anti-hunting fraternity—a fraternity which, amazingly, chooses to ignore biological laws and proven research results when they get up on the stump to blow their horn. They will undoubtedly accept economists and plumbers as being experts in their respective fields, but when a professional biologist opens his mouth to speak of the things he learned, they're likely to punch his teeth out.

Let us recognize first that hunting is indeed a privilege and not an inherent right. Despite what we have done in the past, this doesn't make the land and the animals which reside thereon our exclusive domain. We must share with others. But when these "others" attempt to take over, don't be afraid to cite what we have done. It is a very impressive record and the sportsman should be proud of it.

The foremost reason why hunters conserve and perpetuate game is a purely selfish one. These animals are a necessary part of our sport. But do not be ashamed of this fact. Hunting is a means of recreation, just as is fishing, golf or bowling. It provides a lot of fun for a lot of people. Prohibit hunting, and you eliminate a vital source of recreation which is much needed in this age of increased leisure time. Prohibit hunting, and you eliminate the major influence on keeping game populations at a healthy level in the existing habitat. Prohibit hunting, and even the non-game species will suffer.

How? Consider the following:

The Interior Department reported that 888,000 more hunting licenses were sold nationwide in 1974 than in 1973, raising the total number of licenses to 16,397,369. But this is not a precise indicator of the actual number of hunters because many people—for reasons of age, military service and so forth—can hunt without purchasing a license and are not counted, while many persons buy licenses in more than one state and are therefore counted twice in the statistics. Taking both these factors into consideration, the estimate of hunters is more than 25 million.

In the National Survey of Hunting and Fishing made by the Interior Department a decade ago, it was found that the typical hunter spent 6½ days annually in pursuit of his favorite sport. The average

Good game management is a part of all sport hunting, and sport hunting is a part of good game management. Deer often fall victim to their own habits and starve in winter yards. Proper game harvests and herds in balance with the habitat will reduce this occurrence.

now is around 14 days. Multiply 25 million by 14 and see what you come up with. That's how important hunting is to the recreational picture; and if you consider the money each hunter spends yearly, the figures become even more impressive. (The Interior Department estimates that hunters and fishermen combined spend more than $2.3 billion annually!)

But this is money funneled into the overall economy. How about those funds used directly for the conservation and restoration of wildlife, both game and non-game?

License sales in 1974 provided $142,000,000. Practically every bowhunter owns some type of firearm (there are some 45 million owners of firearms in the United States). When he bought his gun he paid an 11-percent excise tax. Funds raised through this tax on sporting arms and ammunition go to states for approved wildlife restoration projects—under the Pittman-Robertson Act passed in 1937. More than $43 million was distributed to the states last year. This money is used for the benefit of *all* wildlife, not just that which is hunted. It has paid for research stations, management areas and wildlife refuges. Some states now employ a *non-game biologist* on their game and fish department staff, a person who attempts to restore and conserve wildlife which we will never hunt. *This is a bonus from hunting and hunters.*

Beginning this year archery equipment will also be included in the 11-percent excise tax, the same as for firearms. So archers will now be paying their share of the support costs—and receiving their share of benefits.

Waterfowl hunters must purchase a Duck Stamp (which now costs $5). This money is used to buy and restore wetlands, aiding both game and non-game wildlife. Ducks Unlimited donated more than $3.56 million in 1974 to buy waterfowl-breeding areas in Canada.

But providing the necessary money is just part of it. Anyone who knows wildlife has long recognized that it needs management where it can prosper—and effective control to keep it within the limits of what the land can sustain.

Many years ago the Kaibab National Forest of Arizona was recognized as a trophy-deer hotspot. Ideal habitat and balanced natural predation and hunting kept it that way. Then range stock overgrazed it. So hunting was stopped, cattle kept at a minimum, and predators wholesalely killed. As a result, the mule deer population exploded and overbrowsed the area. Belatedly, hunting was allowed again, and with liberal limits. The deer herd and habitat began to recover. Hunting was again restricted, and the deer population expanded and harmed the habitat again. So the seasons were liberalized, skillful management techniques were applied, and today the herd has been brought back down to a stable, healthy level. The North Kaibab now has some of the finest mule deer hunting anywhere.

The same thing happened in the DeSoto National Forest of Mississippi, only this time with whitetail deer. A "doe day" was proclaimed to reduce the number of animals; and when the population was cut back, it became stable and healthy.

A biologist weighs and will then take a stomach sample from this deer in a continuing effort to learn more about deer and gain better game-population balance with the habitat.

Biologists say that ideally at least 25 percent of the deer herd should be harvested annually. Natural reproduction will replace that many. But should the habitat become overpopulated, and man doesn't eliminate the surplus, there will be a die-off during a harsh winter or from starvation or disease. The animals which remain become stunted in physical size and antler development.

Some 80 percent of the quail population will perish each year whether the birds are hunted or not. The mortality rate of doves is something like 65 percent. Hunters take less than 10 percent of both species—which means we could harvest many more and not affect the population. Far more insidious threats are such things as loss of habitat and reckless use of virulent pesticides.

Yet both hunters and qualified wildlife biologists tend to be super-cautious. When studies prove that we could take 20 percent of a certain species, they usually cut that figure in half for practical application. Let wildlife become abused, and the hunter is the first to voluntarily restrict himself.

And still the public continues to be fed the hogwash that the hunter is the enemy of wildlife. If the stakes weren't so high, it almost would be a joke. But the threat is too real to be a laughing matter. Every responsible bowhunter must stand up and be heard. To ignore the problem is certain defeat.

BOWHUNTING'S MAJOR PROBLEMS

We all have problems, individually and collectively. Some are just irritations, others are major threats.

We wanted to find out what various archery and bowhunting groups and individuals regarded as the major problems facing bowhunters and bowhunting—and what the urgency of the situation was. So we asked them.

Here's what they said:

Larry Bamford, president, Pope & Young Club:

1. The anti-hunting groups; the "endangered wildlife" ploy—no species on the endangered list has been brought to that point by sport hunting.
2. Overdevelopment; loss of wildlife habitat. It has been estimated that more than one million acres per year are lost through road development, reservoir construction and urban development.
3. Closing of lands to hunting.
4. Increased costs of hunting, equipment, fuel, licenses, guides and taxidermy.

5. Hunter misbehavior. We must clean up our total image. Hunter education, skill and safety programs will eventually become prerequisite to the issuance of licenses.

There are many things the individual bowhunter can do: Know the facts about the desirability of hunting and its relationship with wildlife management; try to improve the bowhunter's image through your own conduct; exercise good sportsmanship; develop strong personal ethics; obey game laws and report those who do not; respect posted property (improve landowner relations); be safe in the field (learn first aid).

Cooperate with state game commissions and support sound game management practices; promote the concept of selective hunting (trophy hunting), the idea of hunting more and killing less; learn where to hit animals for maximum effectiveness, and practice to become a skillful shot; develop tracking and trailing skills to aid in recovery of wounded game; take the time to tell non-hunters about hunting; explain to others that the hunter is paying for nearly all of the wildlife conservation and management in this country; encourage manufacturers to continue equipment improvement.

We as bowhunters say we are the world's best sportsmen. Now we are going to have to prove it. We are going to have to de-emphasize the importance of the kill and start promoting the hunter as a conservationist, which he is.

Jim Dougherty, Ben Pearson Archery; president, American Archery Council:

While there are several problems facing bowhunting today—and all hunting for that matter—it has occurred to me that one problem alone is most significant. In fact, it very well may be the root of all bowhunting problems.

I'm speaking of the bowhunter himself—our very own ranks —you, me and our buddy down the street.

"Cripple loss" is a term often associated with bowhunting when our opponents take us to task. Our opponents' position that archery tackle is ineffective and inhumane is based on what they contend to be excessive cripple loss.

On the other hand, accredited agencies state that: (1) bow-hunting results in no more cripple loss, or (2) less than other hunting methods. In short, cripple loss is not a significant factor in bowhunting. These observations have in many cases been made after extensive searches have been made in high-use bowhunting areas.

Why is there such a discrepancy between the alleged incidence of cripple loss and what appears to be factual statistics? The answer could very well be the bowhunter himself.

For some strange reason, bowhunters seem to have a habit of wanting to claim a hit when in fact there was none, as if such a statement would elevate his hunting and shooting prowess in the eyes of his fellow bowhunters and companions.

I have hunted extensively throughout the United States in many of the most popular, high-use bowhunting areas. For years, I have listened to the conversations of bowhunters around campfires, gas stations, restaurants, check stations, and so on. I have watched the general hunting and non-hunting public react as they overheard the bowman's conversation, seen game department and Forest Service personnel and local landowners take note of what the bowhunter was saying. The content of what we say is the pulse of our sport, and it is being constantly monitored by many people of diverse temperament and interest.

"Ah, I got a hit, but I lost him." A simple statement, uttered God knows how many times a year by people not pausing to think. A constantly repeated prevarication that creates an illusion—painting archery tackle and those of us who use it as ineffective—adding immeasurably to our problems.

If we can eliminate this problem, we can assuredly cure the rest.

Joe Johnston, Easton Aluminum; president, Archery Manufacturer's Organization:

1. Unification of efforts, with all bowhunters working jointly to attain specific goals and resolving personal differences behind closed doors.

2. The alliance of all hunters and *true* conservationists in an all-out effort to develop the wildlife resource to its fullest.

3. The development of strong, unified state associations that will take positive action to attain these goals—and not be organized only to defend their right to hunt.

4. The development of a national program that will educate the children on the need for hunting as a tool of conservation.

5. The development of coalitions such as the group in Los Angeles which includes hunting and anti-hunting organizations working toward a common goal—healthy wildlife populations.

Fred Bear, president, Bear Archery:

1. The Humane Society of the United States has already taken us to court and will no doubt continue their assault on our sport. We in archery should make every effort to explore all means possible to insure that we take animals in the most humane way possible.

2. Bowhunters must become more tolerant of gun hunters. They should join sportsmen's clubs and develop closer relationships. Game cropping and management cannot be done with the bow alone. *We* are "Johnny-come-latelys," not the gun hunters. Too many bowhunters have an arrogant attitude toward gun hunters, believing that our sport of bowhunting is the only true sport. This is not so, and succeeds only in dividing hunters as a whole at a time when we need unity. Both the ranks of gun hunters and bowhunters contain a few rotten apples that make us all look bad, but percentagewise there are just as many good guys among the gun hunters as there are among us bowhunters.

3. We all must find some way to spread the word that the anti-hunters actually spend their money on propaganda against hunting and very little toward the conservation of birds and animals. Hunters are the only ones who have ever done much for our wildlife, and we must all shout out the message that the best way to do the most for game conservation is to buy a hunting license.

4. The Humane Society of the United States has launched a powerful blow against hunters with their new "KIND" program—a plan to brainwash our small children in the schoolroom. Don't be surprised if your six-year-old comes home from school to point a finger at Dad when he brings home a rabbit. KIND (Kindness In Nature's Defense) is for children and youths, ages six to eighteen, according to the official publication of the HSUS. All hunters, plus those who believe in basic game conservation, should be prepared to combat this propaganda by having the facts at hand.

5. Probably our greatest internal problem is communication. We find that too many hunters are simply not aware of the major issues that face us. Some who are aware of the problems take

them too lightly and do nothing about them. While it is wrong for bowhunters from outside one state to enter into the affairs of another state, there is a great need for an organization to disseminate information on how a particular problem might be solved by the residents of that state. There is a need also for information when one is challenged individually by the anti-hunter. Find this organization and join it as an active, alert member.

Erv Kreischer, president, National Field Archery Association:

There can be no question that the major problem of bowhunting is the rising tide of anti-hunting sentiment. The change from a rural lifestyle to intensified urbanization during the past generation has left the killing and processing of animals far removed from the requirements of everyday living. Now a large segment of our society is repulsed by the very thought of killing an animal.

Anti-hunting organizations are capitalizing on this sentiment and imply the religious, philosophical, ethical and moral degeneration of anyone who would condone the hunting of wild animals. Large sums of money are being spent to inject this propaganda into movies, television and school programs from elementary to college level. School teachers are teaching children that we are murderers for killing the animals. This effort, if allowed to go unchallenged, will eliminate all hunting in one generation.

Other problems will include: continuing pressures to reduce or eliminate hunting seasons; competition with other groups for the use of public lands for recreation; reduction of wildlife habitat due to the encroachment of civilization and the failure of archers and other sporting groups to organize and collectify efforts to provide direction and funding for these issues.

This is why we have a bowhunting and conservation program, a National Bowhunting Defense Fund, public information statements and other such activities within the NFAA.

C. R. Gutermuth, president, National Rifle Association (which is increasing its activities with bowhunting organizations in joint efforts to unify all hunters):

1. Lack of proper and necessary communication with other segments of the hunting fraternity. Hunting is hunting regardless of whether a gun or archery tackle is used to accomplish the kill.

Hunting can be and often is a family event. When people come to understand the place of sport hunting in total wildlife management, as these two young boys undoubtedly will, our sport and our wildlife stand a better chance of healthy survival.

The same basics are necessary in either case: Knowledge of the animal and its habits, stalking skill, familiarity with hunting arms and aesthetic appreciation of the hunt. Yet bowhunters often feel superior to gun hunters, and gun hunters often feel superior to bowhunters. This must change. We must all work together to preserve hunting, or we will simply fight our own separate battles. This will become increasingly important in the future if dwindling habitat and increased preservationist pressures among urban populations are not checked by better education of the public by hunters.

2. Lack of good public image for bowhunting. The idea of an arrow in an animal means a slow, agonizing death to many minds. Bowhunters must educate the public on the humaneness of the method, as well as the sporting aspects of bowhunting, to achieve a higher status in the eyes of the public. An excellent method would be by educating school-age children.

3. Political apathy of the individual. Bowhunters and all hunters must become less afraid of standing up for their rights. They must do so in a courteous, logical fashion and show respect for opposing views, but they must be more vocal. They cannot complain if or when hunting is outlawed because as a group they have been silent. And, more importantly, hunters must set out individually and as a group to educate that major segment of society that is neither pro- nor anti-hunting at the moment. It is truly here that the battle will be won or lost for hunting.

4. Lack of organization of bowhunters. This is not an appeal for a new, all-encompassing organization to step forward. It is a critique of the fact that there are many bowhunting organizations, but few members in each. Collectively, there could be political weight, but only with a unifying relationship so that a few spokesmen could express the views of the majority.

5. Loss of huntable environment. Each mile of highway, each building, each house is that much less habitat to support wildlife. To some extent this cannot be reversed. But the sportsman can insist that the remaining areas of wildlife populations include hunting as a regular and necessary part of their management—instead of idly grumbling as they are turned into preserves because only preservationists spoke up.

George Helwig, president, National Archery Association:

Today it is a rare group of sportsmen who at casual mention of a recent bowhunting trip do not invite comments from other members about their bow efforts. This great number of hunters is possible because of the readily available equipment (as opposed to the old days with fewer bowhunters and more homemade gear).

All this has produced the number-one problem: uneducated novices and once-a-year bowhunters. They generally do not belong to an organized archery group and cause the second problem: inconsideration for private property and the desire to build personal egos by detailing hits that ''got away'' when there most likely were no hits at all. This gives vent to the third problem: untrue stories which give the anti-hunting elements ammunition for their anti-cruelty talks.

The fourth problem is the rapid loss of hunting land and game habitat.

The fifth problem is created by the municipal anti-hunting ordinances that are so inclusive they totally prohibit target archery by saying, ''It is unlawful to discharge any projectile in the limits of this municipality.''

To offset this trend, it will take some well-thought-out programs and strategy directions to disassociate archery from the violence of criminals using guns to carry out their deeds.

There needs to be education of our own participants, as well as education of that great body of people who are currently neither for nor against hunting.

As you have noted, not everyone placed equal weight of importance on the various aspects. But the main themes recur frequently—and frighteningly.

There's work to be done, both organizational and informational—from the grass roots to the upper echelons, individually and collectively.

ARCHERY ORGANIZATIONS

Today, more than ever, it is important that you join an archery organization to help promote and develop our sport. It is especially important for bowhunters to join organized groups, for our sport is undergoing a continual, organized onslaught from the anti-hunting groups who are spreading everywhere their misconceptions about biology, the interrelationships of wildlife and habitat, and the value of hunting.

Bowhunters—*all* hunters—must make sure that the true and accurate story of wildlife and man's positive influences on it reaches every person in the country. To do so demands organization, time, work and money.

Do your very best. Join an organization. Be a sportsman. Get active. Make sure the non-hunting public (which constitutes the major share of the population) hears the real facts and learns and understands why people hunt, the value of hunting *and* the contributions toward the continued good health of *all* wildlife (game and non-game) hunters have made and will continue to make over the years.

Here are some national organizations you may wish to join:

National Archery Association. 1951 Geraldson Dr., Lancaster, Pa. 17601.

National Field Archery Association. Rt. 2, Box 514, Redlands, Cal. 92373.

American Indoor Archery Association. P.O. Box 174, Grayling, Mich. 49738.

Fred Bear Sports Club. Rt. 1, Grayling, Mich. 49738.

Pope and Young Club (Associate Member). c/o Harv Ebers, R.R. 3, Hannibal, Mo. 63401.

National Rifle Association. 1600 Rhode Island Ave., N.W., Washington, D.C. 20036. (They're becoming highly active in cooperative work with bowhunting organizations.)

Professional Bowhunters' Society. c/o Chris Mertz, 2294 'E' Road, Grand Junction, Colorado 81501.

The following groups can provide bowhunting and/or basic archery information:

American Archery Council. 618 Chalmers St., Flint, Mich. 48503.

Archery Lane Operators' Association. 1500 N. Chatsworth, St. Paul, Minn. 55117.

Archery Manufacturer's Organization. 618 Chalmers St., Flint, Mich. 48503.